THE SYSTEMATICITY ARGUMENTS

STUDIES IN BRAIN AND MIND

SERIES EDITORS:

John W. Bickle, *University of Cincinnati, Cincinnati, Ohio*

Kenneth J. Sufka, *University of Mississippi, Oxford, Mississippi*

THE SYSTEMATICITY ARGUMENTS

by

Kenneth Aizawa
Centenary College of Louisiana, U.S.A.

KLUWER ACADEMIC PUBLISHERS
Boston / Dordrecht / New York / London

Distributors for North, Central and South America:
Kluwer Academic Publishers
101 Philip Drive
Assinippi Park
Norwell, Massachusetts 02061 USA
Telephone (781) 871-6600
Fax (781) 681-9045
E-Mail: kluwer@wkap.com

Distributors for all other countries:
Kluwer Academic Publishers Group
Post Office Box 322
3300 AH Dordrecht, THE NETHERLANDS
Telephone 31 786 576 000
Fax 31 786 576 474
E-Mail: services@wkap.nl

 Electronic Services < http://www.wkap.nl >

Library of Congress Cataloging-in-Publication Data

Title: THE SYSTEMATICITY ARGUMENTS
Author: Kenneth Aizawa
ISBN: 1-4020-7271-6

A C.I.P. Catalogue record for this book is available
from the Library of Congress.

Printed on acid-free paper.

Printed in the United States of America.

For my parents, with much love.

CONTENTS

LIST OF FIGURES

PREFACE

This book addresses a part of a problem. The problem is to determine the architecture of cognition, that is, the basic structures and mechanisms underlying cognitive processing. This is a multidimensional problem insofar as there appear to be many distinct types of mechanisms that interact in diverse ways during cognitive processing. Thus, we have memory, attention, learning, sensation, perception, and who knows what else, interacting to produce behavior. As a case in point, consider a bit of linguistic behavior. To tell a friend that I think Greg won a stunning victory, I must evidently rely on various bits of information stored in my memory, including who my friends are, who Greg is, what he won, and what natural languages I share with my friend. I must sense and perceive that my friend is within hearing distance, how loud I need to speak, how loud I am speaking, and whether my friend is paying attention. I must avail myself of what I know about the language I share with my friend, along with innumerable principles about human "folk psychology." This book does not address the full range of contemporary theorizing about cognitive architecture, but only a part. It addresses theories of cognitive architecture that hypothesize that there exist cognitive representations, then begins to explore the possible structure of these representations.

One of the leading hypotheses concerning the structure of cognitive representations is that it is akin to that found in symbolic logic. The representations are thought to be like logical representations insofar as they have a combinatorial syntax and semantics. So familiar is the idea that it is often referred to as "Classicism." Although there are many conceivable alternatives to Classicism, some are more salient than others. One possibility is that cognitive representations are purely atomic, lacking both the syntactic and semantic combinatorial apparatus found in symbolic logic. Another possibility is that cognitive representations represent in the way in which Gödel numbers represent or in the way in which vectors of real numbers represent. This book does not address the full breadth of the issues about cognitive representations, but only a part. This part has to do with a family of productivity and systematicity arguments developed most forcefully by Jerry Fodor and Zenon Pylyshyn.

The common element in Fodor and Pylyshyn's arguments is that some generalization is offered as a putative fact about the nature of cognition, a fact that a theory of cognitive architecture should explain. In the productivity of thought argument, for example, it is alleged that human cognition allows for an unbounded number of distinct thoughts. In the systematicity of inference argument, it is alleged that the capacity for performing a given type of inference is really a capacity for a multiplicity of instances of that type of inference. Also common to these arguments is the Classicist contention that a Classical theory of cognitive representations explains these putative facts, where rival theories, such as those that maintain that cognitive representations are like vectors, do not. This book does not address all the issues that are involved in the systematicity and productivity arguments, but only a part. In particular, it addresses what might be called the "logic" of the arguments.

The systematicity and productivity arguments are ultimately empirical arguments for an empirical theory of human cognitive architecture. One might, therefore, think that we need empirical studies that show that cognition is, in fact, systematic and productive and, if so, just what sorts of systematic and productive regularities there are. Thereafter, one can focus on the extent to which rival theories of cognitive architecture are able to explain such systematic and productive regularities as empirical studies might bear out. Yet, while such studies have their place, the current situation in cognitive science appears to leave room for other work, work that one might think falls more naturally to a philosopher than to a psychologist. In reviewing the literature, one finds a wide range of vagaries, ambiguities, and confusions surrounding what is to be explained in the systematicity and productivity arguments. It is unclear to many, for example, what the productivity of thought is supposed to be and what the systematicity of inference amounts to. One also finds that the basic "logic" of the family of systematicity arguments has gone underappreciated. There has yet to be sufficient attention to Fodor and Pylyshyn's contention that the desired kind of explanation of the various systematic relations in thought requires more than that a theory should fit the data. The consequences of this lack of attention could hardly be greater. Among them is the fact that many non-Classical attempts to explain the systematic relations in thought are quite wide of the mark. More surprisingly, one finds that even Classicism cannot meet the most familiar explanatory challenges posed by the systematicity arguments.

So, the aim of the book is to clarify the premises and the reasoning involved in the productivity and systematicity arguments. The aim, therefore, is well-suited to the exercise of certain basic philosophical skills, such as making distinctions, close reading of texts, and an examination of arguments. It may be tempting, therefore, to object to this work by observing that the nature of cognitive architecture is an empirical matter to be settled by experiment, rather than armchair speculation. This temptation must, of course, be resisted. This book is not meant to resolve all the issues in the debates over cognitive architecture. Instead it is only supposed to be one component of the long-term empirical project of determining the architecture of cognition. The generation of new experimental results is a paradigmatic and crucial scientific activity, but it is not the only paradigmatic and crucial scientific activity. Just as important is the interpretation of the way in which particular experimental and observational results bear on theory. Once the data are in, one must still figure out what theoretical implications they have. Yet another paradigmatic scientific activity is the attempt to clarify scientific issues as an aid to the design of future experiments. Scientists across the disciplines must regularly try to imagine just what sorts of experiment they might design in order to evaluate a theory. The measure of success of the present philosophical exercise will be the extent to which it invites a reconsideration of some of the positions found in cognitive science, stimulates the clarification and resolution of some outstanding problems, and guides the application of relevant experimental results.

ACKNOWLEDGMENTS

For a long time I have seen my life as just my academic life. Thus, I appreciate the various book and journal editors who have accepted my work for publication. I have also enjoyed and benefited from philosophical interactions with people who have read my papers, commented on my papers, and listened to my conference presentations. These people include Fred Adams, Istvan Berkeley, John Bickle, Kevin Falvey, Gary Fuller, Bob Hadley, Jerry Fodor, Jay Garfield, Pim Haselager, Chris Hill, Cory Juhl, Brian McLaughlin, Bob Stecker, Victor Velarde, and Fritz Warfield. I owe a special debt to the Philosophy Department at the University of Maryland, College Park, for a postdoctoral fellowship that gave me time to think about the systematicity of thought, and many other things. Michael Devitt, Michael Morreau, Paul Pietroski, and Georges Rey helped me considerably by pressing for all manner of clarifications and elaborations at an early stage of the present work. Their demands have given me dozens of pages of work. Jay Garfield read and commented on a penultimate draft of the manuscript. Pim Haselager commented on several chapters, especially those with which he disagreed. Brian McLaughlin, both early and late, offered comments and suggestions that changed the character of the work in ways I think he cannot know, perhaps in ways of which he would not approve.

Yet, for a person who has seen his life as his curriculum vita, I do have personal debts I have to acknowledge. There are, of course, my parents, who have always been behind me, supporting whatever I do. I certainly could not have gotten this far without them. For over 20 years, Chris Hill has been reading my papers, encouraging their improvement. Fred Adams, Gary Fuller, Nolan Kaiser, and Bob Stecker were an outstanding group of colleagues in my first years as a professor. I may never have such fine colleagues again. Fred deserves a double thanks for supporting me. Were it not for his intellectual support and being a good bud, I might well have done something like become a physician so I could make a lot more money, live in a much bigger house in a much bigger city. Thanks, . . . I think. Then, there is my brother, Scott "Go for the money!" Aizawa. He's made my drive to work longer, but a helluva lot more fun.

Finally, there is Angie, who has made my life so much more than my curriculum vita. I love her immeasurably.

CHAPTER 1

THE STRUCTURE OF COGNITIVE
REPRESENTATIONS

The most significant area of debate separating Classical and Connectionist theories of cognition has been the family of systematicity and productivity arguments best known from Jerry Fodor and Zenon Pylyshyn's paper, "Connectionism and Cognitive Architecture: A Critical Analysis." These arguments are not the sole basis upon which to try to determine the nature of human cognitive architecture, but they are currently among the most prominent. In roughest outline, the arguments are quite simple. Thought displays certain features, namely, it is systematic, compositional, inferentially coherent, and productive. These features of thought can be better explained by a Classical theory of cognition than they can be by a Connectionist theory, hence there is some defeasible reason to prefer Classicism to Connectionism. Beyond this, however, there are ambiguities, vagaries, and confusions at all levels of detail. At the most general level, therefore, the aim of the present work is simply to clarify and refine the systematicity and productivity arguments, showing how the central ideas of these arguments may be applied to a range of theories of cognitive architecture.

1 SOME THEORIES OF COGNITIVE ARCHITECTURE

A reasonable first step in the work of clarification and refinement is to specify what is meant by "Classicism." The version of Classicism developed here will be the minimal conception that appears to be needed in order to account for the putative systematic and productive features of thought. Some components of this conception will be familiar from the literature and will be set out in this chapter. Other components will be less familiar and will have to be motivated by a consideration of the explanatory needs of the systematicity and productivity arguments. The present use of "Classicism" is, therefore, driven primarily by the nature of the explanatory project under consideration here, rather than by an attempt to be faithful to all uses of the term in the cognitive science literature. Perhaps a better name for the view could be chosen, but there is no obvious, less problematic alternative. Moreover, the view described here will be quite recognizable to many of those who take themselves to be Classicists.

Classicism presupposes that propositional attitudes play a prominent role in cognition.[1] That is, it presupposes that there must be some account of what it is for an agent to adopt a particular attitude toward a proposition. There must be some account of, for instance, what makes it the case that Laurent believes that the race is over and that Greg hopes that he will triumph in the end. What is it about Laurent and Greg that gives them these psychological capacities? Two hypotheses about cognitive architecture loom large here. One hypothesis, Representationalism, concerns the basis of the propositions to which agents are related; the other, the Computational Theory of the Attitudes (CTA), concerns the basis of the attitudes. Representationalists propose that an agent's attitude toward a proposition p is mediated by a representation r that means that p. Thus, underlying Laurent's thought that the race is over is a cognitive representation, a syntactic and semantic object of some sort, that means the race is over. On the Representationalist view, mental representations provide the physical basis for linking material agents to abstract propositions. According to the Computational Theory of the Attitudes, an agent's having an attitude is a matter of having certain computational characteristics. An agent believes something in virtue of one sort of computational characteristic, hopes for something in virtue of another, and fears something in virtue of yet another. At least part of what links a particular computational attitude, such as believing, to a particular proposition p, such as that the race is over, is that the hypothetical computer program of the mind is causally sensitive to the representation r that has the content p. In other words, there must at least be some instructions in the computer program of the mind that respond to the representation r. Putting Representationalism and CTA together, one has it that having an attitude A toward a proposition p is a matter of standing in some sort of computational relation to a representation r that means that p. Thus, Laurent's believing that the race is over amounts to Laurent standing in a "believing" computational relation to a representation r that means that the race is over.

The systematicity and productivity arguments are intended, in the first instance, to discriminate between Representationalist theories of cognitive architecture, leaving the Computational Theory of the Attitudes in a largely supporting role. Nevertheless, some comments clarifying CTA are in order. The Computational Theory of the Attitudes maintains that the hypothetical computer program of the mind is written in some Turing-equivalent, digital computational formalism. A "Turing-equivalent" formalism is one that computes exactly the same set of input-output functions that a Turing machine computes. This class of formalisms includes such familiar programming languages as C, C++, Basic, and Pascal. The notion of digital, as opposed to analogue, computation is more philosophically problematic. Present purposes might tolerate some simplification. Analogue computation allows for representational states being equinumerous with the real numbers. It allows that between any two representational states, there exists a third. By contrast, digital computation allows for representational states being at most equinumerous with the integers and that representational states are discrete. To avoid confusion, we shall always take "computation" to mean Turing-equivalent, digital computation, rather than some less clearly defined notion. So, one consequence of this terminological choice is that "computation" will not cover analogue computation. If we wish to talk about analogue computation, we shall use "analogue computation."

The hypothesis of the Computational Theory of the Attitudes must be contrasted with other claims with which it is often conflated. In particular, CTA does not maintain that the human brain is a von Neumann-style computer with memory registers and a single central processing unit. While one could hold these additional assumptions, they are not of the essence of CTA, hence arguments to the effect that the mind should not be viewed as a von Neumann-style computing device are not challenges to CTA *per se*. Thus, one can accept the argument that, given that electrical activity is distributed across the entire brain, it is unlikely that there is any one region of the brain that serves as a von Neumann-style central processing unit, all the while maintaining the Computational Theory of Attitudes. One can also accept the argument that, given the fact that brain lesion studies show that no one area of the brain is absolutely critical to all cognitive activity, it is unlikely that there is any one region of the brain that serves as a CPU, consisting with defending CTA. The advocate of the Computational Theory of the Attitudes can also accept the view that cognition involves parallel processing. This simply follows from the fact that digital, Turing-equivalent computation comes in both parallel and serial forms. Parallel and serial forms of Turing-equivalent computation allow the very same sets of functions to be computed. Refuting CTA, thus, requires more than arguments whose conclusions are that it is unlikely that the brain is a serial von Neumann style computing device.

As was just mentioned, the systematicity and productivity arguments are intended, in the first instance, to discriminate between Representationalist theories of cognitive architecture. Representationalist theories postulate that there exist vehicles of semantic content, that is, they postulate syntactic items that bear semantic content. Classicism adds to this a theory of the structure of these vehicles. According to Classicism, the vehicles in a system of cognitive representation have a combinatorial syntactic structure that makes a distinction between syntactically atomic and syntactically molecular representations. In a combinatorial syntactic system, one has a specified set of atomic syntactic items and rules or procedures for deriving well-formed, molecular syntactic items. Combinatorial syntactic systems can, thus, differ among themselves in their atomic symbols and in their allowable combinations of atoms. Thus, one system will have the syntactic atoms {A, B, C, D}, where another has {1, 2, 3}. One system will allow any finite string of atoms from the set to count as well-formed, where another will allow only palindromes. Clearly, the syntactically combinatorial systems best known to philosophers are those used in specifying well-formed formulae in systems of propositional and predicate logic.

In contrast to this familiar sort of syntactic combinatorialism, one might advance a species of representationalism according to which the vehicles of semantic content have no internal combinatorial syntactic structure. According to such syntactic atomism, no syntactic items are derived from other syntactic items. Instead, all the syntactic items are specified by an exhaustive list, such as {α, β, γ, δ, ε, ζ, η, θ, ι, κ, λ, μ, ν, ξ, ο, π, ρ, σ, τ, υ, φ, ψ, ω}. Such a system has no provision for deriving any syntactic expressions from any other syntactic expressions. Although such systems of representation are of little interest in most parts of logic, formal language theory, and linguistics, their existence will be relevant to some points of the systematicity arguments.

Just as there is a distinction to be made between combinatorial and atomistic syntax, so there is a distinction to be made between combinatorial and atomistic semantics. In a combinatorial semantic scheme, the meanings of some representations are a function of the meanings of some other representations and the way in which those representations are combined. Combinatorial semantic systems, thus, satisfy what linguists often refer to as the Principle of Semantic Compositionality. For philosophers, the best known semantic combinatorial system is, again, that used in systems of formal logic. By contrast, in an atomistic semantic system, a given syntactic object has the particular semantic content it does independent of the semantic content of all other syntactic objects. As a pragmatic matter, atomistic semantic systems may be found where relatively few diverse contents must be conveyed. So, for example, in baseball, the umpire's signs for ball and strike mean what they do apart from the meanings of any other signs and are not used in combinations. Of the two types of semantic theories, Classicism hypothesizes that cognitive representations have a combinatorial semantics.

With the distinctions we have made so far, we can specify a relatively elementary theory of cognitive architecture that stands in contrast to Classicism, namely, Pure Atomism. This theory endorses the Computational Theory of the Attitudes and is a species of Representationalism that maintains that cognitive representations are both syntactically and semantically atomic. Pure Atomism stands in contrast to two logically possible types of Mixed Atomism. One form of Mixed Atomism maintains that cognitive representations are syntactically combinatorial, but semantically atomic; the other maintains that cognitive representations are syntactically atomic, but semantically combinatorial. As an example of the former type of Mixed Atomistic system, one can envision a system in which one assigns Arabic numerals to propositions. Arabic numerals use a set of ten syntactic atoms, i.e., the set {0, 1, ..., 9}, and have a combinatorial syntax that allows the derivation of larger syntactic molecules. The semantics in this Mixed Atomistic system, however, is atomistic in the sense that the meaning of any given syntactic item is independent of the meaning of any other syntactic item. The meaning of each Arabic numeral is simply specified by an exhaustive list. An example of the latter type of Mixed Atomistic system, where the semantics is combinatorial and the syntax atomic, is a bit more strained. Consider a finite set of syntactic atoms {α, β, γ, δ, ε, ζ, η, θ, ι, κ, λ, μ}. Among these syntactic atoms, some will serve as semantic atoms in the following way.

"α" means Greg will triumph,
"β" means the race is over,
"γ" means conjunction, and
"δ" means disjunction.

The semantic interpretation of the remaining symbols will be determined by a function F,

F (α, α, γ) = ε, meaning Greg will triumph and Greg will triumph,
F (α, β, γ) = ζ, meaning Greg will triumph and the race is over,
F (β, α, γ) = η, meaning the race is over and Greg will triumph,
F (β, β, γ) = θ, meaning the race is over and the race is over,
F (α, α, δ) = ι, meaning Greg will triumph or Greg will triumph,
F (α, β, δ) = κ, meaning Greg will triumph or the race is over,
F (β, α, δ) = λ, meaning the race is over or Greg will triumph, and
F (β, β, δ) = μ, meaning the race is over or the race is over.

In other words, F uses the meanings of the symbols {α, β, γ, δ} and the ordering of these symbols in triplets as a basis for assigning meaning to the symbols {ε, ζ, η, θ, ι, κ, λ, μ}.

While the Mixed Atomistic views are largely mere curiosities, the view we call "Pure Atomism" has been discussed in the literature in different terms. Fodor, (1987), applies the systematicity and productivity arguments to Pure Atomism. In addition, Fodor & Pylyshyn, (1988), implicitly attribute a theory much like Pure Atomism to Connectionism. This gives us some reason to consider Pure Atomism. Another reason, however, is that we can first use the systematicity and productivity arguments to compare Classicism and Pure Atomism. This allows us to put off the specification of more complicated and problematic non-Classical theories of cognitive architecture while we make our first pass through the expository challenges of the systematicity and productivity arguments.

The notions of combinatorial syntax and semantics we have just considered should be familiar to most philosophers. By contrast, the next hypothesis implicit in Classicism is likely to be salient only to those who are familiar with the debate over the systematicity arguments. It concerns an assumption implicit in familiar representational systems, such as propositional and predicate logic. Classicism is said to embody a particular kind of combinatorialism, namely, concatenative combinatorialism. In a concatenative system of representation, a complex representation literally contains as proper parts all the representations from which it is derived. This idea can be applied to both syntactic and semantic combinatorialism. Thus, a syntactically complex expression literally contains as proper parts all the syntactic expressions from which it is derived and a semantically complex expression literally contains as proper parts all the semantic components from which it is derived. Again, the syntactically and semantically complex representations found in formal logic illustrate the idea. Any token of the syntactically and semantically complex representation "P&Q" will contain as literal proper parts, a content-bearing syntactic item "P", a content-bearing syntactic item "&," and a content-bearing syntactic item "Q."

In opposition to Classicism's concatenative combinatorialism, certain non-Classicists have advanced the idea that cognitive representations display what we might call "functional combinatorialism."[2] Functional combinatorialism requires of cognitive representations only a) that there exist a mapping from a set of atoms to any complex expression derived from it and b) that there exist a mapping from a complex representation to its atoms. More restrictive species of functional combinatorialism might require that one or the other or both of the two mappings be computable. Van Gelder's (1990) version, for example, requires computability of both mappings. While one might imagine that a distinction between functional and concatenative combinatorialism could be applied to both syntax and semantics, it appears that the non-Classicists who wish to use a notion of functional combinatorialism in a response to the systematicity and productivity arguments intend to apply the distinction only to semantics. The idea is that in a functionally combinatorial semantics, there need exist only a computable mapping from a complex semantic expression to its semantic atoms and a computable mapping from a set of semantic atoms to any semantic complex derived from it. In order to allow for an unbounded supply of cognitive representations, however, functionally combinatorial representations allow for concatenatively combinatorial syntax. It is this manner of using the notion of functional combinatorialism that we will here designate "Functional Combinatorialism."

As we shall see, the principal motivation underlying functional combinatorialism is to have a theory of the structure of representations that can hope to account for the systematic and productive features of thought, while at the same time not becoming either a Classical theory or a Pure Atomist theory. In fact, the most popular forms of functionally combinatorial theories, those that adopt a concatenative combinatorial syntax and a functionally combinatorial semantics, also avoid being Mixed Atomist theories. Recall that the Mixed

Atomistic theories adopt either an atomistic syntax and a combinatorial semantics, or a combinatorial syntax and an atomistic semantics.

To flesh out our concepts of concatenative and functional combinatorial representations a bit more, we may consider leading examples of each. As examples of concatenative systems, we have already mentioned the propositional and predicate logics, but the category might be thought to embrace more general sentential representations as well as imagistic representations. The core idea behind sentential and imagistic representations is simply that sentential representations represent in the way sentences of natural language do (whatever exactly that amounts to), while imagistic representations represent in the way images or photographs do (whatever exactly that amounts to). As a consequence of their mode of representation, sentential and imagistic representations appear to differ in the range of items they might be used to represent. Sentential representations have syntactic atoms consisting of things for which there can be words, while imagistic representations have syntactic atoms consisting of things for which there can be images. So, one might think there are plenty of words for truth, justice, and beauty, but images of these are a bit of a stretch. A photograph of a blindfolded woman holding a scale might be thought to be an imagistic representation of justice, but, then again, it might be an imagistic representation of a blindfolded woman holding a scale. Sentential and imagistic representations also differ in the way in which they form complex, molecular representations. Sentential atoms can be combined into larger structures via linguistic combinatorial procedures, such as linear ordering, while imagistic representations are combined into larger images by two-dimensional spatial arrangement. Despite the differences just enumerated, linguistic and imagistic representations are concatenative combinatorial representations.

Two popular examples of functionally combinatorial representations are Gödel numerals and representations with vectors.[3] If the syntactic item "1" means "the", the syntactic item "2" means "race", the syntactic item "3" means "is", and the syntactic item "5" means "over," these can be used as the exponents in a function to determine another numeral. Thus, $37,815,750 (= 2^1 \times 3^2 \times 5^3 \times 7^5)$ would mean the race is over. In this case, "37,815,750" retains the familiar concatenative combinatorial syntax of Arabic numerals, but not the familiar concatenative combinatorial semantics. The meaning of the syntactic molecule "37,815,750" will not be a function of the meanings of the tokens of "3", "7", "8", and so forth that appear within it. Instead, the meaning of "37,815,750" is a function of the meanings of the numerals that were the arguments of the arithmetic function used to derive it. In a vector addition model of functional combinatorialism, we might suppose that the vector | 2 7 3 | represents John and the vector | 5 4 3 | represents sleeps. One might, then, represent the proposition that John sleeps by adding the vector representation of John to the vector representation of sleeps thereby producing the vector | 7 11 6 |. In this case, the syntax of the components in the matrices is the usual concatenative combinatorialism found in the Arabic numeral system, but the semantics is not concatenative. The meaning of | 7 11 6 | is not a function of any of the parts which it literally contains.

Classicists and various non-Classicists embrace a notion of semantic combinatorialism according to which the meaning of some expressions is a function of the meaning of the parts of those expressions and the way in which those expressions are derived. In other words, Classicists and some non-Classicists adopt what linguists generally refer to as the Principle of Semantic Compositionality. So described, however, the principle is rather weak, insofar as it does not specify the nature of the function from semantic atoms and the nature of the derivation to semantic molecules. To see this, consider two semantic interpretation functions F_1 and F_2. Both F_1 and F_2 have it that "John" means John, "loves" means loves, and "Mary" means Mary. Both also take into consideration the order of combination of the syntactic items in "John loves Mary" and "Mary loves John" when they assign a content. They differ, however, in the following way. According to F_1 (the "standard" semantic interpretation function),

the syntactic item "John loves Mary" means John loves Mary, and
the syntactic item "Mary loves John" means Mary loves John.

According to F_2 (a non-standard semantic interpretation function), however,

the syntactic item "John loves Mary" means Laurent believes he will win, and
the syntactic item "Mary loves John" means Greg hopes he can triumph.

According to both F_1 and F_2, the meanings of the complex expressions "John loves Mary" and "Mary loves John" are functions of the meanings of their parts and the way in which those parts are put together. Thus, by requiring that a semantic theory meet the Principle of Semantic Compositionality, one does not thereby require a semantic combinatorial function like F_1 rather than F_2.

In truth, all semantic combinatorialists are implicitly interested in something stronger than the Principle of Semantic Compositionality. Classicists, in particular, are interested in a particular specification of the functional relationship between the meaning of complex expressions, on the one hand, and their constituent semantic parts and mode of combination, on the other. They are interested in a principle that requires that the semantic interpretation be like F_1, rather than like F_2. A reasonable candidate in this regard is the hypothesis that a given syntactic item must make the same semantic contribution to each formula to which it makes any contribution. Call this the Principle of Context Independence.[4]   So, if "Greg" provides the content Greg to the expressions "Laurent didn't beat Greg in the race," "Greg loves winning," and "Greg hopes he will win," then these representations will satisfy both the Principle of Semantic Compositionality and the Principle of Context Independence. In all the forms of semantic combinatorialism we discuss, both principles will be in play in some form.

We are now in a position to offer a preliminary accounting of Classicism and Functional Combinatorialism. Classicism maintains that propositional attitudes are constituted by computational relations to representations that have concatenatively combinatorial syntactic and semantic structure that also satisfy the Principle of Context Independence. Functional Combinatorialism, as we shall understand it, maintains that propositional attitudes are constituted by computational relations to representations that have a concatenatively combinatorial syntax, but a functionally combinatorial semantics that respects a version of the Principle of Context Independence. The foregoing is very close to what Classicists have presented in the literature as their theory for explaining the systematicity and productivity of thought. By contrast, what is offered on behalf of Functional Combinatorialism may differ from what these non-Classicists have in mind. This is, in part, because of a lack of clarity on the part of the advocates of the theory. In any event, we shall have much more to say about these theories of cognitive architecture in subsequent chapters.

As a final point of clarification concerning Classicism, it might be worthwhile distancing the form of Classicism developed here from the logically stronger idea that cognitive representations are linguistic. While many Classicists, including Fodor, are committed to the hypothesis that cognitive representations are linguistic, rather than imagistic, this linguistic Classicism is not a view supported by the productivity and systematicity arguments. In other words, the systematicity and productivity arguments do not serve to discriminate between the hypothesis that cognitive representations are linguistic and the hypothesis that they are imagistic. The case for linguistic cognitive representations as opposed to imagistic cognitive representations has to do with expressive power. Those Classicists who champion linguistic representations over imagistic representations typically argue that representational limitations on images indicate that not all cognitive representations can be imagistic. We earlier hinted at the difficulty in representing abstract objects or concepts, such as truth, justice, and beauty. In addition, one might wonder how images might represent both "modal" and "non-modal" thoughts, thoughts such as that it might rain as opposed to that it is raining. Further, one can ask how images could respect the difference between what we might call disjunctive, conjunctive, and conditional thoughts, thoughts such as "John sees rain or John will carry an umbrella," "John sees rain and carries an umbrella," and "If John sees rain, then John will carry an umbrella"? So, to reiterate, we shall mean by "Classicism" simply the view that cognitive representations to which the mechanisms in a Computational Theory of the Attitudes are causally sensitive have a concatenative combinatorial syntax and semantics which respects the Principle of Context Independence. Our "Classicism" is not committed to the thesis that cognitive representations are linguistic in nature. It is formulated this way since our present aim is the articulation of a version of Classicism attuned to the explanatory challenges of the systematicity and productivity arguments.

With our pass through Pure Atomism a few pages back and our current take on Classicism and Functional Combinatorialism, we turn to Connectionism. In the literature, the term "Connectionism" covers a wide range of hypotheses, none of which seems to be canonical and some sets of which are, in fact, mutually inconsistent. Nevertheless, in all the forms of Connectionism that are subject to the productivity and systematicity arguments, there are mathematical structures and relations of the sort laid out in, for example, Rumelhart, Hinton, and McClelland (1986). According to this form of Connectionism, cognition involves networks of nodes with weighted connections between them. The most basic process in these networks is the so-called propagation of activation. In these networks, each node receives an input, produces an activation value, and produces an output value. The relations between inputs, activation values, and outputs are specified by mathematical equations. Thus, more formally, for each node, there exist functions f_1 and f_2 such that f_1(input value) = activation value and f_2(activation value) = output value. Nodes interact with each other by passing output values along weighted connections with the weights on the connections modulating the effect one node has on other nodes to which it is connected. The function,

$g(\text{output}_1, \text{weight}_1, \text{output}_2, \text{weight}_2, \ldots, \text{output}_n, \text{weight}_n) = \text{input}_p,$

provides a more formal description of this relation for the case of the set of nodes 1-n connected to a single node p.

Although, in principle, nodes may be interconnected in any number of ways, in research practice, they are generally grouped into some fairly standard "layered" structures. Figure 1.1 shows a simple feed-forward network in which there is a set of nodes constituting an input layer, another set constituting an intermediate "hidden" layer, and a third set constituting a final output layer. In this network, every node in the input layer is connected to every node in the hidden layer and every node in the hidden layer is connected to every node in the output layer. Figure 1.2 shows a simple recurrent network in which activation propagates from a set of input nodes, to a set of hidden nodes, to a set of context nodes, back to the hidden nodes, and finally to the output nodes. As in the simple feed-forward network, every input node is connected to every hidden node and every hidden node is connected to every output node, but the hidden nodes are mapped one-to-one to the context nodes and the context nodes are connected one-to-one back to the hidden nodes. All the examples of Connectionist networks that we will examine have a simple layered structure of the sort found in the figures.

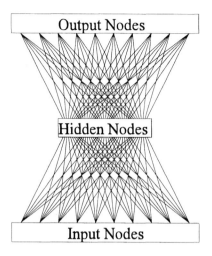

Figure 1.1. A simple feedforward network.

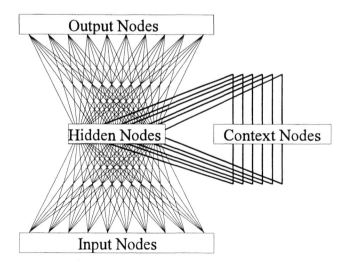

Figure 1.2. A simple recurrent network.

The process of activation propagation in the mathematical hardware of simple feed-forward networks and simple recurrent networks can be deployed in a number of ways in an attempt to model cognitive processing. To take a simple example with the feed-forward network, one might have the activation values of the nodes in the input layer represent the present tense form of a verb and let the output values of the nodes in the output layer represent the past tense form of the verb. With a suitable representational scheme on the input and output layers and a suitable set of functional relations between the inputs, activation values, output values, and weights, such a network could take as input the present tense form of a verb and provide as output the corresponding past tense form. Alternatively, with a different representational scheme and functional relations, the same network might produce a person's name as output in response to a person's face as input. In simple recurrent networks, the most interesting aspect of activation propagation is that the state of activation of the context nodes can act as a kind of short term memory for the network. In other words, the context nodes can store information about a sequence of previous inputs that can in turn be used to determine an output for the network. So, in such a network, a string of words might be sequentially presented to the network so that the pattern of activation on the context nodes comes to represent the entire string. The output of the network after the final word of the string is presented could constitute the network's conjecture as to the grammaticality or ungrammaticality of the input string.

Although all connectionist networks propagate activation, what is much more interesting for practicing Connectionist researchers is the capacity to modify the input-output relations in a network by modification of the weights on the connections. This weight change constitutes the basis for a Connectionist theory of learning and memory formation. By far the most popular method for changing weights has been the family of "back-propagation" weight change procedures. These are most commonly applied to simple feedforward networks, although they are also applicable to simple recurrent networks. Back-propagation can be applied to a network like that in Figure 1.1 whose initial state involves small randomly assigned weights on all the connections. The network will then propagate activation in the manner sketched above. The actual output of the network will then be compared with a target output that the network should have produced. The difference between an output node's actual output and its target output defines an error term for that node. A node's error term provides a basis upon which to modify the weights feeding into the node. Thus, the error terms for the output layer provide a basis for changing the weights on all the connections feeding into the output layer from the hidden layer. In addition, the error terms provide the basis for changing the weights feeding into the hidden layer from the input layer. Thus, activation propagates forward through the network, while error terms and weight changes propagate backwards through the net, hence the name "back-propagation" weight change. By iterating the process of activation propagation and error back-propagation, making small incremental changes on the weights, it is generally possible to have a given network closely approximate any desired input-output mapping. What distinguishes the individual members of the back-propagation family of weight change procedures from each other are various parameter values and functional relations that determine how weights will be in changed in response to errors.

To reiterate, Connectionism will here be understood as the theory that the mathematical hardware of nodes with modifiable weights on connections is a suitable basis for a theory of cognition. Perhaps a more apt description for this view is "Bare Connectionism," since it leaves completely unspecified how the mathematical hardware is to be related to a theory of cognition. In particular, "Connectionism," or "Bare Connectionism," so specified makes no commitment regarding the existence or structure of cognitive representations. Thus, Connectionists may, in principle, be Non-Representationalists, Pure Atomists, Functional Combinatorialists, and even Classical Representationalists. Though this loose understanding of Connectionism does not conform to all estimations of what Connectionism "really" is, this understanding allows us to respect the theoretical flexibility of the various ideas that have gone under the heading "Connectionism," while at the same time addressing it in whatever form it takes. So, we can apply the systematicity and productivity arguments to Fodor and Pylyshyn's relatively narrow conception of Connectionism as embodying Pure Atomism, but we can also see how to apply the productivity and systematicity arguments to other forms of Connectionism and other theories of cognitive architecture that might be developed in support of Connectionism.

2 OUTLINE FOR THE BOOK

In this book, the phrase "the systematicity arguments" will be used, as it has been so far, as a blanket term to cover the family of arguments that Fodor & Pylyshyn, (1988), that appear in their discussions of the systematicity of inference, the systematicity of cognitive representations, and the compositionality of representations, as well as the variations on these arguments. Similarly, the phrase "the productivity arguments" will be used to cover the collection of arguments that have at various times gone under this heading. When we wish to say something about one of the arguments in particular, we shall have recourse to one of the more specific names.

With sketches of the leading theories of cognitive architecture on the table, we might turn to the book's plan for bringing the productivity and systematicity arguments to bear on them. Probably the most important, and least appreciated, feature of the systematicity arguments is the fact that they are meant to embody a particular explanatory standard over and above mere fit of the data.[5] Because of this importance and lack of appreciation, Chapter 2 will be devoted to some history and philosophy of science aimed at cultivating intuitions about the kind of explanatory standard that is at work. Chapter 2 will examine some arguments for Copernican astronomy over Ptolemaic astronomy and for evolution over creationism. This examination will provide some grounds for a theoretical characterization of a class of explanatory confirmations, a characterization that will be helpful when it comes to understanding the systematicity and productivity arguments. Chapter 2 will also begin to make the case for saying that the explanatory standard embodied in these historical examples is the standard that Fodor and Pylyshyn have in mind in their critique of Connectionism.

Chapters 3 through 6 will constitute a first pass through the family of systematicity and productivity arguments as a means of supporting Classicism against Pure Atomism. In these chapters, we compare Classicism and Pure Atomism, because of the simplicity of Pure Atomism. This enables us to focus more single-mindedly on features of the arguments themselves. These features include what is to be explained in the arguments and how the intuitions and analysis developed in Chapter 2 might be extended to the debates over cognitive representation.

Chapter 3 will begin with a look at the way the productivity argument bears on Classicism and Pure Atomism. There we will see that, in the productivity argument, Pure Atomism does not run afoul of the sort of explanatory standard discussed in Chapter 2, since that explanatory standard is not in play in the productivity argument. Instead, Pure Atomism does not account for productivity insofar as it violates certain fundamental principles of computation in physical systems. This discussion of the productivity arguments will delay our examination of the systematicity arguments and the role of explanatory power in these arguments, but is warranted for two reasons. A proper understanding of the productivity arguments promotes, and, at times, is essential to, a proper understanding of the systematicity arguments. In addition, the productivity arguments must be examined at some point in the book and there is no other equally useful place to do this.

Each of Chapters 4 through 6 will focus primarily on one specific component of Fodor and Pylyshyn's case for Classicism. Chapter 4 will examine the systematicity of inference, Chapter 5 the systematicity of cognitive representations, and Chapter 6 the compositionality of representations. All three chapters will share a roughly common structure, beginning with an introduction and explication of what is to be explained in specific arguments (the explananda), followed by Pure Atomist and Classical accounts, and an analysis of the extent to which these theories are able to account for the relevant explananda to the standard that is implicit in Fodor and Pylyshyn's original critique.

While there are commonalities of structure unifying these chapters, they do differ among themselves in matters of emphasis and in their technical dimensions. Chapter 4 has three principal distinguishing characteristics. First, a significant portion of it will be aimed at driving home the analogy between the systematicity of inference argument and the explanatory arguments examined in Chapter 2. In later chapters, the analogy will need less emphasis. Second, another significant portion of the chapter will be devoted to a review of the competence/performance distinction is and how it is involved in these arguments. The third, and probably most surprising, feature of the chapter is the conclusion that neither Pure Atomism nor Classicism explains the systematicity of inference to the standard of explanation that Fodor and Pylyshyn evidently have in mind. At this point, the case for Classicism is made worse.

Chapter 5 repeats many of the observations and conclusions drawn in Chapter 4. It shows how the systematicity of cognitive representations argument might be viewed as sharing a common pattern with the historical examples from Chapter 2 and with the systematicity of inference argument. It also argues for the view that neither Pure Atomism nor Classicism explains the systematicity of cognitive representations to the standard implicit in Fodor and Pylyshyn's critique. To a fair extent, therefore, Chapter 5 may be viewed as consolidating the sorts of considerations and conclusions brought forth in Chapter 4.

The Chapter 6 treatment of the compositionality of representations will contain a surprise or two. Chapter 6 argues that, given the common understanding of what is to be explained regarding the content relations among possible occurrent thoughts, Classicism fares no better at explaining this to the standard implicit in Fodor & Pylyshyn, (1988), than does Pure Atomism. This is the kind of result for which Chapters 4 and 5 prepare us. By the end of Chapter 6, however, the situation for Classicism improves. There we see that some of what Fodor and Pylyshyn have to say in their discussion of the content relations in thought can be developed in such a way that Classicism does explain things that Pure Atomism does not. The idea, in briefest form, is that Classicism, but not Pure Atomism, can explain why it is that agents with counterfactually dependent thoughts also have occurrent thoughts that are content related. Here, we have an argument that will establish a significant theoretical advantage of Classicism over its rivals.

Later chapters in many ways break from the pattern set in Chapters 3 through 6. Where Chapters 3 through 6 apply the systematicity and productivity arguments to Pure Atomism, Chapter 7 applies them to two Connectionist networks more or less explicitly intended as responses to the systematicity arguments. The first of these models is David Chalmers's (1990) model of active-passive transformations; the second is Robert Hadley and Michael

Hayward's (1997) model realizing a conception of strong semantic systematicity. In this chapter, the case is made that, not only do these other theories fail to explain the familiar versions of the systematicity and productivity arguments, they also fail to explain the less familiar argument articulated in Chapter 6.

Chapter 8 shows how one might apply the productivity and systematicity arguments to Functional Combinatorialism. Although there is reason to worry about how Functional Combinatorialism has been characterized in the literature, this issue will largely be finessed by considering the two most popular examples of it. If either species of Functional Combinatorialism fails to explain a given type of productivity or systematicity, then Functional Combinatorialism *per se* does not explain that type. The first example we consider is based on the hypothesis that cognitive representations are Gödel numerals. The idea that cognitive representations are Gödel numerals is generally not offered as a serious hypothesis about cognitive architecture, but instead as an illustration of the potential explanatory power of a theory of Functional Combinatorialism. That is the spirit in which it will be examined here. The second example is the hypothesis that cognitive representations fit the specifications of Paul Smolensky's (1995) Tensor Product Theory (TPT). Fodor and McLaughlin, (1990), and Fodor, (1996), have criticized versions of Smolensky's TPT at length, but not primarily from the angle that is pursued here. Fodor and McLaughlin have been concerned primarily with the causal efficacy of tensor product representations, an idea that does not appear in the original Fodor & Pylyshyn, (1988). Chapter 8, however, pursues a somewhat more conservative line. It uses the explanatory standard implicit in Fodor and Pylyshyn's original critique to show that, not only do Functionally Combinatorial theories fail to explain the explananda to which Fodor and Pylyshyn draw greatest attention, Functional Combinatorialism also does not explain the co-occurrence of counterfactual dependencies and content relations among thoughts.

For the majority of the book, the systematicity and productivity arguments focus on theories of cognitive architecture that are committed to, or at least allow for, the form of Representationalism and the Computational Theory of the Attitudes described above. This may suggest that the systematicity and productivity arguments are applicable only to cognitive theories of this type. Yet, insofar as the systematicity and productivity of thought are *bona fide* features of cognition, they will be features of cognition that, *prima facie*, even those who reject Representationalism and the Computational Theory of the Attitudes must explain. In Chapter 9, we relate the systematicity and productivity arguments to a theory of cognitive architecture that explicitly rejects Representationalism and the Computational Theory of the Attitudes, namely, Robert Cummins's theory of cognitive content. Among the principal conclusions of this chapter is that, although Cummins's theory is in some respects, non-Classical, it succeeds in accounting for the systematicity and productivity of thought insofar as it adopts the kind of semantic and syntactic combinatorialism that is at the heart of Classicism. While this chapter will constitute a kind of digression for those only interested in Connectionism and its associated theories, Cummins's work is of sufficient significance that it merits the attention.

Chapter 10 constitutes a break from the line of exposition of the rest of the book. It provides a kind of motivation for Connectionists to take the productivity and systematicity arguments more seriously. This chapter tries to make more vivid the empirical risks psychologists take when they adopt the Connectionist approach to taking the brain seriously. These risks go beyond those associated with the fact that neuroscience and Connectionism are empirical enterprises, hence fraught with the empirical risks associated with any science. The risk is that, while there must eventually be some alignment between theories in cognitive psychology and theories in neuroscience, there are various reasons to think that the time is not ripe for this. Premature attempts at linking neuroscience and psychology run the risk of misguiding, rather than guiding, psychology. Chapter 10 spells this out in greater detail.

The aim of this book is to contribute to the advancement of the debate over cognitive architecture by clarifying the logic of the productivity and systematicity arguments. Throughout the book, there will be hints about topics that might bear closer or more extended examination. In addition, Chapter 11 concludes the book by drawing attention to a number of the more significant unresolved issues and problems that accumulate over the course of the book. Some of these are more thoroughly philosophical issues, while others are more experimental. Clearly, both components have their role to play in the determination of the architecture of cognition.

NOTES

1. What follows will be familiar to readers of Loewer & Rey, (1991).

2. van Gelder, (1990), develops a version of this idea.

3. In this paragraph, the distinction between numbers and numerals will be ignored for the sake of expository convenience. A proper exposition of the Gödel numerals idea including more technical details will be given later.

4. Although Fodor & Pylyshyn, (1988), refer to this as the "Principle of Semantic Compositionality," this choice is suboptimal. In the first place, linguists use the phrase "Principle of Semantic Compositionality" to refer simply to the idea that the meaning of a complex representation is a function of the meanings of its parts and the way in which those parts are put together. In the second place, the name is not an apt description for what is intended. Discussion in Fodor & Lepore, (1999), suggests that a more apt name for this idea is the "Principle of Context

Independence." It is this latter suggestion that prompts current usage. Thanks go to Barbara Abbott for drawing my attention to Fodor and Lepore's usage. Goschke & Koppelberg, (1991), p. 138, describe what we mean by the Principle of Context Independence in terms of context-free constituents.

5. Cases where it appears that the explanatory standard is ignored include Chalmers, (1990), Garson, (1994), Niklasson and van Gelder, (1994), Cummins, (1996b), and Hadley and Hayward, (1997). Interestingly, McLaughlin, (1993a, 1993b), a defender of the systematicity arguments, develops the arguments in a way that understates, if not entirely omits, this feature of the arguments.

CHAPTER 2

SOME HISTORY AND PHILOSOPHY
OF SCIENCE

One way in which scientific theories are confirmed by data is by finding instances in which observations conform to a theory's law-like generalizations. So, when Newton's theory along with initial and boundary conditions enables an astronomer to accurately predict the successive positions of the planets, one has some measure of confirmation for Newtonian gravitation theory. Such articulation of theory in order to fit the available data is a paradigmatic scientific activity. Yet, it appears that not all scientific reasoning works this way. Sometimes scientific reasoning attempts to show that, even though two theories are able to accommodate a given body of data, one theory can accommodate it or explain it better than can its rival. Copernicans thought they had such reasoning to provide against Ptolemaic astronomy. Charles Darwin thought he had such reasoning against the creationism of his day. In these cases, the Copernicans and the Darwinians thought they had at least a *prima facie* reason to believe that their theory better explains a given body of data. While one paradigmatic scientific activity is fitting theory to data, another paradigmatic scientific activity is showing how one theory better fits a given body of facts than does its rival.

A central contention of this book is that the systematicity arguments involve this latter kind of scientific reasoning. While fitting theory to data is a part of what the systematicity arguments are about, they are also essentially committed to more than this. They involve some notion of a preferred kind of account of the data. The initial motivation for this contention is the need to make sense of various Classicist comments such as the following:

A Connectionist can certainly model a mental life in which, if you can reason from P&Q&R to P, then you can also reason from P&Q to P. . . . But notice that *a Connectionist can equally model a mental life in which you get one of these inferences and not the other* (Fodor & Pylyshyn, 1988, pp.47-48, italics in the original),

The point of the problem that systematicity poses for a Connectionist account is not to show that systematic cognitive processes are *possible* given the assumptions of a Connectionist architecture, but to explain how systematicity could be *necessary* . . . given those assumptions (Fodor & McLaughlin, 1990, p. 202, italics in the original).

More recently, Fodor has added these very suggestive comments,

> Human cognition exhibits a complex of closely related properties–including systematicity, productivity, and compositionality–which a theory of cognitive architecture ignores at its peril. If you are stuck with a theory that denies that cognition has these properties, you are dead and gone. If you are stuck with a theory that is compatible with cognition having these properties but is unable to explain why it has them, you are, though arguably still breathing, clearly in deep trouble (Fodor, 1996, p. 109).

These passages clearly indicate that the Classicists, at least at times, think that something more is needed in the systematicity arguments than merely accommodating the data, hence provide some initial reason to explore the possibility that the systematicity arguments have a structure in common with other explanatory arguments in the history of science. A second, and ultimately more significant, reason to explore the foregoing possibility is that finding this more demanding explanatory standard ultimately indicates a strength that Classicism has against its rivals. This more significant reason will unfold over the course of the next several chapters.

This chapter is the first step in what is meant to be a methodical exploration of the kind of reasoning that underlies the systematicity arguments. It will attempt to clarify the nature and significance of explanatory arguments where scientists have maintained that one theory can explain a given body of data better than can a rival. A reasonable way of doing this is through some examples taken from the history of science. The first pair of examples are taken from the history of Copernican and Ptolemaic positional astronomy. They involve what are now textbook examples of the methodological advantages of explanatory elegance over coverage of data. The second pair of examples is from Charles Darwin's *Origin of Species*. In all these examples we see that there exists an empirical regularity for which two theories provide accounts. One theory, however, provides a better explanation for this regularity, hence giving us some defeasible reason to prefer one theory over another. The examples will be described in a preliminary way in sections 2.1 and 2.2 before a more extensive analysis is advanced in section 2.3. In this more extensive analysis, we see ways to refine what Fodor and Pylyshyn say these explanatory arguments demand. In addition to examining these historical explanatory arguments, we shall make some initial steps to relate them to the systematicity arguments.

1 COPERNICAN AND PTOLEMAIC ASTRONOMY

Quite early in the history of astronomy, it was observed that, in addition to the multitude of stars that remained fixed relative to each other, there exists a small number of bodies that wander through the stars.[1] While it was not possible to describe precisely the motions of these wanderers, the planets, some gross regularities were quite evident. Among the simplest was the fact that, if one traced the motions of Mercury, Venus, and the Sun through the fixed stars over the course of several years, one would find that Mercury and Venus were never found in opposition to the Sun. That is, one could never find the Sun at one point in the sky and Mercury or Venus at another point separated by 180° of arc. More specifically, Mercury could always be found within about 28° of arc from the Sun and Venus always within about 45°. Put in other words, Mercury and Venus displayed a limited elongation from the Sun. In this respect, Mercury and Venus differed from the "superior" planets Mars, Jupiter, and Saturn, which could be found in opposition to the Sun. A second significant qualitative regularity in the motions of the planets was the fact that the superior planets always go through retrograde motion at opposition. Retrograde motion refers to the change in direction of the motion of a planet through the fixed stars. Although usually moving through the sky in a west to east direction relative to the fixed stars, the superior planets periodically slow in their eastward movement, begin to move westward for some time, then again slow and resume their eastward movement. (See Figure 2.1.) Here, then, we have two important astronomical regularities that must be explained: 1) Mercury and Venus are never found in opposition to the Sun and 2) the superior planets always go through retrograde motions while in opposition to the Sun.

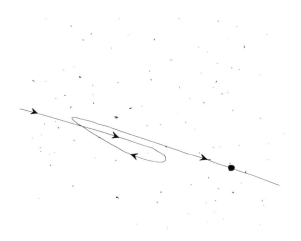

Figure 2.1. Retrograde motion.

Both Copernican and Ptolemaic theories were able to provide accounts of the motions of the planets that were in rough accord with the phenomena, albeit in quite different ways. Consider, first, the accounts available in what is to us the more familiar Copernican heliocentric system. On the heliocentric hypothesis, the ordering of the planets in terms of their distances from the Sun can be fixed as Mercury, Venus, Earth, Mars, Jupiter, and Saturn. Given this order, the two phenomena we have alluded to fall out automatically, of necessity one might say. By visual inspection of Figure 2.2, it is clear why Mercury can never appear in opposition to the Sun. Given that they orbit the Sun with a radius smaller than that of the Earth, the appearances must be as they are. The account of Venus is essentially the same. Further, by visual inspection of Figure 2.2, one can see that retrograde motions must be due to the faster moving Earth overtaking a slower moving superior planet. The superior planets do not genuinely reverse their direction of motion; they only appear to do so against the backdrop of the supposedly fixed stars. Further, it is clear from this why retrograde motions of the superior planets must always occur when the superior planets are in opposition.

Like the Copernican system, the Ptolemaic geocentric system could provide a qualitatively accurate account of the foregoing phenomena using the basic construction of an epicycle attached to a deferent.[2] (See Figure 2.3. The line from the earth to D is the deferent. The line from D to the planet is the epicycle. The epicycles, deferents, and the sizes of the planets and the sun are not drawn to scale.) In order to account for the fact that Mercury is never far from the Sun,

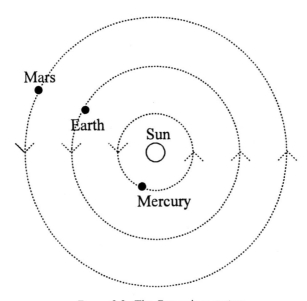

Figure 2.2. The Copernican system.

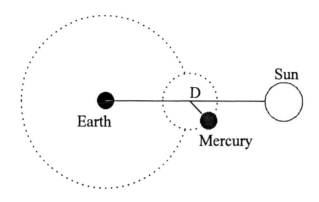

Figure 2.3. A Ptolemaic model.

one supposes that the Sun lacks an epicycle and that the deferents of Mercury and the Sun are collinear. The collinearity of the deferents accounts for the proximity of Mercury and the Sun, while the motion of the epicycle accounts for the deviation of Mercury from the Sun. An analogous account can be given for Venus.

The Ptolemaic account of retrograde motions and oppositions is somewhat more complicated. According to the Ptolemaic account, certain combinations of the relative lengths and rates of rotation of the epicycle and deferent produce retrograde motion. One can get a qualitative sense of what this is like through examination of Figure 2.4. Given epicycles and deferents of roughly the proportions shown in the figure, if one has an epicycle that rotates very slowly relative to the rotation of the deferent, observers on the central Earth will not observe retrograde motion. If, however, one has an epicycle that rotates very rapidly relative to the rotation of the deferent, Earth-bound observers will see numerous periods of retrograde motion. The very phenomenon of retrograde motion, thus, involves some measure of parameter fixing. One has to add yet other adjustments in order to have the superior planets go through retrograde motions at opposition, namely, keeping the solar deferent parallel to the epicycles of the superior planets and keeping the period of the superior epicycles equal to one solar year. One can get a rough qualitative sense of the way this works through Figure 2.4. For ease of illustration, the period of the epicycle is one solar year and the period of the deferent is two solar years.[3] In 2.4a, the planet (gray) is in retrograde motion while in opposition to the Sun (white). In 2.4e, the planet is in normal eastward motion in conjunction with the Sun.

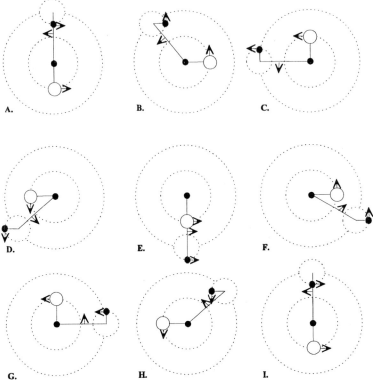

Figure 2.4. The Ptolemaic model of retrograde motion.

Finally, in 2.4i, the planet is again in retrograde motion in opposition to the Sun.

Here we can make some preliminary observations. While both Copernican and Ptolemaic astronomy are able to offer accounts of the phenomena, the Copernican account is superior. Think of the motions of Mercury, Venus, and the Sun. The Copernican heliocentric system explains the fact that Mercury and Venus never stray far from the Sun based on the way the two inferior planets must appear from a planet having a larger orbit. By contrast, in the Ptolemaic geocentric system, one must conjoin to the geocentric hypothesis the hypothesis that the deferents of Mercury, Venus, and the Sun are collinear. The idea, very roughly, is that the heliocentric hypothesis leads naturally, or of necessity, to the phenomena with Mercury, Venus, and the Sun, where the geocentric hypothesis requires the addition of a further arbitrary or *ad hoc* hypothesis about the collinearity of deferents. Still speaking at an intuitive level, the arbitrariness appears to lie in the fact that the Ptolemaic account can as easily allow deferents to be collinear--as in the case of Mercury, Venus, or the Sun--as allow them to move independently--as with Mars, Jupiter, and Saturn.

Think now about the motions of the superior planets. In the heliocentric Copernican system, retrograde motions must occur at opposition, given the proposed nature of retrograde motions. At an intuitive level, one might say that it is a law of nature that the superior planets go through retrograde motions at opposition and the Copernican heliocentric hypothesis necessitates this phenomenon. By contrast, the problem with the Ptolemaic account of these phenomena is that one must invoke geocentrism, along with the hypothesis that the epicycles of the superior planets are parallel to the Sun-earth deferent (along with still other hypotheses relating the relative lengths and speeds of the superior epicycles and deferents). The hypothesis relating the epicycles of the superior planets to the Sun-earth deferent, however, is in some sense an arbitrary hypothesis of Ptolemaic astronomy. While the Ptolemaic machinery can be arranged to allow this parallelism, it can also be arranged not to have this parallelism.

2 DARWINIAN EVOLUTION AND CREATIONISM

Jumping to another historical period and switching scientific disciplines, we can find many additional illustrations of what is apparently the same form of argumentation in the *Origin of Species*. Until 1859, the orthodox scientific theory about the nature of species was that each species had been specially created by a "miraculous" act of God. In the *Origin*, however, Darwin championed the view that new species were transmuted forms of pre-existing species. All living species were the common descendants of one or a few original species. While Darwin was able to convince the majority of his fellow biologists that species do, in fact, evolve, he did not rely primarily on the fossil record. Indeed, the *Origin* treated the fossil record as something of an embarrassment. Rather than relying on the fossil record, Darwin repeatedly applied the strategy we have been discussing to laws or regularities in biogeography, embryology, morphology, and taxonomy. Here we will review two of Darwin's biogeographical arguments.

In Chapter V of the *Origin*, Darwin notes that if one examines the blind animal forms in the deep limestone caves in the United States and in Europe, one finds that the American blind cave forms resemble American sighted surface forms, where the European blind cave forms resemble European sighted surface forms. Here is a biogeographical empirical regularity: blind cave forms resemble the sighted forms from the spatially adjacent surface. Why is there this biogeographical regularity? What explains it? Darwin envisioned two accounts, an evolutionary account and a creationist account. According to the evolutionist, the patterns of resemblance between cave and surface forms is due to the fact that the blind forms in American caves are transmuted descendants of the sighted forms on the American surface, where the blind forms in the European caves are transmuted descendants of the sighted forms on the European surface, and descendants tend to resemble their ancestors. According to the creationist, God created all life forms and chose to distribute animals on the surface according to some plan whose pattern is only vaguely manifest in the biogeographical data. The distribution of surface and cave forms is merely one component of this overall plan. Which account is superior? Evidently, the evolutionary account. The deep limestone caves in Europe and the United States are about as similar environments as one could imagine, says Darwin. So, there is reason to think that God could as easily have placed the *same* blind forms in both the American and European caves, as he could have placed *different* blind forms in the caves. Indeed, it would have been just as much within God's infinite power to place the blind forms that resembled European sighted surface forms in American caves and the blind forms that resembled the American sighted surface forms in European caves. The problem for the Creationist account appears to be that, even supposing God to have created the world, He could have done what the creationist purports He did as easily as He could have done something else. The creationist account, while it is able to save the phenomena, after a fashion, does not save the phenomena *in the right way*. The creationist theory has what appears to be an arbitrary assumption about it, namely, that God chose to distribute life forms in one way, when He could as easily have chosen to distribute them in another way. The evolutionary account does not have this sort of arbitrariness about it. This gives us a defeasible reason to prefer the evolutionary account to the creationist account.

As a second example, consider Darwin's account of the biogeography of Batrachians, given in Chapter XII of the *Origin*:

> Bory St. Vincent long ago remarked that Batrachians (frogs, toads, newts) have never been found on any of the many islands with which the great oceans are studded. I have taken pains to verify this assertion, and I have found it strictly true. I have, however, been assured that a frog exists on the mountains of the great island of New Zealand; but I suspect that this exception (if the information be correct) may be explained through glacial agency. This general absence of frogs, toads, and newts on so many oceanic islands cannot be accounted for by their physical conditions; indeed it seems that islands are peculiarly well fitted for these animals; for frogs have been introduced into Madeira, the Azores, and Mauritius, and have multiplied so as to become a nuisance. But as these animals and their spawn are known to be immediately killed by sea-water, on my view we can see that there would be great difficulty in their transportal across the sea, and therefore why, on the theory of creation, they should not have been created there, it would be very difficult to explain (Darwin, 1859, p. 393).

Here we have to do some reconstruction to see why Darwin thinks that evolution provides a better explanation of batrachian biogeography than does creation.

According to the theory of evolution, batrachian forms first appeared on the relatively old mainland, rather than the relatively young oceanic islands. But, because sea-water kills batrachians and their spawn, thereby hindering their migration across oceans, one finds that (almost without exception) there are no batrachians on oceanic islands. Evolutionary theory has a story to tell about batrachian biogeography, but so does creationism. Creationism can simply maintain that God brought life to the planet and distributed it according to a plan. The problem with the creationist account, even allowing for the existence of God, is that it appears that God's plan could as easily have placed batrachians on oceanic islands as not. The evidence for this latter claim is that naturalists had already observed that it is possible for humans to transport batrachians to Madeira, the Azores, and Mauritius and have them survive quite well. The creationist can invoke some plan to try to explain the distribution of batrachians across the surface of the earth, but the hypothesis of a plan is a kind of arbitrary addition to the creationist hypothesis. Again, speaking intuitively and very roughly, the idea in these explanatory arguments is that some regularity must occur as a kind of natural consequence of a central hypothesis, not as the product of a central hypothesis conjoined with an additional arbitrary hypothesis.

3 WHAT THESE EXPLANATORY ARGUMENTS HAVE IN COMMON

In the foregoing two sections, the morals of the story were described in rough and intuitive terms not chosen entirely at random. As we shall see, the intuitive terms were of the sort that Fodor & Pylyshyn, (1988), at times, used to describe what is involved in the systematicity arguments. What we would like to do now is try to move beyond these rough and ready analyses to a more refined analysis. At the outset, it is worth noting that drawing attention to interesting and suggestive explanatory arguments from the history of science is one thing, providing a philosophically adequate analysis of them is quite another. While the examples might be on to something methodologically important, exactly what constitutes this importance may be quite elusive. Thus, while it is reasonable to predict that there will be philosophical problems with the analysis, it would be rash to infer from that alone that there is nothing to the explanatory intuition underlying these historical cases and the systematicity arguments. In other words, a maximally compelling rejection of the significance of our arguments taken from the history of science would not only explain what is wrong with the analysis that is about to be offered, it would also indicate how the intuitions that they involve are ill-founded. So, on to work.

As there are a number of potentially problematic dimensions to these arguments, it is perhaps best to begin with some simple, less controversial observations, observations that are not the less important for their simplicity and obviousness. Clearly one of the most obvious features of these arguments is that in each case we have two theories, both of which have some story or account to give regarding the things to be explained (the explananda). The theories in each debate–both heliocentrism and geocentrism, both evolution and creationism–have stories to tell about why the putative astronomical and biogeographic facts are the way they are. The arguments are not about fitting the data or which theory saves the phenomena; they are not about which theory is able to exhibit the desired regularities. Rather, they are about the ability of one theory to provide a superior kind of account. In the astronomical cases, the point is not that there are various facts about the motions of the planets that Ptolemaic astronomy cannot accommodate. Some Copernican arguments--such as the changing apparent brightness of Mars at opposition--are about a theory being able to provide some account of the data, but the explanatory arguments involving the limited elongation of Mercury and Venus and the retrograde motions of the superior planets are not like that. In the biogeographical cases, Darwin certainly knew that the creationist could call upon God's infinite power to distribute life across the surface of the planet in any number of ways, so he knew that the challenge he was issuing was not to accommodate the facts. The challenge was to explain them in a desired way.

Consider, now, something about the elements of the foregoing arguments. In each of our historical cases we have two theories which offer accounts of putative regularities. In the astronomical cases, we have the regularity that Venus and Mercury are never found in opposition to the Sun and the regularity that the superior planets go through retrograde motion while in opposition to the Sun. In the biogeographical cases, we have it that blind cave forms tend to resemble the forms of the surrounding environment and that Batrachians are not found on remote islands. What is the status of these generalizations? Are they mere empirical generalizations or perhaps laws of nature? In various developments of the systematicity arguments, it is held that one must explain why systematicity is lawful or nomologically necessary.[4] No reason is given for this requirement nor is there any obvious reason for it. Nor does anything in the foregoing examples motivate this requirement. In fact, the foregoing examples suggest that it may be enough that the regularities be mere empirical generalizations. Recall that the textbook examples of empirical generalizations are Kepler's laws.[5] The first Keplerian law states that planets move in ellipses with the sun at one focus, the second states that the radius of a planet sweeps out equal areas in equal times, while the third states that the square of the period of a planet is proportional to the cube of its distance from the sun. Each of these generalizations describes the motions of the planets or some feature of the motions of the planets without any implications regarding the causes of these motions. In the goodness of time, Newton's laws provided the causal underpinning to these generalizations. Like Kepler's laws, the generalizations concerning the limited elongation of Mercury and Venus, the retrograde motion of superior planets at opposition, and the biogeography of Batrachians and cave forms appear to be mere empirical generalizations awaiting some mechanism that would account for them. Geocentrism and evolution provide these mechanisms. Thus, Classicist contentions notwithstanding, there is reason to think that the explananda in these arguments need not be lawful regularities, but may be mere empirical generalizations.

Having said something about the nature of the generalizations (the explananda) in these sorts of arguments, we ask about the relationship between the thing to be explained (the explananda) and the thing doing the explaining (the explanans).[6] We may begin with Fodor and McLaughlin's suggestion that the explanans must necessitate the explanandum in these sorts of arguments. The very first thing to observe is that the kind of necessity involved here is not clear. The so-called "received view" of explanation in the philosophy of science, the tradition of Hempel and Oppenheim's (1948) Deductive-Nomological (DN) model of explanation, had it that explanations are a kind of deductive argument, hence that the explanans logically entails the explanandum, hence that the relation between explanans and explanandum is one of logical necessity. Yet, one of the persistent problems of the Deductive-Nomological model was the attempt to have logical relations, which the Logical Positivists took to be relatively unproblematic, do duty for nomological relations that seem to underlie genuine explanations. That is, the DN model was constantly threatened by counterexamples in which a set of premises allowed one to deduce some explanandum, but not thereby explain it.[7] Given these problems, it appears that we should examine the conjecture that, in these explanatory arguments, the explanans nomologically necessitates, rather than logically necessitates, the explanandum.

If we look to our examples from positional astronomy, we may observe that, given only the Copernican configuration of the sun, Mercury, Venus, and earth, it does *not* nomologically follow that Mercury and Venus must never appear very far from the sun. The Copernican system of hypotheses generates the relevant appearances only given certain other auxiliary hypotheses, such as the rectilinear propagation of light and the absence of obstructions that might prevent the propagation of light from the sun to the earth. So, as things stand, the explanans does not nomologically necessitate the explanandum. We may, however, try to defend the Fodor-McLaughlin view that the explanans should necessitate the explanandum if we take the foregoing historical examples to present mere explanation sketches in Hempel's sense (Hempel, 1965, pp. 423-424). That is, we may suppose that the Copernican narrative mentioned only some of the salient factors that will figure in a true, complete explanation. Pursuing this line, we might, therefore, reformulate or perhaps flesh out, the Fodor-McLaughlin idea of the explanans nomologically necessitating the explanandum in terms of complete explanations: in a complete explanation (one in which no relevant hypotheses are omitted from the explanans) the explanans nomologically entails the explanandum. With this refinement in place, it appears that, given a complete Copernican account, including the hypothesis that light is propagated rectilinearly and that there are no occluding objects, it is nomologically necessary that Mercury and Venus never appear very far from the Sun. Further, given the rectilinear propagation of light and the absence of occluding objects, the hypothesis that a period of retrograde motion consists of the earth overtaking a slower-moving superior planet does nomologically entail that retrograde motions will appear only at opposition. So, there is reason to believe that, in a complete explanation of the kind under consideration here, the explanans nomologically necessitates the explanandum.

But, what about the evolutionary cases? Insofar as biological evolution is fundamentally a probabilistic process, the evolutionary cases seriously threaten the present formulation of the Fodor-McLaughlin analysis. Even given the assumption that Batrachians first appeared on the mainland and that saltwater constitutes a barrier to their migration to remote islands, it is not nomologically necessary that there will be no Batrachians on remote islands. A lack of Batrachians on remote islands is at most rendered unlikely by the background facts. It is possible, as Darwin himself suggests, that vigorous glacial action could provide an effective means by which Batrachians might safely traverse the ocean to remote islands. Similarly, given that sighted organisms live on the surface near limestone caves, it is not nomologically necessary that they will migrate into the caves and lose their eyes. The gradual reduction in the eyes is subject to the probabilistic vicissitudes of the selection process. So, provided that the evolutionary and astronomical cases involve arguments of the same form, it appears that we *cannot* say that a complete explanans nomologically necessitates its explanandum.

The evolutionary cases show that an explanans nomologically necessitating or entailing the explanans is not itself a necessary features of these arguments. The Ptolemaic explanations, however, further show that hypotheses nomologically necessitating the explanandum is also not sufficient for the desired form of explanation. If we think of the complete set of Ptolemaic hypotheses relating to the motions of Mercury, Venus, and the Sun, it turns out that they nomologically necessitate the explanandum. The same holds for the set of Ptolemaic hypotheses relating to the retrograde motions of the superior planets. Further, one might be tempted to argue that the Creationist's set of hypotheses relating to God's creation of life on earth nomologically necessitates a pattern of distribution of blind cave forms and Batrachians.

If an explanans nomologically necessitating the explanandum is neither a necessary nor a sufficient condition in these explanations, what else, or what more, contributes to the presumed superiority of the Copernican and Darwinian explanations? In our initial commentary on these cases, we suggested that the Ptolemaic and Creationist accounts relied on arbitrary hypotheses. Perhaps something can be made of this idea. It is, of course, not a problem that explanations have recourse to auxiliary hypotheses for explanation and confirmation. Perfectly good explanations quite freely make use of auxiliary hypotheses. Perhaps the problem has to do with the auxiliary hypotheses being in some sense arbitrary. One way to try to unpack this arbitrariness is to say that arbitrary hypotheses are those that one could as easily take as leave, consistent with one's central scientific hypothesis.[8] In Ptolemaic astronomy, we might identify geocentrism as the central hypothesis. Given this hypothesis, one can as easily have the deferents of Mercury, Venus, and the Sun collinear as not. Further, given the Ptolemaic hypothesis of geocentrism, one can as easily have the superior planets go through retrograde motions at opposition as not. Similarly, it appears that the problem with the creationist explanations of biogeography is that, within the creationist framework, one hypothetical plan of divine creation is just as good as another. The rough idea, then, is that the preferred kind of explanation does not rely on arbitrary auxiliary hypotheses, where by an arbitrary hypothesis we mean something like a hypothesis such that both it and its negation are consistent with the central hypothesis of the theory.

This initial analysis, inspired by comments from Fodor, et al., requires some refinement. The Copernican account of the apparent planetary motions relies on the background assumption that light is propagated rectilinearly. But, a heliocentric theory can as easily take as leave the hypothesis that light is propagated rectilinearly. The Darwinian account of Batrachian biogeography relies on the background assumption that saltwater constitutes a migration barrier. But, of course, the theory of evolution is consistent with salt water being a barrier to Batrachian migration and with it not being such a barrier. So, if we are to sustain the intuition that Darwin and Copernicus were on to something with their explanatory arguments, it cannot be that the arbitrariness of an auxiliary hypothesis consists of both it and its negation being consistent with a central theoretical hypothesis. Such a standard of arbitrariness would disqualify even the Copernican and Darwinian accounts from counting as genuine explanations.

There are, however, other features of the Copernican and Darwinian auxiliary hypotheses that set them apart from their Ptolemaic and Creationist counterparts. The Copernican and Darwinian auxiliary hypotheses were confirmed independently of the explanations in which they were deployed, where the Ptolemaic and Creationist hypotheses were not. Sixteenth century scientists had reasons, independent of geocentrism, heliocentrism, and the motions of the planets, for thinking that light travels in straight lines. Darwin assumes that it is a (relatively) well-known or well-established fact that seawater kills Batrachians and their spawn. By contrast, there were no independent checks on the Ptolemaic hypothesis regarding the collinearity of the deferents of Mercury, Venus, and the Sun. Nor were there independent checks on the plan of God in creation. So, one reasonable conjecture is that independently confirmed auxiliary hypotheses are acceptable for explanatory purposes, where auxiliary hypotheses that are not independently confirmed are not acceptable.

Unfortunately, this analysis has a subtle weakness. Were this the source of the superiority of one account over the other, one might suppose that the Ptolemaic and Creationist accounts were simply not as strong or compelling as they might be. They would be better if each of the hypotheses invoked were independently confirmed. In other words, all things being equal, the more evidence an explanatory argument has for each of its constituent hypotheses the better the explanation. The superiority of one account over the other would, thus, be a matter of degree. This, however, seems not to be the nature of the dissatisfaction found in the Ptolemaic and Copernican case. The common take on these historical episodes is that one account constitutes an explanation, where the other does not--period. In fact, examination of these cases often provokes the much stronger claim that Ptolemaic astronomy *cannot* explain why Venus and Mercury are never found in opposition to the Sun and that Ptolemaic astronomy *cannot* explain why retrograde motions occur only at opposition. Consideration of biogeography often provokes the charge that Creationism *cannot* explain the facts. This sort of commentary suggests that more is going on than that the accounts are not as well-grounded as they might be. It suggests a deeper dissatisfaction with the accounts.

In order to capture this deeper dissatisfaction, we might venture the following: the problem is that the auxiliary hypotheses are arbitrary in the sense that one cannot confirm the auxiliary short of establishing the truth of the theory. In the Ptolemaic case, there is no way to confirm the hypothesis that the deferents of Mercury, Venus, and the Sun are collinear, short of confirming the Ptolemaic geocentric system. Perhaps more obviously, there is no way to confirm the nature of God's plan in distributing life across the surface of the globe, short of confirming the Creationist theory that God in fact had a plan in creation. Put in other words, the various arbitrary auxiliary hypotheses are arbitrary in the sense that they can state whatever needs to be stated in order to get the explananda to come out as they should. They are to this extent *ad hoc*, "free parameters".

So, in these inference to the best explanation arguments about empirical generalizations, it appears that the principle that favors one explanation over another is that an explanation must not rely on hypotheses that can only be confirmed given the truth of the theory. If this is the correct analysis of these arguments, then it makes some sense of these explanatory showdowns. If the entire aim of these sorts of showdowns is to confirm one theory against its rivals, then the fact that one theory cannot provide this sort of confirmation, without relying on a hypotheses that presupposes the independent confirmation has to seem deeply problematic. This seems to capture the sense in which arbitrary or *ad hoc* hypotheses are methodologically suspect.

To this point, we have talked of central and auxiliary hypotheses without having offered any characterization of them. This terminology is, of course, common in the philosophy of science, capturing to some extent the pragmatics of science. The central hypotheses are those that are of most pressing interest to a scientist, while the auxiliaries are of lesser concern. The central hypotheses are those of such importance that they bear names, such as evolution, creationism, heliocentrism, geocentrism, uniformitarianism, and corpuscularianism, where auxiliary hypotheses are typically specified by descriptions. Here it should be noted that the distinction between central and auxiliary hypotheses is required to do no philosophical work, hence that its invocation is innocuous. What we have found to be problematic in Ptolemaic and Creationist cases is some feature of the set of hypotheses. The set of hypotheses is problematic insofar as one (or more?) of them might be varied to fit the explanandum without independent check. The problem that some theories have in explaining certain regularities is that they must rely on free parameters.

We have just said that what matters in separating the "good" explanatory accounts from the "bad" is something about the set of hypotheses invoked in the explanation. In particular, it is something about one set of hypotheses relying on a hypothesis that is in some sense arbitrary or *ad hoc*. It does not matter how we identify particular hypotheses as either central or auxiliary. In this same vein, we should add that it does not matter how we name groups of hypotheses. It does not matter whether by the name "Ptolemaic astronomy" we mean simply the hypothesis of geocentrism or some more extensive set including the hypothesis that there are epicycles and deferents or some still more extensive set including hypotheses about the particular position, lengths, and rates of rotations of each epicycle and deferent. The same holds for use of the name "creationism." A given set of hypotheses has or lacks whatever explanatory power it has, quite apart from how they are grouped under various names. While obvious at this point, it may be less than obvious in the later, more contentious, context of systematicity arguments.

The last few paragraphs have offered a range of reasons for analyzing particular episodes in the history of science in a particular manner. The proposal is that there are various empirical regularities that call for accounts in which a central theoretical hypothesis, in conjunction with confirmed auxiliary hypotheses, bring about the desired regularity. Furthermore, the account may not rely on hypotheses that cannot be confirmed short of confirming the hypothesis under test. The ability of a theory to provide explanations meeting these conditions seems to be an important indicator of the truth. This is not to say that the ability guarantees the truth of the theory; only that the ability is a defeasible bit of evidence for the truth of the theory. This feature bears emphasis. In his discussion of systematicity, Robert Cummins, (1996b), describes the explanatory standard we have in mind in terms of explanations that are "principled" versus those that are not. He, then, has this to say about principled explanations:

Being principled is a virtue in explanation. But the virtue is purely methodological. Principled explanations are easier to test, but they are no more likely to be true. If there are independent reasons for preferring a connectionist architecture (as clearly there are), then the methodological weakness of the ensuing explanations of our sensitivity to systematicity in language must simply be swallowed. If you are convinced that the mind is a network, you should not be dismayed by the fact that your explanation of our sensitivity to linguistic systematicity is not as easily tested as the other guy's (Cummins, 1996b, p. 608).

If, in fact, the systematicity arguments share a form with the arguments we have just reviewed, then the examples have something to say about Cummins's analysis. Cummins claims that "principled" explanations are more easily tested, but they are no more likely to make their background theories true. The idea about ease of testability is an interesting idea, perhaps correct, and surely worthy of further exploration. Yet, the examples from biogeography and positional astronomy do suggest that explanations of the sort that Darwin gave provide us with good reasons to think that evolution actually took place. Explanations of the sort that Copernicus could have given, give us reason to think that heliocentrism is really true. Cummins is, of course, correct in pointing out that explanatory arguments are not the only sort of evidence that may be brought to bear in a scientific dispute and that other evidence may lead to an alternative assessment of rival theories. He is right insofar as he is reminding us that theory choice must be made on the basis of all the available evidence. Perhaps Connectionists, for example, can give us good reason to believe in their theory of cognition, even if Connectionism does not explain the systematicity of thought. One might also suggest that theories can have methodological virtues other than those displayed in the kinds of arguments we are here exploring. These are points to which we shall return. Here, however, we may note that these points only show what should have been evident all along, namely, that these "principled" explanatory arguments are merely *defeasible* indicators of the truth. Observations about defeasibility, however, do not show that "principled" explanations are to be preferred only for methodological reasons. From the historical cases surveyed so far, it appears that "principled" explanations are guides to the truth.

To emphasize the defeasibility of this form of argument, we might note a curious example where the argumentative strategy lead to a false theory. An 18th Century evolutionist, Demaillet, apparently asked why it is that

To every species of parrot, whose plumage is the most diverse, the rarest and the most singularly marked of all the birds, there corresponds a fish colored like them, in black, brown, grey, yellow, green, red, violet, gold, and blue, and these markings appear on the same parts of the fish as they do in such a bizarre manner on the plumage of these very birds (cited by Richard Owen in his review of Darwin's *Origin.*, reprinted in Hull, 1973,

p. 199).

Demaillet's implication was that the birds had evolved rather directly from the fish, which provides a neat diachronic explanation of the regularity. Demaillet's argument can go wrong, if it turns out that, in fact, there is no bona fide icthyo-ornithological regularity of the sort that Demaillet offers. As we shall see, a number of critics of the systematicity arguments argue that there is no *bona fide* explanandum involved in these arguments.[9] Yet another moral is that we should allow for the possibility of even true regularities turning out to be mere coincidences. Be all of this as it may, the final conclusion to draw seems to be that there is only some presumption in favor of the need to provide the preferred style of explanation for a given regularity. An unexplained regularity is a kind of anomaly for a theory. A theory may survive an anomaly, but it must recognize them, especially anomalies of the form that have helped topple well-entrenched theories, such as Ptolemaic astronomy and creationism.

Having sketched a proposal for a structure to these explanations, it is important to observe that not all scientific explanations in good standing have this structure.[10] Four kinds of cases come to mind. A first and obvious illustration is the explanation of particular events, such as the crash of the Hindenberg or the extinction of the dinosaurs. In the arguments that have been at the focus of this chapter, the explanandum has been supposed to be some empirical generalization and empirical generalizations are not particular events. So, explanations of particular events may not fit this model. In addition, there are instances of structural facts whose explanations are properly explained by recourse to a thing's substructure. Why does water expand when it freezes? This has to do with the structure of the water molecule and the arrangement of its molecules into a crystal. Molecules in the liquid water are able to move about freely and independently which allows them to move closer to each other than is possible when the molecules must assume the fixed arrangement of the solid crystalline form. A third class of explanations that appears not to fit this model are explanations of particular processes, such as how proteins are made. The story in this case is that DNA, in conjunction with certain nucleotides and enzymes, makes RNA which, in conjunction with amino acids and other enzymes, give rise to the proteins. A fourth class involves explanations of what things are, for example, what the Krebs cycle is, what sunspots are, and what structure of DNA is. These explanations, as well, seem not to have the form of the arguments from biogeography and positional astronomy. There is no reason to think these four cases constitute a mutually exclusive and jointly exhaustive taxonomy of possible scientific explanations. They almost certainly do not. The point here is simply that there are multiple reasons for thinking that not all scientific explanations must be like those found in the Copernican and Darwinian examples we have reviewed.

The existence of legitimate scientific explanations that do not fit this pattern does not, of course, diminish the importance of the kind of explanation we have seen in astronomy and biogeography. Nor do they show that the particular examples we have seen have been incorrectly analyzed. They do, however, raise other sorts of difficult questions. To begin with, it is unclear exactly how we are to categorize explanations and explanatory demands. This is, to some extent, an unavoidable consequence of the lack of a sound general theory of explanation. If we are to have a philosophically satisfactory classification of explanations, it must divide them into theoretically interesting classes. Yet, in the absence of a satisfactory general theory of explanations, we don't know what the theoretically interesting classes are. Another significant question raised by explanations that do not fit our pattern is when the demand for our preferred type of explanation must be met. If not all explanations must fit this pattern, which explanations must?

Alas, no answer to these questions will be forthcoming here. Nevertheless, it would be rash to dismiss the scientific challenge the Copernican and Darwinian explanatory arguments pose. Good judgement would suggest that the Copernican and Darwinian arguments ought not be ignored simply for lack of a philosophical theory to ground them. Science should not have to wait for a philosophical seal of approval on its reasoning. It appears that whatever is going on in the Copernican and Darwinian arguments, it is an important indicator of truth. We should take as relatively fixed points in our debate the idea that the Copernican and Darwinian theories are on to something that philosophers would do well to characterize, in spite of local failures to characterize them properly. So, as far as cognitive science is concerned, we need to attend to what the Copernican and Darwinian cases have to tell us.

4 SOME BROADER IMPLICATIONS OF OUR EXPLANATORY STANDARDS

Our principal concern with the history of science has been to illuminate the structure of the systematicity arguments. Yet, the explanatory standard found in these episodes would be worth reflecting upon, even were we not to be concerned with the systematicity arguments. There are other regularities in cognitive science that might also benefit from scrutiny in the sorts of terms we have found operative in the history of science. To close out this chapter in support of this contention, this section digresses to review two contemporary and completely unrelated areas in which explanatory standards make a difference. For those only interested in the Classicism/Connectionism debate, this section can be skipped without loss.

Developmental psychologists often recognize domains of cognitive development, such as language, mathematics, and physics. Annette Karmiloff-

Smith, (1992), however, postulates, in addition, *microdomains.* As the name would suggest, a microdomain covers a part of some domain. Thus, Karmiloff-Smith suggests that, within the domain of language acquisition, we might recognize three microdomains corresponding to noun, verb, and pronoun acquisition. Karmiloff-Smith also proposes that development might, or might not, take place at different rates in different microdomains.

By hypothesizing multiple, independently developing microdomains, Karmiloff-Smith has more parameters to use in fitting available developmental data. Microdomains can be isolated and timed to fit many, many patterns. Yet, the potential weakness in this flexibility in data coverage looks to be comparable to Ptolemaic astronomy's weakness in its flexibility in fitting the data of planetary positions. Judicious selection of microdomains and the freedom to vary independently the time course of development in diverse microdomains leaves one with auxiliary hypotheses with enough flexibility to allow the theory to fit essentially any pattern of development without thereby providing a genuine explanation.

Karmiloff-Smith's discussion of the developing child as physicist bears out this point. If a 4-month old infant visually observes the joint and continuous movement of parts of an occluded object, this suggests to the infant the presence of a single object. If a 4-month old cannot see the joint and continuous movement of an object, but can use two hands to feel two parts of an unseen thing move together continuously, this also suggests to the infant the presence of a single object.[11] Here is a fact to be explained: Why is it that continuous movement in both the visual and tactile modalities leads a 4-month old child to postulate a single object? One possible answer is that the ability to use continuous motion in the visual modality and the ability to use continuous motion in the tactile modality are two microdomains that arrive at the same developmental stage at the same time. Another possible answer is that the ability to use continuous motion is one domain, so it must happen that the ability to use it in one modality goes with the ability to use it in another. Either way, however, it seems that Karmiloff-Smith's theory must rely on auxiliary hypotheses about the individuation of microdomains and (perhaps) the timing of development of microdomains, auxiliary hypotheses that seem to admit of no independent confirmation. Here we have a puzzle worthy of further examination.

Not to lay the burden for meeting this explanatory standard too heavily with more experimentally oriented cognitive psychologists, a second example challenges Classicism with a homely folk psychological hypothesis. Folk psychology appears to have it that, as a matter of nomological fact, actions require an agent to have both a belief and a desire. So, suppose that an agent believes that there is water in the refrigerator. If the agent has no desires, folk psychology has it that the agent will perform no action. By the same token, suppose that the agent desires a drink of water. Without any beliefs about how the agent might go about getting a drink, the agent will again perform no action.

So, here is some regularity to be explained: in normal cognitive agents, actions require both beliefs and desires. A viable form of this requirement, if there really is one, might well add something about the relationship between the content of the belief and the desire somehow being related, so that a belief about water being in the refrigerator and a desire for a cup of coffee will produce no action. But, for present purposes we may forbear this refinement. All we care about is why both beliefs and desires are required for action.

Perhaps such a folk psychological regularity will be denied, but if not, we may ask how, for example, Classicism might explain such a regularity. To begin with, we recall that, according to Classicism, believing that p is a matter of standing in some sort of computational relation to a mental representation r that means that p and that desiring that q is a matter of standing in some sort of computational relation to a mental representation that means that q. The natural thing to do, then, is to build upon the metaphor of a "belief box" and a "desire box". This metaphor might be cashed out in terms of something like a two-tape Turing machine. One tape has the mental representations that represent the objects of belief, while the other tape has representations that represent the objects of desire. The read-write head in our hypothetical two-tape Turing machine will simultaneously scan both tapes and will process information only if the head scans something on both tapes. So, rather than having Turing machine instructions, such as "s_0 1 0 s_2" (which are interpreted to mean "if in state s_0 scanning a 1, write a 0 and go into state s_2"), our new two-tape Turing machine will have instructions such as "s_0 0 1 0 0 s_2" (which are interpreted to mean "if in state s_0 scanning a 0 on the first tape and a 1 on the second tape, then write a 0 on the first tape, a 0 on the second tape, and go into state s_2"). In a two-tape Turing machine of the sort just described, there will be no processing, no cognition, no action, if there are not representations on both tapes. If either beliefs are totally lacking or desires are totally lacking, then there will be no action. This conforms to the explanandum before us.

Having an account, of course, is not all there is to the explanatory standard we have surveyed. We need to consider whether or not we have had recourse to an arbitrary hypothesis and the worry is that we have. Given the hypothesis that propositional attitudes are matters of standing in computational relations to mental representations, we can as easily have it be the case that processing depends on both beliefs and desires as that it depends on beliefs alone or desires alone. That is, we have already seen how we might have a computational theory of mind realized in a system in which both beliefs and desires are necessary for processing, but, of course, the standard case involves the equivalent of only one Turing machine tape. That is, Turing machines compute given only very localized information about what is on a tape. When a Turing machine computes simple arithmetic functions, there are only markers on the tape. It need not be the case that there is something corresponding to a belief and something corresponding to a desire in order for processing to take place. Now, it is, of course, true that "belief boxes" and "desire boxes" can be realized on a single Turing machine tape. That is beside the point. The problem is that there need not be any functional realization of both a belief and a desire in order to get a Turing machine to compute. Further, what holds for Turing machines holds for other Turing-equivalent computing devices. So, given Classicism as a central hypothesis, it appears that only by the addition of a problematic auxiliary hypothesis--one that can be tested only given the truth of the theory under question--will we generate the desired empirical generalization about the need for both beliefs and desires. If this is so, however, then we don't have the sort of explanation we have seen to be so important in a range of scientific episodes.

5 TAKING STOCK

The present chapter has an important moral. It is that there is good reason to believe that not all ways of saving the phenomena are equally good. At some level, both Copernicus and Ptolemy were able to save the phenomena regarding the motions of the planets. At some level, both creationism and evolution were able to save the phenomena regarding the distribution of life forms across the surface of the planet, the nature and distribution of vestigial organs, and the commonalities in morphological structures. Yet, at a deeper level, the Copernican and Darwinian theories appear to provide superior explanations of commonly accepted empirical regularities. The intuition is, roughly, that the accounts provided by some theories do not amount to genuine explanations because they are *ad hoc* or rely on arbitrary hypotheses.

The history of science suggests that there are explanations, then there are explanations. The history of science tells us that there is something of epistemic interest going on in these historical episodes. What it doesn't tell us is just how to characterize what is going on in these episodes. Providing such a characterization is a job for the philosopher of science. The core of the analysis proposed here is that, in these cases, there are empirical generalizations for which we want some explanation. An explanation will involve a single "central" hypothesis that may, in itself, lack any confirmation other than that which it might obtain via its role in the explanation at hand. In addition, the single "central" hypothesis may have recourse to any number of additional, independently confirmed "auxiliary" hypotheses. If a theory is able to provide an explanation meeting these criteria, this will provide a rather strong, but still defeasible, reason to think that the theory providing the explanation is true.

Such arguments, however they are characterized, cannot constitute the whole of scientific reasoning that might be offered in support of a theory. In fact, given the apparent structural features of these arguments, where two theories are both able to provide accounts of a single empirical generalization, such arguments are bound to be relatively rare in the history of science. Such arguments must, therefore, constitute only a rarely used means of confirming a theory with much o the confirmatory work being done elsewhere. Moreover, such scientific virtue as these explanatory arguments may embody need not be assumed to constitute the whole of the scientific virtues. No reason at all, for example, has been given to think that there are no "supra-empirical" virtues, such as beauty, simplicity, or parsimony, that might support one theory over another. No reason at all has been given to think that there might not be some other feature of a theory to recommend it over its rivals. Rather, the present sort of argument appears to constitute a rarely used, but nonetheless extremely important, defeasible indicator of the truth of theories. In subsequent chapters, we will have the opportunity to explore some of the alternative empirical and "supra-empirical" bases upon which one might try to evaluate competing theories of cognitive architecture.

NOTES

1. The following discussion owes much to Kuhn, (1957), and Glymour, (1980).

2. The Copernican system also postulated epicycles and deferents, but these were not needed in the explanations of the motions of Mercury and Venus relative to the Sun or the occurrence of retrograde motion of superior planets during opposition.

3. This is very roughly the situation with Mars for which the period of its epicycle is ~365 days and the period of its deferent is ~687 days.

3. Cf., e.g., Fodor & McLaughlin, (1990), p. 202.

4. The phrase "Kepler's laws" merely reflects common usage and should not be taken to indicate that Kepler's laws are genuine nomological laws, rather than mere empirical generalizations.

5. Fodor and McLaughlin threaten to conflate these two issues in the following passage:
   The point of the problem that systematicity poses for a Connectionist account is not to show that systematic cognitive processes are *possible* given the assumptions of a Connectionist architecture, but to explain how systematicity could be *necessary*--how it could be a *law* that cognitive capacities are systematic--given those assumptions (Fodor & McLaughlin, 1990, p. 202).
Here the proposed lawlike status of the explanandum is not clearly distinguished from the relationship between the explanandum and the explanans.

6. A nice account of this may be found in Ruben, (1990).

7. Recall Fodor & Pylyshyn, (1988), pp. 47-48.

8. For example, Dennett, (1991), van Gelder and Niklasson, (1994), Cummins, (1996b), and Hadley & Hayward, (1997).

9. In defense of a model of certain systematic relations in thought, Hadley, (1997), sketches cases of explanations that he supposes do not have this structure.

10. For the details of how these conclusions are reached experimentally through a habituation paradigm, the reader is referred to Karmiloff-Smith, (1992), pp. 67-72.

CHAPTER 3

THE PRODUCTIVITY OF THOUGHT

The standard expository approach to the systematicity and productivity arguments has come to be that one examines them in the context of a debate between Classicism and Connectionism.[1] Our approach in Chapters 3 through 6, however, will consider the arguments as a debate between Classicism and Pure Atomism (PA), the view that cognitive representations are syntactically and semantically atomic. Chapter 3 will handle productivity, Chapter 4 the systematicity of inference, Chapter 5 the systematicity of thought, and Chapter 6 the compositionality of representations. While the present approach differs from what has come to be standard in the literature, there is a respectable precedent. Fodor, (1987), introduces the productivity and systematicity arguments as a kind of in-house debate between Classicism and what we have here called Pure Atomism. These views share a commitment to Representationalism and the Computational Theory of the Attitudes (CTA), but differ in the structure they attribute to cognitive representations. This manner of setting up the debate is sustained in Fodor & Pylyshyn, (1988). There Fodor and Pylyshyn identify two Classical hypotheses. The first is that cognitive representations have combinatorial syntax and semantics and the second is that cognitive processes are sensitive to the combinatorial syntax and semantics of cognitive representations.[2] By contrast, Connectionism is supposed to embody representations that are essentially syntactic and semantic atoms. In fact, Fodor and Pylyshyn dedicate several pages to arguing that various features of Connectionist networks do not constitute Classical combinatorial structures. More specifically, they spend several pages arguing that the labels on nodes in networks, the graph structural representations of networks, distributed representations, and representations distributed over microfeatures do not constitute Classical syntactically and semantically combinatorial representations.[3]

There are a number of advantages to proceeding in the expository mode established in Fodor, (1987), and sustained in Fodor & Pylyshyn, (1988). In the first place, it simplifies the exposition. The contrast between Classicism and Pure Atomism is easily drawn, so that we can focus initially on the logic of the productivity and systematicity arguments as illuminated by the analysis of the preceding chapter. In particular, we can postpone the exposition of matters relating to Connectionism and Functional Combinatorialism. Second, many cognitive scientists find it easier to accept the conclusion that purely atomistic representations cannot explain the productivity and systematicity of thought than they can that Connectionism cannot explain the productivity and systematicity of thought. This allows us to bring the intuitions cultivated with the examples in Chapter 2 into the context of cognitive science, so that the arguments will seem less foreign when the "serious" contenders in cognitive science face off starting in Chapter 7. Third, once we accept the conclusion that Classicism is explanatorily more powerful than Pure Atomism we will have a further constraint on how we analyze the explanatory power of Classicism, Connectionism and Functional Combinatorialism in subsequent chapters. In other words, the Copernican arguments against Ptolemaic astronomy, the Darwinian arguments against Creationism, and the Classicist arguments against Pure Atomism will constrain how we analyze the Classicist arguments against other rival theories of cognitive architecture. By having another example of our explanatory strategy in play in the field of cognitive science, it will be more difficult to defend *ad hoc* theories of explanation in more contentious contexts.

The present chapter's examination of the productivity argument will follow a pattern to be used in Chapters 3-6. It will begin with an exposition and clarification of what is to be explained in the argument, then move on to consider Classical and Pure Atomistic attempts to explain the regularity at issue. The principal conclusion of this chapter is that the strongest version of the productivity argument does not rely on the principle of explanatory power explored in Chapter 2. The problem with a Pure Atomistic account of productivity is not that it relies on *ad hoc* hypotheses, but that it violates certain principles of effective computation. Thus, insofar as the present treatment of productivity does not invoke the explanatory principle explored in Chapter 2, it interrupts the line of development begun in Chapter 2. This interruption is, however, warranted insofar as it serves some important expository needs that will emerge in later chapters.

1 THE PRODUCTIVITY OF THOUGHT

At the heart of the productivity argument is a putative psychological regularity that merits an explanation. Stating just exactly what this regularity is requires some attention. To begin with, we may observe that, in Fodor, (1985), the productivity of thought is introduced as the fact that, during the course of a normal human lifetime, any given human will entertain only a finite subset of all the possible thoughts she appears to be capable of entertaining. Or, to put the matter in another way, normal humans seem always to be capable of entertaining new thoughts. So, for example, Fodor invites us to consider that we have probably never before thought that no grass grows on kangaroos, but that once this idea is presented to us, it is perfectly intelligible. We may not believe it, but we certainly can comprehend that, or entertain the thought that, no grass grows on kangaroos. Perhaps a more apt name for this hypothetical feature of cognition would be "the persistent possibility of novel thoughts," hence that an argument based upon it would be "the persistent possibility of novel thoughts argument."[4]

By whatever name, this feature of cognition merits an explanation. Yet, it would seem to admit of a perfectly good explanation by either Classicism or PA: so many possible representations, so little time.[5] In other words, either sort of Representationalist is free simply to maintain that the stock of possible or available mental representations is much greater than the stock of representations that are ever actually used during the course of a normal lifetime. Given this analysis, the structure of the representations is entirely irrelevant to the matter. So, the productivity of thought in the foregoing sense–in the sense of the ever present possibility of novel thoughts–provides no basis for a rational theory choice between Classicism and Pure Atomism.

Formulating productivity in terms of the persistent novelty of thought is a false start for Classicism, since this understanding of productivity provides no reason to be a Classicist as opposed to a Pure Atomist. Another possible interpretation of productivity, however, is the idea that a system is productive if it is capable of processing an unbounded number of distinct inputs. While a perfectly well-defined conception, it too fails to serve Classical ends insofar as it is clearly not an explanandum that requires the hypothesis of a Classical system of representation. Two examples–one relatively simple and informal, the other relatively more complex and formal–show this. Take the relatively simple case: a temperature warning system. A red light's being on might mean "overheated," where a green light being on means "normal". Each light constitutes a syntactic atom which has its meaning independently of the meaning of any other syntactic item. The representational system is, thus, Purely Atomic. Yet, it is able to handle an unbounded number of inputs insofar as it can handle a range of real-valued temperatures. Now consider the relatively more complex and formal case. It involves a finite state automaton (FSA). Our FSA is in many respects like a Turing machine. It has an unbounded tape divided into squares and that may contain either a single 0 or a single 1. It also has a programmable, read-only head that scans the contents of individual tape squares and is capable of assuming two distinct states, S_1 and S_2. The FSA's program is such that, if it is in state S_1 and is given a 1, then it moves one square to the right and goes into state S_2, while if it is in state S_2 and is given a 1, then it moves one square to the right and goes into state S_1. After a finite sequence of 1's is presented, the

FSA will halt in either S_1 or S_2. Since this FSA begins with its read-only head in state S_1 scanning the leftmost 1's of a non-null string of 1's, if its halts with its scanning head in S_1, then it has seen an even number of 1's, while if it halts with its scanning head in S_2, then it has seen an odd number of 1's. It is clear that the FSA is able to determine whether an input string is even or odd in length and that there is no bound on the length of input this FSA is capable of handling. Yet, this FSA lacks Classical representations. So, the need to handle an unbounded set of diverse inputs can be met without recourse to a Classical system of representations.

The structure of the preceding example is obvious, but the claim that the FSA lacks Classical representations might bear a bit of argumentation. More specifically, one might wonder whether either the states of the read-only head, S_1 and S_2, or the 1's and 0's on the tape might constitute Classical representations. As for the states S_1 and S_2, they are non-concatenative and syntactically atomic, hence non-Classical. Perhaps one can argue that the S_1 can only be co-ordinated with even inputs and S_2 can only be co-ordinated with odd inputs in virtue of the inter-relations between S_1 and S_2, hence that their meanings are mutually dependent, hence that S_1 and S_2, are not semantically atomic. Be this as it may, S_1 and S_2 also count as being non-Classical in virtue of their lacking concatenative combinatorial syntax. So, neither S_1 nor S_2 counts as a Classical representation. In addition, the incoming strings of 1's and 0's need not be Classically structured representations either. Although there are finite state automata for which input strings are Classically structured, there are also finite state automata for which the input strings have no semantics, hence no Classical semantic structure. Many finite state acceptors are like this. So, even though not every finite state automaton will serve to guide us away from a conception of productivity that does not confirmatory work for Classicism, it is fortunate that some will.

To make a case for Classicism using some conception of productivity, the Classicist needs more than the claim that a person's possible thoughts greatly outnumber a person's actual thoughts and more than the claim that a normal person is capable of handling an unbounded number of distinct inputs. Rather, the Classicist needs the idea that there is a sense in which people are capable of entertaining arbitrarily many possible thoughts, that there is a sense in which there is no upper bound on the number of possible thoughts one could entertain. This is, in fact, the explanandum we find in Fodor & Pylyshyn, (1988). To make this idea more concrete, we may develop it by reference to the following infinite set of sentences

the successor of 0 is 1
the successor of 1 is 2,
the successor of 2 is 3, and so on.

No matter how long scientists observe human thinking regarding successors, they will only observe a finite number of distinct thoughts. This finite human performance, however, admits of at least two possible interpretations.[6] One possibility is that underlying this finite performance is a bounded and strictly finite representational capacity. That is, there will be some largest number such that a human will not be able contemplate its successor. So, normal humans might be such that they can think that, say,   the successor of 11,342,985,014,103,759,200 is 11,342,985,014,103,759,201, but not for the life of them be able to think that the successor of 11,342,985,014,103, 759,201 is 11,342,985,014,103,759,202. Here one might recall handheld calculators that can compute the sum of 555,555 and 444,444, but not compute the sum of 555,555 and 444,445. The other possibility is that underlying the observed thoughts of successors is an unbounded representational capacity masked to a considerable extent by a host of other factors that come into play in actual human thought and action. Among these other factors are, most obviously, the simple facts that humans have only finite life spans and that entertaining a thought takes at least a small amount of time. Yet, the limitations on human performance are more severe than this. There are also limitations on available memory and attention.[7] Personal reflection strongly suggests that thinking that 923,463,213 is the successor of 923,463,212 makes considerable demands on attention and memory.

Since we have invoked a distinction between competence and performance and this distinction often meets with resistance, something should be said in its defense.   In   particular,   we   should   be   sure   to   separate   the competence/performance distinction *per se* from particular theories of what might constitute any particular cognitive competence. In its essence, something like the competence-performance distinction has to be accepted by any serious experimental psychologist. Beyond any reasonable scientific doubt, human behavior or performance is the product of a very large number of psychological and biological factors whose precise effects are sometimes only vaguely understand. The recognition of this multitude of factors affecting actual behavior is precisely what Chomsky urged in his famous review of Skinner's *Verbal Behavior*. Take what we might call verbal behavior. The production and comprehension of a sentence in English is the product of the interplay of numerous factors. The amount of caffeine and nicotine in one's system, along with one's tolerance for these drugs, is a factor. Physical fatigue, as from lack of sleep or intense physical exertion, is a factor. One's emotional state–whether it is extreme depression, extreme joy, nervousness, or anxiety–influences speech production. One's attentional mechanisms come into play as well. A sudden loud noise, bright light, or rapid motion can interrupt normal speech production or comprehension. Memory limitations have a role to play as well. During the course of producing a long sentence, a normal speaker may forget how she began a sentence, thereby leading her, inadvertently, to utter a non-sentence.

Similarly, a normal hearer may lose track of how a sentence began, hence be unable to understand what is uttered. There are indefinitely many other factors, but one that cannot pass without mention is what one knows about the language one is speaking or hearing. This factor is what has traditionally been understood as linguistic competence. It is one among many factors that figure into linguistic behavior or linguistic performance.

So framed, a respect for the competence-performance distinction is little more an essential feature of good experimental design. Respecting the distinction comes down to controlling variables. In the psycholinguistic case, if a scientist wishes to ascertain a human's capacity to understand English sentences, the scientist must be sure to control for such things as the presence of stimulants or depressants in the person's blood stream, fatigue, emotional state, attention, motivation, memory limitations, and so forth. Concern for such controls is thoroughly commonplace. If a scientist wishes to determine something like a short-term memory capacity, she must control for such features as "chunking." She may, for example, use as test items random strings of digits or letters. She will not use "organized" strings of digits, such as "1, 2, 3, 4, 5", or organized strings of letters, such as FBI, CIA, or USSR. What holds in the general experimental situation holds for determining a normal human's representational capacity. If one wishes to explore the limits of a human representational capacity for numbers, one has to control for the effects of attention, memory, recognition, and motivation.

As the competence/performance distinction has been described here, it seems to be entirely unobjectionable. To keep it in this uncontroversial status, it is important to distance the competence/performance distinction from specific theories of what constitutes competence. In other words, objections to particular hypotheses about what constitutes a specific cognitive competence should not be mistaken for objections to the distinction between competence and performance. In the case of human representational capacities, we have on the table two theories about the nature of these capacities. One theory says that these capacities are strictly finite, the other says that they are unbounded. While one might doubt that representational capacities are unbounded, one should not for this reason think that this, in itself, constitutes a basis for the rejecting the competence/performance distinction *in toto*.

To better distance particular theories of cognitive competence from the competence/performance distinction, we might consider another example. Another potentially worrisome theory of competence is the hypothesis that linguistic competence involves what are called "derivations." Consider the rough form derivations take in the transformational grammars inspired by Chomsky, (1957, 1965). In this kind of grammar, a derivation begins with an S as a root node. This root node might then branch to an NP and a VP. The NP might in turn branch to a det and an N, each of which might then undergo lexical insertion. The VP might have a V appended to it and this V have a lexical item inserted. A linguistic derivation is, thus, the construction of a kind of tree structure, which Chomsky maintained was a part of linguistic competence. This theory of competence has met with skepticism in some quarters because of its apparent dissociation from linguistic performance. In particular, sentence parsing and production have generally been thought *not* to consist of first constructing a tree with a root node S, adding an NP and VP, then appending a det, N, and V, and finally inserting lexical items. So, a source of scepticism about the role of derivations as part of human linguistic competence stems from the fact that derivations bear only a vaguely specified, at best indirect relation to performance. In other words, Chomsky's theory of linguistic competence is thought to be problematic insofar as it is too far removed from linguistic performance.

Be skepticism about particular theories of cognitive and linguistic competence what they may, such skepticism should not be allowed to spread from those particular theories of competence to doubts about the viability of the distinction between competence and performance. Once we recognize the absolute necessity of some form of competence-performance distinction in any remotely plausible psychological theory and separate it from less psychologically essential theories of what constitutes a specific linguistic or cognitive competence, we are better prepared to see how to make an empirical determination of the productivity of human thought.

In the productivity argument, Fodor and Pylyshyn, (1988), maintain that the proper extrapolation from actual human performance is to an unbounded thought capacity. The need for this extrapolation means that the productivity of thought is not a phenomenon in the sense of something that is relatively directly available to sensory examination.[8] The productivity is not open to direct sensory inspection, but must be detected by more careful experimental means. It is an extrapolation that Fodor and Pylyshyn justify on the basis of the ways in which variations in memory and attentional demands can extend the range of actual performance. In other words, by providing incentives for greater attention to a task, one enables subjects to contemplate larger successors. By providing increased memory resources, such as those allowed by paper and pencil, subjects are capable of thinking about larger successors.

Thus, the explanandum that appears to be required for the productivity argument to begin to serve Classical ends is that there exists an unbounded capacity for entertaining distinct thoughts. At the least, there is no obvious reason to think this is not the explanandum that will serve Classicist ends. Moreover, there is at least some *prima facie* reason to think that human thought does have this unbounded capacity. Thus, insofar as human thought has this unbounded capacity, there is a feature of human cognition that bears explanation. If there is such a competence, its basis merits an explanation.

As a final note of clarification of our explanandum, it may be worth noting that nothing in the foregoing begs any questions in favor of Classicism and against Pure Atomism. Classicism and Pure Atomism both agree that there exist cognitive representations, but differ in the structure they attribute to these representations. Classicism attributes to them combinatorial syntactic and semantic structure, where Pure Atomism postulates only atomic syntactic and semantic structure. We might add as well that nothing in the foregoing development of the explanandum begs any questions in favor of Representationalism. We began by postulating a finite repertoire of actual human thoughts regarding successors. As was mentioned, one Representationalist interpretation of this is to postulate a finite underlying representational capacity, another is to postulate an unbounded underlying representational capacity. Focusing on these two interpretations is consistent with the fact that the productivity argument is intended primarily as a means of adjudicating between Representationalist theories, Classicism and Pure Atomism in particular. Logically speaking, however, one could opt for a species of Non-Representationalism that postulates either a finite or an unbounded underlying capacity that does not consist of representations. Exactly how and why one might choose these options is tangential to our present concerns. They are mentioned here only to indicate the extent to which a relatively theory-neutral explanandum might be developed here.

2 EXPLAINING UNBOUNDED REPRESENTATIONAL CAPACITIES

We have before us the explanandum. Now for the Classical explanation. Much of this explanation is familiar from the literature, but there are also some background assumptions that need to be spelled out in order to have a complete explanation, rather than a mere explanation sketch. Consider, first, the familiar hypotheses that were reviewed in Chapter 1. Classicism invokes the Computational Theory of the Attitudes and Representationalism, hence that thinking (believing, hoping, fearing) that p amounts to standing in a thinking (believing, hoping, fearing) computational relation to a representation r that means that p. Then, of course, there is the hypothesis that r has syntactic concatenative combinatorial structure to which the computer program of the mind is causally sensitive. Further, there is the hypothesis that cognitive representations have a concatenative combinatorial semantics. Finally, there is the hypothesis that cognitive representations satisfy what we called the Principle of Context Independence, according to which a given syntactic atom makes the same semantic contribution to each syntactic and semantic molecule to which it makes any semantic contribution. These are the Classical hypotheses one finds explicit in the literature.

One additional assumption that is only implicit in the Classical account is that, not only must r be part of a syntactically and semantically combinatorial representational system, r must be a part of a syntactically and semantically *recursive* combinatorial representational system. By this, we suppose that the grammar of the cognitive representations contains the functional equivalent of recursive syntactic rules, such as,

S → It is not the case that S,

S → NP VP, and

VP → VP S,

along with corresponding recursive semantic rules. If the system of representation were not syntactically and semantically recursive, then there would be no computational means of generating arbitrarily large representations. Or, to put matters in another way, it cannot be merely in virtue of the Computational Theory of Attitudes, Representationalism, and having syntactically and semantically concatenative combinatorial representations that respect the Principle of Context Independence that thought is productive, for even if these hypotheses were true, it need not be the case that thought is productive. One also needs the hypothesis that cognitive representations are recursive.

Four points of clarification about the recursivity of cognitive representations should be noted. First, the Classicist is often taken to assert that in order to explain the productivity of thought, one needs to postulate combinatorial or structured representations. This is in some sense correct. However, the foregoing shows that postulating combinatorial or structured representations is not sufficient for accounting for the productivity of thought. In addition, one must postulate recursive mechanisms. This point might not be worth mentioning were it not for the numerous responses to the productivity and systematicity arguments that devote tremendous efforts to showing how Connectionist networks might use a non-Classical combinatorial system of representation without thereafter devoting sufficient attention to specifying how this non-Classical combinatorial structure might account for the productivity and systematicity of thought.[9] Second, the sense in which we here describe a language as recursive differs from the standard usage found in formal language theory. In formal language theory, even grammars not containing recursive formation rules are considered recursive, so that merely combinatorial languages are by definition also recursive. So, on standard usage in formal language theory, an extremely simple grammar, such as

S → NP VP

NP → det N

VP → V

det = {the}
N = {dog}
V = {runs},

would count as recursive, where on our usage it would be counted as merely combinatorial, but not recursive. As a third point of clarification, we should note that the Classical hypothesis that the system of cognitive representation is syntactically and semantically recursive in the sense used here is logically stronger than the hypothesis that it is syntactically and semantically combinatorial. If a language is syntactically and semantically recursive, then it must be syntactically and semantically combinatorial. By contrast, even if a language is syntactically and semantically combinatorial it need not be syntactically and semantically recursive. The very simple grammar mentioned above illustrates this point. Fourth, a syntactically and semantically recursive language allows for arbitrarily large representations, but does not allow for literally infinitely large representations. No computer program writes a sentence that is infinitely long. At any point in a computation, a system can have executed only finitely many steps. Further, if a computation halts, it halts in a finite number of steps. So, although there may be no finite bound on the length of a sentence a given program may write, there is no infinite computation in Turing-equivalent digital computation. While this may now appear to be merely a technical point, it will prove to have important theoretical consequences in a moment.

Classicism, thus, offers a complete explanation of the productivity of thought by hypothesizing that attitudes are computational relations to mental representations, that mental representations have recursive (hence combinatorial) syntactic and semantic structure, that the system of mental representations involve context independent content, and that the computational mechanisms of the mind are causally sensitive to the syntactic structure of the cognitive representations. These are the minimal requirements for specifying what it is in virtue of which thought is productive. Once these hypotheses are in place, it follows that thought must be productive, so Classicism discharges its explanatory obligation.

Turn now to a Pure Atomistic account of productivity. As noted in Chapter 1, PA relies on some of the same hypotheses that Classicism does, namely, the Computational Theory of the Attitudes and Representationalism. Where Classicism supposes that cognitive representations have a combinatorial syntax and semantics, PA hypothesizes that cognitive representations are syntactically and semantically atomic. Thus, PA does not have to be concerned about the Principle of Semantic Compositionality, the Principle of Context Independence of Content, or recursivity, since these hypotheses presuppose a framework of combinatorial representations. To account for productivity, therefore, PA supposes that there is an infinite set of syntactically and semantically atomic representations, one for each possible thought.

The purported problem for PA is that an infinite set of syntactically and semantically atomic representations is untenable. Without the syntactic recursivity of representations, it is argued, PA has no tenable means for generating arbitrarily large representations. How can a finite structure, such as the brain, have the capacity to recognize denumerably many distinct syntactic states that have nothing syntactically in common? How can a finite structure, such as the brain, recognize denumerably many distinct states, without decomposing that recognitional capacity into a finite set of recognitional capacities that constitute a) recognitional capacities for a finite set of syntactic atoms and b) recognitional capacities for a finite set of syntactic combinatorial operations? Further, how could a finite structure, such as the brain, have the capacity to generate the semantics of denumerably many syntactically distinct states having no common syntactic elements? The only known way of generating an unbounded set of representations is through the use of some sort of combinatorial syntax and semantics, such as that postulated by Classicism.

This is about as far as expositions of the productivity argument go. Yet, it does not address some of the possible responses. The logic of the productivity argument is not strictly speaking that of an impossibility argument. Oversimplified exposition and overstated rhetoric aside, the productivity arguments offer no positive account of why an alternative to Classicism is impossible. Rather the point is that the Classical way to account for productivity is the only known feasible way. This leaves the door open for a Pure Atomist to provide some account of the way in which denumerably many syntactically and semantically atomic representations are possible. Here the most salient possibility is analog representation. Perhaps some real-valued physical quantity, such as the firing rate of a neuron, might constitute the syntactic vehicles of cognitive content. Digital representations of magnitudes, such as decimal expansions in Arabic numerals, will not suffice, as this system is itself syntactically and semantically combinatorial. What is needed instead is the actual real-valued physical quantities themselves. This proposal makes for an unbounded supply of discrete syntactic states that are not combinatorial, hence suitable for use by a Pure Atomist. Further, it is possible to have these real physical quantities be semantically atomic. Further, we can embody the non-denumerably many physical quantities in a finite amount of physical material. So, real-valued quantities might be a viable starting point for the Pure Atomist.

The real-valued quantities version of PA is a sketch of a solution to the problem of explaining the productivity of thought, but it faces a number of challenges. In the first place, there is the challenge of providing a plausible account of the way in which the non-denumerably many distinct syntactic states receive a semantic interpretation of the sort one expects to find in a cognitive economy. Exactly what this amounts to is not completely clear, but something like the following is involved. The challenge here is not merely to have real-valued quantities constitute representations. One can envision how real-valued quantities such as, say, the firing rate of a neuron, might represent, say, a range of temperatures. The range of firing rates has a structure and organization that can be mapped in a relatively natural way onto the structure and organization of temperatures; the higher the firing rate, the higher the temperature. By contrast, it is much less clear how the structure and organization of real-valued neuronal firing rates might be related to the contents of propositional attitudes, such as that the race is over, that the moment of truth is at hand, that it all comes down to the race of truth. So, it is one thing for real-valued quantities to get some semantic interpretation; it is another for them to receive the range of semantic interpretations that might do duty in a cognitive economy. The challenge is the latter.

A second challenge is to address the possibility of entertaining the same thought twice. On the real-valued theory, even the slightest discrepancy in the values of two distinct real-valued quantities would apparently constitute a syntactic and semantic difference. Thus, any two distinct firing rates in a neuron, for example, would correspond to two distinct thoughts. So, unless a neuron could precisely reproduce a given firing rate with complete precision, a neuron could not precisely reproduce the same thought. If such a theory of cognitive representation were true, it would appear to be quite rare that an agent with that system of cognitive representation would think the same thought twice. This is simply one way of understanding the problem of noise in analog representational schemes, the problem of requiring unbounded precision in a system of limited precision.

A third challenge would be to develop a plausible theory of cognitive processes or sequences of cognitive states. Consider the sorts of cognitive states that one passes through when playing a game of chess. One considers, say, the knight and one of its possible moves. One then entertains possible responses from one's opponent, then one considers how one might respond to the opponent's response. Or think of the sequences of cognitive states involved in channel surfing. Perhaps this involves recognizing what is showing on a given channel, spending a greater or lesser amount of time determining whether what is showing is a commercial or part of a program. One then evaluates whether it is worthwhile to continue watching what is on the given channel or whether the next channel might have something more interesting. How can one relate sequences of cognitive states such as this with changes in real-valued physical quantities, such as the changes in rates of firing of a given neuron? After all, when a neuron changes from one firing rate to another, doesn't it pass through non-denumerably many distinct firing rates, hence through non-denumerably many distinct representational states, hence non-denumerably many distinct cognitive states? There is no reason to think that this or the other challenges are insuperable, but at the very least much more will have to be said in order to get this version of Pure Atomism in working order.

The upshot of our examination of the productivity argument is that, while Classicism has a relatively clear, plausible account of productivity, a Pure Atomistic account faces significant obstacles. The only Pure Atomistic account on offer, some version of the theory of analogue representation, is not sufficiently well-developed so as to have an account of the class of cognitive representations that might constitute a cognitive economy. Nor do analogue representations have a means for addressing the problem of reliable reproduction of a given representational state. Nor does the theory of analogue representation have a plausible theory of cognitive processes. This gives us some defeasible reason to think that, insofar as thought is productive, we have some reason to think that cognition involves a recursive system of syntactically and semantically combinatorial representations.

NOTES

1. Cf., e.g., Matthews, (1994), Niklasson and van Gelder, (1994), van Gelder and Niklasson, (1994), Cummins, (1996b).

2. Cf., Fodor & Pylyshyn, (1988), pp. 12-13.

3. Cf, Fodor & Pylyshyn, (1988), pp.17-28.

4. Braddon-Mitchell & Fitzpatrick, (1990), p. 6f, examine this version of the productivity argument.

5. Fodor, (1987), p. 148, implicitly draws attention to this weakness in this way of formulating the productivity argument.

6. Cf., Fodor, (1987), p. 148.

7. Cf., Fodor & Pylyshyn, (1988), p. 34.

8. This feature of productivity motivates the present consistent use of the technical term "explanandum", rather than the more familiar term "phenomenon." Similar considerations motivate talk of the systematicity explananda, rather than the systematicity phenomena.

9. Smolensky, (1987), for example goes on at great length about how one might have non-Classically structured representations, but says very little about how this non-Classical structure is to explain the productivity or systematicity of thought.

CHAPTER 4

THE SYSTEMATICITY OF INFERENCE

Moving on to the systematicity of inference argument, we begin to collect on our investment in the history and philosophy of science made back in Chapter 2. Here we hope to see how Fodor and Pylyshyn think that structural features of the accounts offered by Classicism and Pure Atomism provide some defeasible reason to think that human cognition is Classical. The principal problem for Pure Atomism is that, while it is able to develop a system that displays systematic relations among inferences, this is not all that has to be accomplished in order to explain the systematic relations. In this chapter, we begin with a relatively lengthy discussion and defense of the truth of the explanandum, then turn to an examination of the Classical and Pure Atomistic accounts of the explanandum. The surprising conclusion in this chapter will be that, while Pure Atomism does not meet the explanatory standard Fodor and Pylyshyn are aiming for, neither does Classicism.

1 WHAT IS THE SYSTEMATICITY OF INFERENCE?

As Fodor and Pylyshyn present it, the explanandum in the systematicity of inference argument is the following putative fact:

inferences that are of similar logical type ought, pretty generally, to elicit correspondingly similar cognitive capacities. You shouldn't, for example, find a kind of mental life in which you get inferences from P&Q&R to P but you don't get inferences from P&Q to P (Fodor & Pylyshyn, 1988, p. 47).

In a footnote to this they add that

The hedge ["pretty generally"] is meant to exclude cases where inferences of the same logical type nevertheless differ in complexity in virtue of, for example, the length of their premises. The inference from (AvBvCvDvE) and (¬B&¬C&¬D&¬E) to A is of the same logical type as the inference from AvB and ¬B to A. But it wouldn't be very surprising, or very interesting, if there were minds that could handle the second inference but not the first (ibid., fn. 28).

Although the explanandum here would seem to be relatively straightforward, there are many features that bear elaboration.

1) As with all of the systematicity arguments, the explanandum is supposed to be a property of a finite set of cognitive states. Unlike the third version of the productivity argument discussed above, the explanandum here does not involve an idealization or extrapolation from actual finite performance to an unbounded cognitive capacity. Thus, in a finite set of sentences, a normal human who can infer one instance of a given type of logical inference, say, inferring Q from P and (P → Q), has the capacity to perform another instance of that type of inference, say, inferring Q from P&R and ((P&R)→Q) or from (PvR) and ((PvR)→Q).

2) The foregoing point has implications for what we say about an ambiguity in Fodor and Pylyshyn's exposition of the systematicity of inference. On the one hand, the letters P, Q, R, etc., might be treated as abbreviations for particular natural language sentences that identify particular cognitive states. On the other, the letters P, Q, R, etc., might be treated as schematic letters that might correspond to a range of natural language sentences that identify sets of cognitive states. On the former interpretation, the capacity to infer P both from P&Q and from P&(Q&R) would amount to a relatively limited capacity, something like the capacity to infer that John loves Mary both from John loves Mary and Mary loves John and from John loves Mary and Mary loves John and John is married to Mary. By contrast, on the latter interpretation, where the letters are schematic letters or metalinguistic variables, the capacity to infer P both from P&Q and from P&(Q&R) would amount to a relatively more robust capacity. It might amount to, say, the capacity to infer that John loves Mary from

a) John loves Mary and Mary loves John,
b) John loves Mary and Mary loves John and John is married to Mary,
c) John loves Mary and John is tall,
d) John loves Mary and John is tall and John is married to Mary,
e) John loves Mary and John is tall and Mary is not tall.

In fact, if the letters are treated as schematic letters, there appears to be no upper bound on the number of distinct premises from which a conclusion, such as that John loves Mary, might be inferred. If the letters are treated as schematic letters, then the capacity to infer P both from P&Q and from P&(Q&R) will be a kind of general capacity.

Point 1) above, however, renders the distinction between P, Q, R, etc., as abbreviations and as schematic letters much less momentous. Since the systematicity of inference is a strictly finite inferential capacity, there is no implicit unbounded generality. When P, Q, R, etc. are schematic letters, they still express only a finite capacity. So, in truth, there are no significant philosophical/scientific consequences to this ambiguity. We discuss the ambiguity simply to show that it is innocuous.

3) Even though Fodor and Pylyshyn eschew an *explanandum* involving an unbounded representational capacity, this does not mean that the *theory* they invoke to explain this explanandum does not involve an unbounded representational capacity. That is, in limiting the nature of the explanandum, they are not thereby limiting themselves regarding their theory of cognitive architecture. In fact, insofar as Classicists are committed to the explanation of productivity presented in Chapter 3, they are committed to a system of cognitive representations with an unbounded generative capacity. Fodor and Pylyshyn simply do not bring this unbounded capacity into play in explaining the systematicity of inference, or indeed any of the systematicity explananda. For purposes of the systematicity arguments, the Classicist's hypothesis of an unbounded representational capacity of human thought is assumed to be explanatorily idle.

4) The explanandum in this argument is about cognitive competence or cognitive capacities. The explanandum is not that any normal human who, at some point in her life, infers P from P&Q will, at some other point in her life, go on to infer P from P&Q&R, or vice versa. The claim is not about performance; it is about competence. In fact, the hedge mentioned in Fodor and Pylyshn's footnote quoted above is supposed to draw attention to one of the many possible performance factors, such as memory or recognitional limitations, that might have differential impacts on the capacity to infer A from (AvBvCvDvE) and (¬B&¬C&¬D&¬E), on the one hand, and the capacity to infer A from AvB and ¬B, on the other.

5) The systematicity of inference need not be a capacity that all human beings can immediately exercise. The point here might be spelled out through a rough and ready distinction Chomsky, (1980), has drawn between first- and second-order capacities. A first-order capacity is one that a person can currently exercise, provided that there are no occurrent impediments. A second-order capacity is one that a person can exercise given appropriate training or conditions for development. Thus, most citizens of the United States have a first-order capacity to speak English. They can immediately speak English provided they are not gagged, sleeping, sedated, and so forth. By contrast, most citizens of the United States have only a second-order capacity to speak Chinese, run ten miles, prove theorems in topology, or play the piano. The average U.S. citizen can speak Chinese, run ten miles, prove theorems in topology, or play the piano only with appropriate training, under certain conditions conducive to development. Applied to the systematicity of inference, it is possible that the

average human being does have the capacity to draw inferences in keeping with the principles of sentential logic, provided only that limitations of memory, salience, recognitional capacities, and so forth, are taken into account. It is also, however, probable that the systematicity of inference is a kind of capacity that requires certain conditions for development, conditions such as proper education. While it is an important theoretical question how one might demarcate the two kinds of capacities and an important empirical question as to which type of capacity the systematicity of inference might be, for present purposes of making the case for a Classical system of representation, the Classicist need only establish that the systematicity of inference is a second-order capacity. If it is possible for normal human beings, given potentially specifiable developmental conditions, along with occurrent environmental conditions, to carry out systematic inferences, then there exists some regularity that merits scientific attention.

6) The systematicity of inference is supposed to be a feature of a "normal" human cognition. It is not to be expected that this human capacity is beyond the reach of disease or injury. Just as disease and injury can impair human capacities for speech, vision, and facial recognition, so disease and injury can impair human reasoning capacities.

7) It is possible to decompose the systematicity of inference into a cluster of different explananda based on the type of inference involved. Thus, we might recognize the systematicity of conjunction elimination, the systematicity of *modus ponens*, and the systematicity of *modus tollens*. So, were a normal human to have the capacity to infer P from P&Q and the capacity to infer P from P&Q&R, then that human would display at least some limited degree of systematicity for conjunction elimination. Further, were a normal human to have the capacity to infer Q from P and P→Q, and from P&R and ((P&R)→Q), then that person would display systematicity for *modus ponens*. In principle, a Classicist might appeal to any one of these types of systematicity of inference to formulate an explanandum in a defeasible argument for the existence of a Classical system of mental representation

8) In Chapter 1 we drew attention to the fact that the systematicity arguments are initially designed to adjudicate between competing theories of the structure of cognitive representations, namely, Classical and Pure Atomist theories. In Chapters 5 and 6, we shall see that the explananda in Fodor and Pylyshyn's discussion of the systematicity of cognitive representations and the compositionality of representations draw attention to supposed features of possible cognitive states; these explananda make no presuppositions–or at least relatively minimal presuppositions–regarding the transitions among possible cognitive states. By contrast, the systematicity of inference in any of its subspecies presupposes certain features of the possible cognitive states and certain features of the transitions between the possible cognitive states. In order

for a device to display, say, systematicity of conjunction elimination, it must be capable of entering certain representational states corresponding to the premises and conclusions of conjunction eliminations. One set of such states might be described schematically as

P, Q, R,
P&P, P&Q, P&R,
Q&P, Q&Q, Q&R,
R&P, R&Q, R&R,
P&(P&P), P&(P&Q), P&(P&R),
P&(Q&P), P&(Q&Q), P&(Q&R),
P&(R&P), P&(R&Q), P&(R&R).[1]

Similarly, in order for a system to display systematicity of *modus ponens*, a system must be capable of assuming states with contents corresponding to the premises and conclusions of inferences involving *modus ponens*. An example of such a set of possible occurrent states might be described schematically as

P, Q, R,
P→P, P→Q, P→R,
Q→P, Q→Q, Q→R,
R→P, R→Q, R→R,
P→(P→P), P→(P→Q), P→(P→R),
P→(Q→P), P→(Q→Q), P→(Q→R),
P→(R→P), P→(R→Q), P→(R→R).

This much is obvious. Less obvious is that the systematicity of inference also involves conditions on transitions among the foregoing types of possible cognitive states. In principle, it is possible to program a digital computer, such as a Turing machine, such that it is possible for it to enter a state that represents P&Q, a state that represents P, and a state that represents Q, without it being possible for it to go from a state that represents P&Q to a state that represents P or a state that represents Q. In other words, there are computing devices programmed such that they perform computations that pass through a representational state with the content P&Q, other computations that pass through representational state with the content P, and still other computations that pass through the representational state with the content Q, but they do not perform computations that pass through the representational state P&Q, then proceed to a computational state with the content P or a computational state with the content Q. If, however, the computing device is systematic for conjunction elimination, it must be possible for it to go from a state in which it can represent P&Q to a state in which it can represent P and a state in which it can represent Q. This is simply part of the requirement of a system being able to perform conjunction elimination. Thus, the systematicity of conjunction elimination places certain conditions on the patterns of possible state transitions, while the systematicity of *modus ponens* places other conditions and the systematicity of *modus tollens* still others. We shall return to this feature of the systematicity of inference in later chapters where we consider the systematicity of cognitive representations and the compositionality of representations.

9) In an extensive examination of the systematicity arguments, Robert Cummins (1996) argues that Fodor relies on some dubious/dubitable (?) philosophical assumptions about the nature of propositions. He claims that

> there is an undefended assumption here that standard logical notation does, in fact, provide a structural representation of propositions and other inferentially related contents. This assumption is bound to remain undefended pending an independent account of the structure of propositions and other inferentially related contents (Cummins, 1996b, p. 612).[2]

Although Fodor does, in fact, believe that propositions have structure,[3] this is incidental to the workings of the various systematicity arguments. There is simply no need to appeal to propositions or their structure in order to state the explanandum in the systematicity of inference argument or even any other systematicity argument.[4] The point should be clear from an examination of the systematicity of conjunction elimination. Whenever a person is in some cognitive state that has what we identify as conjunctive content and can perform a conjunction elimination, then, whenever that person is in another cognitive state that has what we identify as conjunctive content of greater or lesser complexity, then the person has the cognitive capacity to perform another conjunction elimination. Here we haven't had recourse to any presuppositions about the structure of propositions or semantic contents, yet we have stated an empirical generalization that merits an explanation. If conjunction eliminations correspond to a class of inferences such that a person can perform a conjunction elimination of a given degree of complexity just in case she can perform one of another degree of complexity, then there exists a regularity that deserves an explanation. What holds for the systematicity of conjunction elimination holds for the systematicity of various other inferences forms, *mutatis mutandis*.

10) One of the more common reactions to the explananda in the systematicity arguments is to suggest that they somehow beg some question in favor of a Classical theory of the structure of cognitive representations. We have already encountered this idea once in our discussion of the productivity arguments. Here we consider other versions of this claim that appear to be most relevant to the systematicity of inference. Mark Rowland observes that "The demand that connectionism postulate and account for logically or sententially structured representations is simply not a legitimate demand" (Rowlands, 1994, p. 495). Quite right.[5] It should be clear, however, that Classicists do not demand that

non-Classicists postulate or account for logically or sententially structured representations. To demand that non-Classicists postulate or account for sententially structured representations *in the mind* would just be to demand that they be Classicists. Not a very philosophically or scientifically interesting demand. Further, to demand that non-Classicists postulate or account for sententially structured representations in the environment, as in the sentences of natural or artificial language, is not an essential element of the systematicity of inference argument. We just reviewed this point in our consideration of Cummins's worry about the logical structure of propositions. What Classicists demand in the systematicity of inference argument is that non-Classicists explain why inference is systematic, why it is, for example, that a normal human being who has the capacity to infer John loves Mary from John loves Mary and Mary loves John also has the capacity to infer that John loves Mary from John loves Mary and Mary loves John and John is married to Mary.

11) It has sometimes been thought that the systematicity arguments beg the question against non-Classicists by making certain metaphysical assumptions about the nature of the cognitive or in supposing that there in fact exist cognitive representations. Common worries notwithstanding, it is relatively easy to see that the premise that inference is systematic makes no presuppositions regarding the metaphysical nature of thought or how thoughts might be constituted in the brain. Classicism, of course, advances hypotheses about the way thoughts are constituted in the brain, but the explanans in the systematicity of inference argument does not. To see this, we can as before state the explanandum without presuppositions as to what constitutes a cognitive state. Again, consider just conjunction elimination. What we suppose needs to be explained here is such things as that Antoine can infer that John loves Mary either from John loves Mary and Mary loves John or from John loves Mary and Mary loves John and the Pope is Catholic. Supposing that Antoine has this pair of inferential capacities makes no presuppositions about the nature of thought, the existence of mental representations, or the nature of mental representations. To take an extreme case, we may take a (Dennettian?) instrumentalist account of cognitive states according to which Antoine's being in a particular cognitive state is a matter of someone taking a particular stance toward Antoine. On such a view, Antoine's cognitive state may be supposed to be a matter of someone finding it practically convenient to treat Antoine in a particular manner. On such a view of the nature of cognitive states, there need be no mental representations. From this instrumentalist perspective, the systematicity of inference simply comes to a feature of the patterns in our attributions of cognitive capacities: any time we are willing to treat someone such that she can infer P from P&Q then we are also willing to treat her in such a way that she can infer P from P&Q&R, and vice versa. There is nothing logically inconsistent about such a form of instrumentalism admitting the systematicity of conjunction elimination, or any

of the other forms of systematicity for that matter. Of course, if thought is in fact systematic in this or any other sense, then the instrumentalist will be obliged to provide some explanation of the patterns in our attributions of cognitive capacities.[6]

In each of the three foregoing issues, we have seen that the way to deal with objections that the systematicity of inference makes certain dubious philosophical presuppositions or begs certain philosophical questions is to restate the essential elements of the explanandum in such a way that these presuppositions are eliminated. In other words, formulate the explananda in such a way as to eliminate the dubious assumption and render them logically neutral between Classicism and Pure Atomism.

2 THE CASE AGAINST THE SYSTEMATICITY OF INFERENCE

To this point, we have been considering what is thought to constitute the systematicity of inference. Now we turn to the case that some non-Classicists have made for doubting the existence and/or pervasiveness of the systematicity of inference. Tim van Gelder and Lars Niklasson, (1994), with Robert Cummins (1996b) following their lead, have argued that the human reasoning literature shows that inference is not systematic.[7] If, however, there is no systematicity of inference, then there is nothing to explain in the systematicity of inference argument, hence no argument that might favor Classicism over its rivals. The problem with the evidence van Gelder and Niklasson cite is simply that it only establishes the existence of certain content effects in inference, not the non-existence of systematic effects in inference. This is not a criticism of the literature cited; it is a criticism of van Gelder and Niklasson's and Cummins's attempt to press these results against Classicism.

The van Gelder & Niklasson, (1994), challenge to the systematicity of inference relies on experimental results involving conditional reasoning. In particular, their criticism focused on the putative systematicity of *modus tollens*.[8] They begin by arguing that,

> classical architectures predict that, since mental processes are sensitive to structure, such features of the inference instance as the *content* of the constituent symbol or their *frequency of prior occurrence* should be irrelevant, since such features make no difference to the combinatorial structure (van Gelder & Niklasson, 1994a, p. 907).

In other words, van Gelder and Niklasson argue that Classicism predicts that there should be no content or familiarity effects in conditional reasoning. They then proceed to review experimental results that show that there are content and familiarity effects. In Kerns, Mirels, and Hinshaw, (1983), the investigators presented scientists with inferences in abstract form (which asked such things as "Do $P \rightarrow Q$ and *not-Q* imply *not-P*?") and in concrete form (which asked such things as "Do *If Rex is a terrier, then he likes apples*, and *Rex does not like apples*, imply *Rex is not a terrier?*") The study found a disparity in performance between the abstract and concrete instances. Only 41% of scientists in one group correctly recognized the validity of *modus tollens* in the abstract case, while 69% of the scientists in another group recognized its validity in the concrete case. So, contrary to what van Gelder and Niklasson say Classicism predicts, subjects did not render their decisions only on the basis of sentential structure or logical form. The content of the inference made a difference.

Van Gelder and Niklasson also draw attention to a comparison of the results of the Wason card selection task with the results on a similar task involving more familiar items. In the Wason card selection task, subjects are shown four cards and given a rule as shown in Figure 4.1. They must then report which cards must be turned over in order to test the rule. It is well established that subjects perform very poorly on this task. By contrast, they are much better if the subject matter of the task involves something familiar, e.g., a rule such as "If a person is drinking beer, then that person must be over 19 years of age" (Griggs & Cox, 1982, cited in van Gelder and Niklasson, 1994). In this case, familiarity with the subject material, not just formal structure, appears to function in human reasoning, hence,
according to van Gelder and Niklasson, provides a refutation of a putative prediction of Classicism.

To begin to address van Gelder and Niklasson's concerns, we must recall the role of the competence/performance distinction in the Classical conception of the mind. As we have said before, it is beyond any reasonable scientific doubt that human performance on cognitive tasks, such as the Wason card selection task, will require the co-ordinated interaction of a wide range of distinct, often poorly

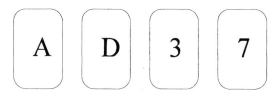

If there is an A on one side,
there is a 3 on the other.

Figure 4.1. A Wason card selection task.

understood, capacities. Thus, when a normal literate person sits in a quiet room, under good lighting conditions, looking at an image like the one shown in Figure 4.1, many capacities come into play. The subject must be sufficiently motivated in order to attend to and undertake the task. Attention must be involved to a greater or lesser degree. The subject's recognitional capacities must enable her to recognize the various marks printed on the paper in front of her. Her reading ability must be deployed. In solving the task, certain memory demands must be met. Further, the subject's inferential reasoning capacities, whatever they are, must be engaged. All this, and possibly more, must interact smoothly in order for the subject to ascertain which card(s) must be inspected in order to justify a correct answer the question that has been posed. It is clearly not the Classical position to maintain that only the logical form of a proposition a subject encounters will influence the course of information processing.

Now van Gelder and Niklasson recognize that Fodor and Pylyshyn will invoke the competence/performance distinction here, so they try to minimize its role. For present purposes, only two of van Gelder and Niklasson's three arguments are relevant. They write,

> Second, note that in Connectionism and Cognitive Architecture, Fodor & Pylyshyn *explicitly declined* to rely on the competence/performance distinction, acknowledging that the hypothesis of ideal competence was held in suspicion in the opposing camp (connectionists) (van Gelder and Niklasson, 1994, p. 908, italics in original).

Here van Gelder and Niklasson simply overstate what Fodor and Pylyshyn propose to do without in moving from the productivity argument to the systematicity arguments. Fodor and Pylyshyn *do not* explicitly decline to rely on the competence/performance distinction. They do not propose to abandon the distinction, but only one component of their theory of what constitutes human cognitive competence, namely, the assumption that it includes an unbounded generative capacity. The text of Fodor and Pylyshyn's critique is relatively clear about this:

> In the meantime, however, we propose to view the status of productivity arguments for Classical architectures as moot; we're about to present a different sort of argument for the claim that mental representations need an articulated internal structure. It is closely related to the productivity argument, but it doesn't require the idealization to unbounded competence. Its assumptions should thus be acceptable even to theorists who - like Connectionists - hold that the finitistic character of cognitive capacities is intrinsic to their architecture (Fodor & Pylyshyn, 1988, pp. 36-37).

Note, in the final sentence, the explicit reference to a finite cognitive capacity. Later, Fodor and Pylyshyn add,

> The point isn't that phrase books are finite and can therefore exhaustively specify only *non*-productive languages; that's true, but we've agreed not to rely on productivity arguments for our present purposes (ibid., p. 37).

Then, later,

> Notice that you can make this argument for constituent structure in sentences without idealizing to astronomical computational capacities. There are productivity arguments for constituent structure, but they're concerned with our ability–in principle–to understand sentences that are arbitrarily long. Systematicity, by contrast, appeals to premises that are much nearer home (ibid., p. 38)

Then, yet again,

> Productivity arguments infer the internal structure of mental representation from the presumed fact that nobody has a *finite* intellectual competence (ibid., p. 40).

All these passages uniformly indicate that what Fodor and Pylyshyn propose to do without in the systematicity arguments is the hypothesis that there is an unbounded representational capacity. None of the foregoing passages, nor any others in the Fodor and Pylyshyn critique, indicate that they wish to abandon any more than this. In particular, none indicate that they wish to abandon the competence/performance distinction *per se*. As a final indication of Fodor and Pylyshyn's continued commitment to the competence/performance distinction, we should recall the passage cited above:

> The hedge ["pretty generally"] is meant to exclude cases where inferences of the same logical type nevertheless differ in complexity in virtue of, for example, the length of their premises. The inference from (AvBvCvDvE) and (¬B&¬C&¬D&¬E) to A is of the same logical type as the inference from AvB and ¬B to A. But it wouldn't be very surprising, or very interesting, if there were minds that could handle the second inference but not the first (ibid., fn. 28)

If this passage does not invoke one dimension of the competence/performance distinction, then van Gelder and Niklasson owe us some explanation of what

Fodor and Pylyshyn are up to here. The cental point here is that van Gelder and Niklasson simply conflate the competence-performance distinction with one component of the Classical theory of the nature of cognitive/linguistic competence. We discussed this kind of confusion in the defense of the competence/performance distinction back in Chapter 3. Given what has been said above about the crucial role of the competence/performance distinction in psychology, Fodor and Pylyshyn could hardly be expected to abandon it.

Van Gelder and Niklasson's other comment on the Classicist appeal to the competence-performance distinction is that,

> explanations of facts of performance that begin from a competence and degrade that competence by means of contingent limitations must be able to give *plausible* explanations of *how* those contingent limitations give rise to the observed performance. In the case of deductive inference, there is no obvious plausible way to do this. Classicists are welcome to take up the challenge (van Gelder & Niklasson, 1994, p. 908).

Here the argument appears to be that, even if Fodor and Pylyshyn wanted to avail themselves of a competence/performance distinction, the distinction would be more of an empirical burden that it is worth. Yet, what is the alternative to accepting the explanatory burden of maintaining a competence/performance distinction? Surely the view that there is *no* cognitive reasoning capacity is indefensible. Surely, whatever cognitive reasoning capacity there is must interact with such things as capacities for recognition, memory, and attention. One can, of course, have a fair chance of refuting a particular view of the nature of human inferential capacities, some view such as that they are systematic. Yet, that does not suffice to show that there is no cognitive capacity for reasoning that ought to be separated from other performance factors.

In this passage, there is also the implication that Classicists are in more of a bind explaining the role of performance factors in behavior than are non-Classicists. Once one appreciates the Classicist's view that behavior is the product of multiple interacting factors, however, the basis for supposing that Classicism is in an especially difficult situation is not obvious. Why can't Classicists simply appeal to the same performance factors, such as abstractness and familiarity, as do non-Classicists? To answer this, we should recall that van Gelder and Niklasson argue that

> classical architectures predict that, since mental processes are sensitive to structure, such features of the inference instance as the *content* of the constituent symbol or their *frequency of prior occurrence* should be irrelevant, since such features make no difference to the combinatorial structure (van Gelder & Niklasson, 1994a, p. 907).

At first glance, this passage appears to be nothing but fallacious reasoning. When Fodor & Pylyshyn, (1988), p. 13, claim that cognitive processing is sensitive to the structure of cognitive representations, they do *not* claim that cognitive processing is sensitive *only* to the structure of cognitive representations. Further, while it is true that content and frequency effects do not influence combinatorial structure of cognitive representations, it does not logically follow from this that Classicism can admit no content or frequency effects. This is no better than arguing that, since friction does not change the mass of a pendulum, friction is irrelevant to the behavior of a pendulum. Content and frequency can have their effects on cognition through means other than influencing combinatorial structure, just as friction has its effects on pendula through means other than by influencing a pendulum's mass.

The foregoing might suffice to turn back van Gelder and Niklasson's argument, were it not for the existence of certain comments that Fodor makes that seem to endorse the van Gelder and Niklasson line. Fodor often says something like the following:

We can therefore build machines which have, again within famous limits, the following property: The operations of the machine consist entirely of transformations of symbols; in the course of performing these operations, the machine is sensitive solely to syntactic properties of the symbols; and the operations that the machine performs on the symbols are entirely confined to altering their shapes. (Fodor, 1987, p. 19).

Such claims might well suggest the view that van Gelder and Niklasson argue for, namely, that there is no room for such content effects as abstractness and familiarity in a Classical architecture. All that exists in a computational model of cognition are syntactic effects.

Yet, such comments must be read in context. In the case of the foregoing claims, that context includes these claims:

Yet the machine is so devised that it will transform one symbol into another if and only if the propositions expressed by the symbols that are so transformed stand in certain *semantic* relations—e.g., the relation that the premises bear to the conclusion in a valid argument. Such machines—computers, of course—just *are* environments in which the syntax of a symbol determines its causal role in a way that respects its content (Fodor, 1987, p. 19).

So, properly understood, the Classical view is not that there are no content effects, such as those that might be attributed to abstractness and familiarity. Rather, it is that such of these content effects as are genuine must be accommodated within a computational framework by the interaction of combinatorial representations and computational operations that are causally sensitive to the combinatorial structure of these representations. In other words, all *bona fide* cognitive effects must ultimately be the product of underlying syntactic processes.

Now, it is true that Fodor's first comments above do not lend themselves to the idea that there are such things as frequency effects in cognition. Nevertheless, one can imagine ways in which such effects could be embedded in a syntactic engine roughly meeting Fodor's specifications. For example, a consistent Classicism might suggest that frequency effects are due to the way in which a list of syntactic objects is searched. More frequently used syntactic items are moved higher up on a list. Alternatively, a consistent Classicism might propose that frequency effects arise because of an order in which complex syntactic objects are generated. Changes in frequency of use are reflected in changes in the procedure for generating complex syntactic objects. All of this respects the Fodorian sense that the machinery of the mind is ultimately purely syntactic. Thus, if van Gelder and Niklasson are to establish their thesis that Classicism cannot admit content and familiarity effects, they need the conclusion that such content effects cannot be captured by the interaction of syntactically combinatorial representations and a syntactic computational apparatus. Granted, Classicists cannot, at present, provide the reduction of all putative content effects to syntactic processes. Nevertheless, van Gelder and Niklasson give no reason to think that such a reduction is impossible either.

Having, at long last, addressed van Gelder and Niklasson's use of the human reasoning literature, we may turn to Cummins's use. Cummins's critique of the systematicity of inference argument, though very brief, has much the same gist and many of the same weakness as does the van Gelder and Niklasson critique. Here is what Cummins has to say:

> there is ample empirical evidence that our sensitivity to the inferential relations captured by standard logic is extremely limited. Humans are a good deal better at modus ponens than they are with modus tollens, a fact that classical schemes will have to explain in some relatively ad hoc way. For similar reasons, it is an embarrassment to classical schemes that structure sensitive processing, unless constrained in some way, will treat "(A v B v C) & (D v E v F)" in the same way it treats "(P&Q)". I am not sure about this particular example, but no one who is up on the human reasoning literature could think that humans are very good at detecting sameness of logical form. Classical schemes based on standard logical notation appear to predict far more sensitivity to entailment relations than humans actually exhibit (Cummins, 1996b, pp. 612-613).

There are a number of weak points in this passage, some of which should be familiar at this stage of our discussion. In the first place, the systematicity of inference arguments have nothing to say about humans being very good at detecting sameness of logical form. As has been noted, actual human performance in detecting logical form is what Chomsky might call a second-order cognitive capacity, a capacity that is developed to a greater or lesser degree based on experience. It is also a capacity that presumably interacts with a multitude of factors. Among these factors are recognitional and attentional capacities, not to mention motivation, fatigue, memory capacity, and so forth. The systematicity of inference requires of humans only that they *be capable of* detecting and responding to sameness of logical form given appropriate training and opportunities for development, not that they normally do detect or respond to (sameness of) logical form or that they are normally very good at it. Some of the positive evidence for the hypothesized second-order human capacity for systematic inference is that at least some undergraduate students can be taught first-order predicate logic.

The second weak point in Cummins's critique is his observation that humans are not as good at *modus tollens* as they are at *modus ponens*. The systematicity of inference, however, is not a claim comparing distinct inference types at all; it is about comparing different instances of identical inference types. This should be pretty obvious from Fodor and Pylyshyn's claim, cited above, that "inferences that are of similar logical type ought, pretty generally, to elicit correspondingly similar cognitive capacities. You shouldn't, for example, find a kind of mental life in which you get inferences from P&Q&R to P but you don't get inferences from P&Q to P."

A third point to note in response to Cummins is that, even if it were to turn out that *modus tollens* were not systematic in the way Fodor and Pylyshyn suggest--even if there were nothing to be explained in this regard--all would not be lost for the systematicity of inference argument. As we suggested above, one might get much the same argumentative force by appeal to the systematicity of other inference forms, such as the systematicity of conjunction elimination.[9] Even if the only systematic patterns of inference in human reasoning were in conjunction elimination, this would be an explanandum that would figure in a version of the systematicity argument.[10] In fact, even some extremely limited degree of systematicity in conjunction elimination would serve. Thus, one could ask why it is that any person who can infer P from P&Q can also infer P from P&Q&R? Why is it that these capacities co-occur? As Fodor puts it,

Just a little systematicity of thought will do to make things hard for [Pure Atomism] since, as previously remarked, [Pure Atomism] is compatible with there being no systematicity of thought at all. And this is just as well, because although we can be sure that thought is somewhat systematic, we can't, perhaps, be sure of just how systematic it is (Fodor, 1987, p. 153).

It is, of course, more convenient for the Classicist to have the effects of combinatorial syntactic and semantic structure all over the place, just as it was convenient for Darwin to have biogeographical, morphological, and embryological regularities all over the place. Pervasiveness makes the relevant explanandum more salient and less open to doubt, but, for all that, pervasiveness is not essential to the efficacy of the argument.

A fourth problem arises when Cummins claims that the fact that humans are better at *modus ponens* than they are at *modus tollens* is a fact that must be explained in some relatively *ad hoc* way. This puts a sharper point on van Gelder and Niklasson's invitation to Classicists to take up the challenge of explaining how various performance factors interact with inferential competence to produce human behavior in various reasoning tasks. This is not directly an attack on the systematicity of inference arguments, but it need not pass without comment for that reason. Cummins gives no reason in support of his claim about what will be relatively *ad hoc*, but there is at least some reason to think it untrue. One proposal for explaining the disparity between *modus ponens* and *modus tollens* begins with the observation that *modus tollens* in some way involves processing an embedded negation, where *modus ponens* does not. In a *modus tollens*, one must recognize that the consequent of the conditional is the negation of the unconditional premise. This implicates something like the hypothesis that embedded negations are normally hard for humans to process. This hypothesis, however, is not simply an unconstrained *ad hoc* conjecture introduced merely to handle the superiority of *modus ponens* processing over *modus tollens* processing. We have independent corroborating evidence from human reasoning with disjunctive syllogism. Johnson-Laird, (1975), found that a high percentage of children can draw the appropriate inference from the following:

John is intelligent or he is rich.
He is not rich
=======================
???,

but even adults have considerably more difficulty with seeing what, if anything, follows in:

John is intelligent or he is not rich
He is rich.
=============
???

Some adults inferred that John is not intelligent, where others concluded that nothing follows from these premises. While Classicists maintain that normal humans can be made sensitive to logical form, they are free to accept the view that embedded negation is difficult to process. The difficulty could stem, for example, from the syntactic operations that are involved in searching for pattern matches. All of this, and considerably more, is perfectly consistent with the view that there are syntactic effects to be detected among a multitude of factors interacting to produce cognitive behavior. The point is not, of course, to defend this particular analysis of the difference between *modus ponens* and *modus tollens*. Perhaps the recourse to an hypothesis regarding the difficulty of embedded negation will not ultimately work out. Perhaps the weight of evidence will undermine the foregoing line of analysis. The point is that there is at least some reason to think that, Cummins's unsupported contentions notwithstanding, Classicists are not hopelessly bound to *ad hoc* hypotheses regarding the performance difference between *modus ponens* and *modus tollens*.

To wrap up this discussion we may reiterate the principal points concerning what the systematicity of inference is. Fodor and Pylyshyn suppose that humans have an inferential reasoning capacity–perhaps a second-order inferential capacity–that allows them to draw many inferences of a given logical type, provided that they are able to draw one inference of that logical type. Detecting this reasoning capacity can be a subtle experimental matter of controlling for such things as recognition, attention, memory, motivation, fatigue, content, familiarity, and abstractness, as well as conditions of proper training and development. Controlling such factors in an experimental setting in order to detect the effects of an underlying syntactic combinatorial apparatus is simply part of good scientific procedure. Perhaps one can make a solid case that inferential cognitive capacities are not systematic, but, to date, the efforts by van Gelder and Niklasson and Cummins do not succeed.

3 EXPLAINING THE SYSTEMATICITY OF INFERENCE

Having clarified the nature of the explanandum and eliminated some of the reasons for doubting its verity, we can examine why it is that providing an explanation of it is a problem for Pure Atomistic theories of cognitive representation. Suppose, for the sake of simplicity of exposition, that all that must be explained is why it is that a normal human who can infer that John loves Mary from the fact that John loves Mary and Mary loves John can also infer that John loves Mary from the fact that John loves Mary and Mary loves John and John is married to Mary; that is, consider only a limited degree of systematicity in conjunction elimination. Pure Atomism shares with Classicism an adherence to the Computational Theory of the Attitudes, Representationalism, and the hypothesis that the computer program of the mind is sensitive to the structure of representations. It remains for Pure Atomism to account for the systematicity of thought using only syntactically and semantically atomic representations. So, Pure Atomism will say something like the following. There exists a set of syntactic items $\{\alpha, \beta, \gamma\}$ such that

α means John loves Mary,

β means John loves Mary and Mary loves John,

γ means John loves Mary and Mary loves John and John is married to Mary,

0 is a null symbol,

and there exists a Turing machine program of the mind,

(TM1)   s0 β α s1,

        s0 γ α s1,

that replaces either β or γ with α. The first instruction is such that if the Turing machine is in state s0 scanning a β, it will replace it with an α and go into state s1. The second instruction is such that if the Turing machine is in state s0 scanning a β, it will replace it with an α and go into state s1. Since there is no instruction for the Turing machine to act upon when in state s1, it halts. Such a system can infer that John loves Mary from either John loves Mary and Mary loves John or from John loves Mary and Mary loves John and John is married to Mary.

The basic idea here can be extended in obvious ways to handle wider, but still finite, classes of propositions. So, for example, the basic scheme that enables the Turing-equivalent computer to infer that John loves Mary from two other propositions, can also enable the computer to infer that, say, Greg won from two other propositions. The scheme would suppose that there exists a set of syntactic items $\{\alpha, \beta, \gamma, \delta, \epsilon, \zeta\}$ such that

α means John loves Mary,

β means John loves Mary and Mary loves John,

γ means John loves Mary and Mary loves John and John is married to Mary,

δ means that Greg won,

ϵ means that Greg won and Laurent lost,

ζ means that Greg won and Laurent lost and Laurent will try again,

0 is a null symbol,

and that there exists a computer program of the mind,

(TM2)   s0 β α s1,

s0 γ α s1,
s0 ε δ s1,
s0 ζ δ s1.

In this system, the second pair of instructions functions in a manner analogous to the first pair. Clearly, the approach can handle any finite number of instantiations of the capacity to infer P from both P&Q and P&Q&R. There are also obvious ways to give a Pure Atomistic system the capacity to infer P from both P&Q and P&(QvR), or to infer P from both P&(Q&R) and P&(Q&(R&S)). Given this, an interest in convenience leads us to consider only simplest case without incurring any loss of argumentative power.

Notice that, in this argument, Pure Atomism has some story to tell. Fodor and Pylyshyn explicitly discuss this possibility.[11] This point is significant for both critics and supporters of the systematicity of inference argument. Critics and supporters alike cannot presume to have explained the systematicity of inference simply in virtue of having some mechanism that exhibits the explanandum. Even if a theory does have some account, one must still consider whether the account relies on arbitrary hypotheses. In fact, the burden at many points throughout this book will be to show just how arbitrary hypotheses have figured into the kinds of accounts that have been offered by both Classicists and Non-Classicists of various stripes. In other words, the burden will be to show how accounts of the sundry forms of systematicity are like the Creationist account of batrachian biogeography or like the Ptolemaic account of the limited elongation of Mercury and Venus.

So, what auxiliary hypotheses do Pure Atomists invoke? In addition to the hypotheses of Representationalism and the Computational Theory of the Attitudes, the Pure Atomist account relies on an hypothesis about the computer program of the mind, namely, that the program should contain the instruction "s0 β α s1" as well as the instruction "s0 γ α s1." This enables the program to carry out the pair of conjunction eliminations, hence display some systematicity in conjunction elimination. Yet, one might observe that one could just as easily program a computer to have both instructions, as well as just one or the other or neither. On this point, nothing hinges on the particular programming language used in our example, since the variability in programmability is found in all Turing-equivalent programming languages. Consider how the sorts of locutions that Fodor, et al., have used might be applied to criticize the Pure Atomist account. It is not enough in these cases to show that a Pure Atomist architecture is compatible with our limited degree of systematicity of conjunction elimination; the relevant kind of explanation requires something more. One might say that, while it is true that the Pure Atomist account shows how our limited degree of systematicity of conjunction elimination is *possible*, it does not show how it is *necessary* given Pure Atomism. It is possible for a Pure Atomist system to be programmed so that it infers John loves Mary both from John loves

Mary and Mary loves John and from John loves Mary and Mary loves John and John is married to Mary, but there is no necessity in it being so programmed. Although it is possible for a system to contain both "s0 β α s1" and "s0 γ α s1" as instructions, there is no reason why it must be this way. Or to make the point in yet another way, a Pure Atomist system could as easily be programmed to perform conjunction elimination only on sentences with exactly 1, 3, or 5 conjuncts, but not conjunction elimination on sentences with exactly 2, 4, or 6 conjuncts (Cf. Fodor & Pylyshyn, 1988, p. 48). These are the locutions Fodor and Pylyshyn use, but consider, now, the way in which the discussion in Chapter 2 suggests a slightly different analysis of way the Pure Atomist account relies on arbitrary hypotheses. According to this analysis, we appear to have the arbitrary hypothesis that the computer program of the mind has an instruction, or instructions, that insure that it can infer John loves Mary from both John loves Mary and Mary loves John, on the one hand, and John loves Mary and Mary loves John and John is married to Mary, on the other. It is arbitrary in the sense that it cannot be confirmed independently of the theory that cognition involves the stated system of Purely Atomic representations. That is, one cannot know that the computer program of the mind contains the instructions in (TM1), rather than some others, without knowing whether or not Pure Atomism holds in the cognitive economy. Thus, Pure Atomism has no genuine explanation of the systematicity of thought, hence there is some defeasible reason to think that the architecture of the mind does not use syntactically and semantically atomic representations. Here again, it is worth emphasizing that the distinction between central and auxiliary hypotheses is doing no work. Instead, the trouble lies in a feature of the set of hypotheses in the proffered account.

Consider, now, how Classicism might try to come to grips with our bit of systematicity in conjunction elimination. As with the productivity argument, the complete Classical argument for the systematicity of inference invokes the Computational Theory of the Attitudes, Representationalism, the syntactically and semantically concatenative combinatorial structure of representations, and the context independence of content. For the purposes of explaining our limited degree of systematicity of conjunction elimination, Classicism need not appeal to the recursivity of thought, but it must suppose that there exists a cognitive computer program that is sensitive to the syntactic structure of the representations and manipulates them so as to have them respect valid principles of conjunction elimination. Thus, the Classicist's program may scan sentences for a main-clause conjunction and, if a conjunction symbol is found, erase all the symbols save for those in one conjunct. In all instances of a given inference, the same formal operations apply, so that if a cognitive agent can infer one instance of a given inference, it can infer another. To make the point slightly more concrete, one might postulate a set of syntactically atomic representations, {α, β, γ, 0, &}, such that

α means John loves Mary
β means Mary loves John
γ means John is married to Mary
& means conjunction, and
0 is a null symbol,
along with a cognitive computer program, say, the Turing machine program,

(TM3) s0 α R s1
   s1 β 0 s2
   s1 γ 0 s2
   s1 & 0 s2
   s2 0 R s1.

The first instruction of (TM3) has the read-write head scan over α to the next square on the right and go into state s1. The remaining four instructions erase the symbols "β" "γ" and "&" replacing them with blanks.

We now have a *prima facie* complete Classical account of the systematicity of conjunction elimination, so we can now consider whether or not the account relies on some arbitrary hypothesis. But, of course, it does. Just as Pure Atomism relies on some hypothesis about the computer program of the mind in order to generate the explanandum, so Classicism must rely on a comparable hypothesis. The computational architecture of a Turing machine, or any other Turing-equivalent programming system, is such that it can just as easily allow a computer to perform systematic inferences as not. So, a combinatorial system might have the computer program (TM3) listed above, or it might have the program,

(TM4) s0 α R s1
   s1 & R s2
   s2 β R s3
   s3 0 L s4
   s4 β 0 s5
   s5 0 L s6
   s6 & 0 s7.

The first three instructions in this program cause the read-write head to scan right across an input string "α&β". If, when in state s3, the read-write head scans something other than a blank "0", it simply stops. So, on input "α&β&γ" the program does not change any of the tape contents. If, however, when in state s3, the read-write head scans a blank "0", then it moves back right across the tape erasing the symbols "&β", before finally halting in state s7. Thus, this computer program infers that John loves Mary from John loves Mary and Mary loves John, but not from John loves Mary and Mary loves John and John is married to Mary. Whatever would confirm the hypothesis that the system has one program, rather than the other, would confirm the hypothesis that the system uses combinatorial representation. So, the Classical hypothesis fails to explain the systematicity of inference in just the way that the Pure Atomist hypothesis did.

We have just seen that there is reason to think that Classicism and Pure Atomism fail to satisfy Fodor and Pylyshyn's explanatory standard insofar as both must rely on arbitrary principles concerning the nature of their hypothetical computer program of the mind. Yet, Classicism seems to run afoul of this explanatory standard in other ways as well. Consider the Principle of Compositionality and the Principle of Context Independence. These are well-recognized elements of Classicism. More important given the standard by which we chose to formulate Classicism in Chapter 1, they are clearly essential to the Classicist account of the systematicity of inference. The fact that the symbol, or string of symbols, "John loves Mary" has one and the same meaning when it occurs in "John loves Mary and Mary loves John" and "John love Mary and Mary loves John and John is married" enables a Classical system to infer that John loves Mary from both the fact that John loves Mary and Mary loves John and the fact that John love Mary and Mary loves John and John is married given only syntactic operations, such as erasing symbols on a Turing machine tape. The Principles of Compositionality and Context Independence have to be in force in order for a Classical system to process information by reference to logical form. This suggests that Classicism may, in fact, be in deeper trouble than Pure Atomism when it comes to meeting the explanatory challenges of the systematicity of inference. Then again, it may be that this sort of explanatory argument does not admit of degrees. One either has an explanation of the systematicity of some form of inference or not. Be this as it may, these additional violations of the explanatory scruples that Fodor and Pylyshyn invoke are not good news for Classicism.

Now that we have applied the explanatory standard described in Chapter 2 to a debate in cognitive science, there are two objections/responses that seem to arise rather naturally. First, one might object to the usefulness of the explanatory standard we have invoked because of a suspicion that neuroscientific evidence can provide some independent confirmation of some of the otherwise *ad hoc* cognitive architectural hypotheses involved in Classicism or Pure Atomism.[12] After all, both Classicism and Pure Atomism make commitments that must be realized in the underlying structures in the brain. Perhaps facts about these underlying structures can guide us to the truth about the structure of cognitive representations. The point of this objection is not to support either Classicism or Pure Atomism against its rival. Rather, it is to question the assumption that neither Classicism nor Pure Atomism can meet the explanatory standard that we have taken to be at work in the systematicity of inference argument.

This kind of objection has considerable intuitive appeal. Yet, it appears to involve a misunderstanding of what the explanatory principle we have in play requires. This was discussed in Chapter 2, but its significance may not have then been apparent. The principle requires not that there be independent confirmation of the auxiliary hypothesis. Rather, it requires that it be possible to confirm hypothesis H short of confirming the truth of the theory that relies upon H. The idea might be made more vivid by recalling the examples from Chapter 2. It is, perhaps, possible to provide independent confirmation of some hypothesis about God's plan in distributing life across the surface of the earth, including some hypothesis about the distribution of batrachians. Yet, any such confirmation would already confirm the Creationist account of biogeography, against an evolutionary account. If one knew that God had some biogeographical plan in creating life forms, one would already know that Creationism is true. Similarly, if one definitely knew that the deferents of Mercury, Venus, and the Sun were collinear, one would definitely know that the Ptolemaic theory of the planets is true. Similarly, were one to know by appeal to neuroscientific evidence that there is a computer program of the mind that uses the instructions in (TM1) to compute conjunction elimination, one would already know that the system of cognitive representation is Purely Atomic, rather than Classical. Likewise, were one to know through appeal to neuroscientific evidence that there is a computer program of the mind that uses instructions like those found in (TM3) to compute conjunction elimination, one would already know that the system of cognitive representation is Classical, rather than Purely Atomic. So, initial appearances to the contrary, an appeal to neuroscience does not undermine our analysis of the explanatory standard at work in the systematicity arguments.

A second response to the use of our explanatory standard in cognitive science is to invoke evolution by natural selection. In fact, this is quite a popular approach. It has been proposed by Braddon-Mitchell & Fitzpatrick, (1990), Sterelny, (1990), and Hadley, (1997). Roughly, the idea is that the capacity for systematic reasoning confers greater fitness than does either a capacity for non-systematic inference or a lack of a capacity for systematic inferences. Natural selection, therefore, will favor systematic reasoning. Since, however, natural selection can show how features of cognition, such as the systematicity of inference, might be necessary, there is no need to rely upon a theory of cognitive architecture to do this work.

Despite its popularity, the evolutionary response remains quite sketchy and unconvincing. To begin with, we should observe that the existence of an historical account of how some system came to be is not, in and of itself, sufficient to discharge the explanatory burdens in these sorts of arguments. Clearly, there was some history detailing how the solar system came to be as either Copernican or Ptolemaic astronomers observed it to be. Nevertheless, the obvious existence of such a history, unknown to astronomers of the day, was clearly insufficient to meet the explanatory burdens of the day. Similarly, we know that there is *some* historical account of human cognitive architecture involving evolution, but this cannot be sufficient to discharge either Classicism's or Pure Atomism's explanatory obligations. So, presumably, those who would explain the systematicity of inference via an appeal to evolution must have in mind some *selectionist* historical account of why human cognitive capacities are inferentially systematic. There must be some story about the way in which natural selection favored some organisms over others. Yet, there is reason to doubt that we have a selectionist account that is up to the task. The systematicity arguments are meant to provide some measure of confirmation. The fact that the hypotheses in a putative *explanans* stand in a particular relation to the systematicity regularities is meant to provide some measure of confirmation for some of the hypotheses constituting the *explanans*. Yet, it appears that for this type of confirmation, we cannot rely entirely on unconfirmed hypotheses. There must exist some independent confirmation for such things as the fact that salt water constitutes a migration barrier to batrachians, for the fact that light is propagated rectilinearly, etc. The problem for a selectionist account of the systematicity of inference is that the account is about as thin a selectionist explanation as one can get. What selectionist offer us regarding the systematicity of inference is hardly distinguishable from "just so" stories about evolutionary adaptations. Surely the idea that systematicity of inference confers fitness upon their possessor's has some intuitive plausibility, but other than that the actual scientific evidence is non-existent. We know nothing about the relevant genotypic and phenotypic alternatives, nor the environments in which they were found, nor how the forces of selection were supposed to drive some traits to (near?) fixation. This is particularly clear if we wonder about what species might display systematic inferential capacities. So, while we cannot rule out the existence of an evolutionary explanation of the systematicity of inference, a *bona fide* selectionist account is not really available.[13]

To this point we have urged a symmetry between Classicism and Pure Atomism vis a vis the systematicity of conjunction elimination. Both Classicism and Pure Atomism generate accounts that rely on some presupposition about the nature of the computer program of the mind that both hypothesize. This symmetry, by itself, leaves open the question as to whether both Classicism and Pure Atomism explain the systematicity of inference or whether neither explain it. If an explanation of an empirical generalization requires merely developing a set of hypotheses upon which the explanandum follows, then we should say that both Classicism and Pure Atomism explain the systematicity of inference. If, however, an explanation of an empirical generalization requires more, then this is an invitation for us to say that neither Classicism nor Pure Atomism explains the systematicity of inference. If we view the systematicity arguments in a vacuum, isolated from the rest of the history of science, it appears we can take either road. If, instead, we avail ourselves of some historical examples, we find reason to believe that more is required than having a set of hypotheses that exhibits the explanandum. When Ptolemaic astronomy is given all the auxiliary hypotheses it needs, then it does follow that Mercury and Venus will never be found in opposition to the sun and that the superior planets will always go through retrograde motion when in opposition. When Creationism is given all the auxiliary hypotheses it needs, including hypotheses about God's plan in creation, then it follows that there will be no batrachians on remote oceanic islands and that blind cave forms will resemble the sighted surface forms in the local area. Nevertheless, both the Ptolemaic and Creationist accounts are flawed. The historical cases also lead us to conjecture that this something extra is that the explanans must not rely on "arbitrary hypotheses" and that by "arbitrary hypotheses" we should mean something like any auxiliary hypotheses that cannot be confirmed short of securing the truth of the theory that relies upon it to meet its explanatory burdens. In short, the history of science provides reason to say that neither Classicism nor Pure Atomism explains the systematicity of inference, rather than simply that they are in the same explanatory situation or that both explain the systematicity of conjunction elimination.[14]

By and large, most philosophers and cognitive scientists are willing to let Pure Atomism go by the wayside, but there are many Classicists who hold out hope of having Classicism explain the systematicity of inference. So, we may consider five responses that might be ventured toward this end. As we consider defenses of Classicism, however, we must bear in mind that if some response works for Classicism, there is the possibility that it will also be pressed into service by a non-Classicist, thereby undermining the usefulness of the systematicity of inference as an argument for Classicism over non-Classicism.

1) One such response begins with the observation that, in order to explain the systematicity of inference, Pure Atomism must postulate that each possible conjunction elimination uses a specific instruction, or set of instructions, where a Classical architecture need not. In fact, a Classical architecture can function in the same way for arbitrarily large domains.[15] In terms of our Turing machine example, the Pure Atomist will have to say that the capacity to infer that John loves Mary from Mary loves John and John loves Mary will take one instruction, the capacity to infer that John loves Mary from John loves Mary and Mary loves John and Mary is married will take another instruction, the capacity to infer that John loves Mary from John loves Mary and John is married will take another instruction, and so forth. By contrast, it is possible, roughly speaking, for a set of instructions computing over a set of Classical representations to compute over any finite size set of conjunction eliminations. Perhaps the ability to account for the systematicity of conjunction elimination in this way constitutes a "supra-

empirical" virtue that Classicism has over Pure Atomism. For convenience, we might call this the "objection to punctate inferential capacities." Perhaps this objection can be construed as an extrapolation from what Fodor and Pylyshyn actually say; perhaps it can be construed as a separate, but nonetheless significant, argument for Classicism. What should be said about these possibilities?

There seem to be good reasons to stand by the analysis of the systematicity arguments introduced in Chapter 2 and pressed into service in this chapter. To be sure, the objection to punctate inferential capacities is not a far-fetched extrapolation of what underlies the Classicist critiques. To be sure, it is reasonable to pursue alternative arguments for Classical architecture. Nevertheless, this does nothing to undermine the sort of analysis developed in Chapter 2. All of the systematicity arguments are being explored here as merely one (important) component in the debates over cognitive architecture. Other psychological, neuroscientific, and evolutionary facts, and other methodological principles must be weighed in as part of the effort to determine the nature of human cognitive architecture. So, the existence of another argument for Classicism gives us no reason to abandon the line of argumentation to which we have devoted so much attention. These are merely logical considerations about the proposal, having little to do with the substance of the proposal. There are, however, substantive challenges to be faced by the "objection to punctate inferential capacities".

Formulating the objection so that it cuts against Pure Atomism, but not against Classicism is a matter of some delicacy. This is clearer if we look more closely at the way in which Classical models deploy individual instructions. Recall program (TM3) above, the one that infers John loves Mary both from John loves Mary and Mary loves John and from John loves Mary and Mary loves John and John is married to Mary. Suppose that we want a system with greater inferential capacities. We want a system that, in addition to the capacities of (TM3), has the capacity to infer that Ted loves Mary both from Ted loves Mary and Mary loves John and from Ted loves Mary and Mary loves John and John is married to Mary. Schematically, we want a system that, in addition to the capacity to infer P from both P&Q and P&Q&R, has the capacity to infer S from both S&Q and S&Q&R. To this end, we add the symbol δ, which will mean that Ted loves Mary, to the alphabet over which our Turing machine computes so that we have

α means John loves Mary
β means Mary loves John
γ means John is married to Mary
δ means Ted loves Mary
& means conjunction, and
0 is a null symbol.

Then we replace (TM3) with one that has one additional instruction, the one for handling the symbol δ,

(TM5)   s0 α R s1
          s0 δ R s1
          s1 β 0 s2
          s1 γ 0 s2
          s1 & 0 s2
          s2 0 R s1.

(TM5) functions in essentially the same way as does (TM3): it simply scans across symbol α (which means that John loves Mary) or a symbol δ (which means that Ted loves Mary), then erases the remainder of the input. Thus, it performs the new task simply by adding a single instruction to our old system. Further, it is obvious how this scheme could be extended, if we wished to have a system that can do with Mark loves Mary what the current system, (TM5) can do with John loves Mary and Ted loves Mary. We simply let, say, ε mean that Mark loves Mary, alongside our other semantic conventions, then give our Turing machine the program

(TM6)   s0 α R s1
          s0 δ R s1
          s0 ε R s1
          s1 β 0 s2
          s1 γ 0 s2
          s1 & 0 s2
          s2 0 R s1.

Now notice that in following this schema, there is a sense in which one gives the Turing machine a new inferential capacity by the addition of a single instruction that one might say is dedicated to just that particular inferential capacity. This suggests that one challenge to the "objection to punctate inferential capacities" lies in articulating very precisely what is supposed to be methodologically problematic and what is not. If there is some kind of principle of best explanation or some principle of methodological virtue at work here, we have to face this dimension of articulating the principle that is being invoked. If this is to help Classicism, we have to articulate it in such as way as to make it cut against Pure Atomism and in favor of Classicism.

A second dimension of the articulation problem concerns the generality of the methodological principle being invoked in the objection to punctate capacities. Once we have formulated a criterion of "supra-empirical" virtue or explanatory virtue or explanatory power that discriminates between Pure Atomism and Classicism, we will want to see how this virtue applies to a range of scientific theories. How do principles concerning the way in which instructions are added to computer programs relate to principles in physics, biology, or chemistry? How are we to think of this weakness in such a way as to recognize it in other scientific enterprises?

Finally, there is the question of what reason there is to think that adhering to this "supraempirical" virtue or explanatory virtue will lead to the truth. Surely the principle is defeasible at best, but what is there, if anything to recommend it.

In Chapter 2, we attempted to address these sorts of issues for the kind of explanatory argument we expected to be at work in the sundry systematicity arguments. The analysis in Chapter 2 is relatively clearer than what Fodor and Pylyshyn had on offer. Its general applicability is suggested by its derivation from historical episodes in other sciences, namely, positional astronomy and biogeography. Finally, we can at least point to the success of evolutionary theory and Copernican astronomy as a bit of inductive evidence for the value of the explanatory strategy as a touchstone for truth. These points give us some reason to stand by the version of the systematicity arguments we have developed so far.

2) As a second attempt to save some form of Classicism, one might contend that we know that the computer program of the mind must be such as to generate our limited degree of systematicity in conjunction elimination, hence that there is confirmation of the auxiliary hypothesis regarding the computer program of the mind. To evaluate this line of response we do well to consider how it would fare in our historical episodes. After all, one of the motivations for having these examples is that they might constrain our present analyses. Suppose Ptolemy were to say that, given the motions of Mercury, Venus, and the Sun, we have reason to think that the deferents of Mercury, Venus, and the Sun are collinear. Of course, given that Mercury and Venus are always found near the Sun, we know that on a Ptolemaic account their deferents must be collinear, but the problem is that we need to be able to provide some *independent* confirmation of the arrangements of the deferents. That is, it must be possible to confirm these auxiliary hypotheses short of having secured the truth of the theory that relies upon them. Or, suppose that the Creationist were to say that, given the distribution of life forms across the planet, we have reason to think that the plan of God included having no batrachians on remote oceanic islands and blind cave forms resembling local surface forms. Again, we must say that the auxiliary hypothesis about the plan of God must be *independently confirmable*. So, what fails for the Ptolemaic astronomer or the Creationist biogeographer, fails for the Classicist as well.

3) Consider another possible defense of Classicism. Suppose we admit that Classicism as hitherto defined does not explain the systematicity of inference. Instead, we can look to a more extensive definition of Classicism than we have seen so far. Perhaps we can maintain that it is part of the very definition of this refined Classicism-perhaps it is implicit in what has always been meant by "Classicism"- that the computer program of the mind is such that it produces

systematic patterns of inference.[16] In such a case, an hypothesis about the computer program of the mind would not be an auxiliary hypothesis, nor would it be arbitrary. Such a hypothesis would then be of the essence of Classicism. Again, in meeting this response it is useful to consider how it would fare in the context of the debate between Copernican and Ptolemaic astronomers or between evolutionists and Creationists. Suppose the Ptolemaic astronomer were to claim that it is part of the very definition of "Ptolemaic astronomy" that the deferents of Mercury, Venus, and the Sun be collinear, or that the epicycles and deferents of the superior planets and the sun be such that the superior planets go through retrograde motion at opposition. Surely we would reject this defense of Ptolemaic astronomy. So, we should just as surely reject it as a defense of any species of "Classicism". Suppose the Creationist were to maintain that it is part of the very essence of the Creationist theory of biogeography that God distributed organisms across the surface of the globe in such as way as to have no Batrachians on remote oceanic islands. Such a distribution is part of God's plan for creation. Darwin was fully aware that Creationists might advance this thesis, but was also prepared to reject it as an inadmissible kind of account. So, we should reject any "Classical" theory that attempts to defend itself in this way. Here we need to recall that the problem with the Ptolemaic and Creationist accounts has nothing important to do with what is or is not part of the "definition" of the theory. Instead, the crucial feature is the extent to which the hypotheses invoked in the putative explanation admit of independent confirmation. Perhaps this paragraph amounts to simply a long winded way of saying that we cannot take a non-explanatory set of hypotheses and make it explanatory simply by changing its name.

4) At this point, one might admit that *as the systematicity of conjunction elimination argument has been laid out here* it does not work. What is needed is some further specification of, or perhaps modification of, the explanandum. What needs to be emphasized, or added to the explanandum, is that the capacity for systematic conjunction elimination is a *general* capacity.[17] It is not a feature of cognition limited simply to pairs of inferences. Although the details of this revised systematicity of inference argument have not been fleshed out, it appears that the putative explanandum suffers from a confused set of intuitions concerning generality. To make the point, consider a story. A computer science professor tells his class to write a program that generates all the prime numbers between 0 and 100. One student writes a program of the form

write "2"
write "3"
write "5"

. . .

write "97".

When the student turns in the assignment, the professor is irritated with the student, because the procedure she used is not general. But, the student is puzzled about the relevant concept of generality. The Pascal program she has written is perfectly well-formed and it provides all and only the primes between 0 and 100. The professor couldn't really want a program that generates arbitrarily large prime numbers, the student reasons, since the assignment specifically said that only the prime numbers between 0 and 100 had to be written. By stipulating that only a finite number of primes need be printed, she thinks, the professor seems to have cut himself off from the notion of generality. The student's reason is sound. Generality in computational systems applies to infinite or unbounded domains. In the systematicity of inference argument, however, Fodor, et al., specifically limit themselves to properties of finite capacities for thoughts, sentences, and inferences. This is equivalent to the computer science professor specifying a finite range from which all the primes should be reported. By limiting themselves to finite domains, both the Classicist and the computer science professor are denied access to the notion of generality they want. In fact, one of the morals of our examination of the systematicity arguments will be that the move to finite domains is of greater consequence that Fodor and Pylyshyn seem to realize.

5) It might be maintained that we have misinterpreted another dimension of the explananda in the productivity and systematicity arguments.[18] There is a difference between computation over an infinite domain and computation over an arbitrarily large domain. In the productivity argument, the explanandum involves an infinite domain, but in the systematicity arguments we require only generality defined in terms of arbitrarily large domains. In the move from the productivity argument to the systematicity arguments, we renounce any recourse to an infinite domain, but not to arbitrarily large domains. So, the Classicist is not in the same situation as the computer science professor, so, the formulations we have given of the productivity and systematicity of conjunction elimination arguments do not really capture what is going on.

This argument, however, falters on both textual and conceptual grounds. In the only passage that clearly bears on this distinction, Fodor and Pylyshyn align productivity with arbitrarily large representations:

> Notice that you can make this argument for constituent structure in sentences without idealizing to astronomical computational capacities. There are productivity arguments for constituent structure, but they're concerned with our ability - in principle - to understand sentences that are arbitrarily long. Systematicity, by contrast, appeals to premises that are much nearer home (Fodor & Pylyshyn, 1988, p. 38).

So, looking at the relevant texts, we find no basis for saying that productivity relies on infinite generative capacity, where systematicity relies merely on an unbounded generative capacity. More important, on the conceptual side, we simply cannot say that, in the productivity argument, systems are supposed to be able to compute, say, infinite sums. No computer program writes infinitely long numerals or sentences. This is why in our exposition of the productivity argument we always had it that there is no bound on the size of numbers that a program might produce or no bound on the length of a sentence it might write. A computer can have an unbounded representational capacity, but it cannot literally have an infinite representational capacity. It is only loose talk to say that a computer program computes over an infinite domain. Or, to put things another way, the only sense in which a computer program can be said to compute over an infinite domain is the sense in which it can compute over arbitrarily large instances of the domain. Or, to put things yet another way, the only sense in which a computer program computes over an infinite domain is the sense in which there is no upper bound on the size of representations which it can process. This being the case, therefore, one cannot have it that in the productivity argument one abandons infinite domains, while retaining in the systematicity argument the idea of arbitrarily large domains. Such a distinction cannot be pressed into service to aid the systematicity of inference arguments.

4 TAKING STOCK

The majority of the present chapter was dedicated to articulating what the systematicity of inference is supposed to be, namely, a capacity perform one instance of a given type of inference given the capacity to perform another instance. It is supposed to be a feature of cognitive competence that must teased out of a plethora of interacting factors contributing to actual human behavior. One can surely venture a case against a cognitive capacity for systematic inference, but that case must do justice to the sophistication of the Classical hypothesis and the difficulties of isolating the multiple factors contributing to produce behavior.

The remainder of the chapter brought the ideas introduced in Chapter 2 into the context of cognitive science. Chapter 2 drew attention to certain explanatory/confirmatory episodes in the history of science and provided an analysis of them. This chapter has built on that work by drawing a contrast between the explanatory standard involved in the productivity argument and the standard invoked in the systematicity of inference argument. Where the challenge in the productivity argument is to provide some account of the explanandum, the challenge in the systematicity of inference argument is to provide a particular kind of account, one that does not rely on arbitrary hypotheses. Roughly speaking, Fodor and Pylyshyn's idea was that one could drop a problematic assumption in the productivity argument, namely, the assumption about an unbounded representational capacity, but maintain compelling alternatives in the systematicity arguments by taking up the slack with a principle of good scientific explanation. What we have found, however, is that, contrary to Fodor and Pylyshyn's initial conceptions, the combination of a weaker explanandum regarding cognitive capacities and a principle of best explanation do not mesh to create a compelling systematicity of inference argument. Given the explanatory standard evidently at work in the systematicity of inference argument, we appear to be forced to the conclusion that neither Classicism nor Pure Atomism explains the systematicity of inference.

NOTES

1. To those who are familiar with what Fodor and Pylyshyn mean by the semantic relatedness of thought, this set of cognitive states suggests semantic relatedness. The relations between the state presuppositions of the systematicity of inference and the semantic relatedness of thought will be discussed in more detail in Chapter 6. The relations between the state presuppositions of the systematicity of inference and the systematicity of cognitive representations will be explored in Chapter 5.

2. Cf., Rowlands, (1997), who also supposes that an isomorphism between representations and propositions is also supposed to underlie various arguments for combinatorial/linguistic representations.

3. Cf. Fodor, (1987), p. 136, p. 138.

4. In his discussion the systematicity of cognitive representations, Cummins, (1996b), p. 595-6, appears to recognize that systematicity does not require the view that propositions have structure.

5. Recalling the discussion in Chapter 1, we may note that Rowland may mean by "logically or sententially structured representations" something more than what we have here called Classical representations. Sentential representations are a species of Classical representations; they are Classical representations that are "linguistic" or "sentential" whatever exactly that amounts to.

6. Perhaps a desire to avoid such an obligation is the reason why Dennett is sometimes inclined simply to deny that there is such a thing as the systematicity of inference that merits an explanation. Cf., Dennett, (1991).

7. Dennett, (1991), p. 27, appears to want to run this sort of argument using research on vervet monkeys. Unfortunately, Dennett's discussion is not sufficiently clear or extensive as to indicate whether the evidence is supposed to show that vervet thought is not inferentially systematic or that vervet thought is not compositional in the sense to be explained in Chapter 6. Nor is his discussion sufficiently detailed as to enable one to ascertain exactly what the evidence is supposed to be.

8. van Gelder and Niklasson have a rhetorically unstable view at this point. In much of their paper (and in Niklasson and van Gelder, (1994)) they complain about a lack of clarity in Fodor and Pylyshyn's concept of systematicity, but when it suits their purposes they are able to formulate a

perfectly reasonable definition of the systematicity of *modus tollens*.

9. Van Gelder & Niklasson, (1994), p. 906, also suggest this idea.

10. Both Cummins, (1996b), and van Gelder and Niklasson, (1994), are in a rhetorically unstable position here. On the one hand, they both complain of Fodor and Pylyshyn's inattention to the literature on human inference, but, on the other hand, when it comes to citing literature relevant to substantiating their skepticism about the systematicity of conjunction elimination, they have nothing to cite. Recall that Cummins writes,

> it is an embarrassment to classical schemes that structure sensitive processing, unless constrained in some way, will treat '(A v B v C) & (D v E v F)' in the same way it treats '(P&Q)'. I am not sure about this particular example (Cummins, 1996b, p. 613).

Van Gelder and Niklasson for their part give us this:

> Fodor & Pylyshyn single out the *systematicity of inference* as a key component of the wider phenomenon of systematicity. It is, roughly, the idea that the ability to make some inferences is intrinsically connected to the ability to make other, logically related inferences. They offer no precise definition of the phenomenon and cite no literature in its support, but do anecdotally illustrate what they have in mind the following way:
>
>> You don't, for example, find minds that are prepared to infer John went to the store from John and Mary and Susan and Sally went to the store and John and Mary went to the store but not from John and Mary and Susan went to the store. (p. 48).
>
> Perhaps; perhaps not (van Gelder & Niklasson, 1994, p. 906).

If they wish to take Fodor and Pylyshyn to task for armchair speculation about human inferential capacities, they would do well to cite experimental literature when advancing their own claims about human inferential capacities. Certainly more than "I am not sure about this particular example" and "Perhaps, perhaps not" is in order.

11. Fodor & Pylyshyn, (1988), p. 47-48.

12. This issue was raised by an anonymous reviewer for the book.

13. Suppose, however, that we were to have a full-fledged, detailed, well-confirmed selectionist account of the way in which evolution gave rise to systematic inferential capacities. Would that relieve Pure Atomism of its explanatory burden? McLaughlin, (1993b), has claimed that an evolutionary account would not meet the Classicist's challenge and, surely, the Classicist can issue whatever challenges he may like. Still, one might wonder about the legitimacy of the challenge. While one can see that there must be *some* explanation of the systematicity of inference, it is not clear what it must be an architectural explanation. If the explanandum must be architectural, why must it be architectural? This is a rather subtle question in the philosophy of science that would bear further exploration.

14. The foregoing addresses Hadley, (1997), who observes the symmetry between Classicism and Connectionism, but draws the inference that both are explanatory. He does this on the ground that both theories, when given appropriate auxiliary hypotheses, necessitate the explanandum. Contrary to Hadley, however, Chapter 2 argued that necessitation of the explanandum is still not sufficient for explanation in the sense at work in the systematicity arguments. Both theories rely on arbitrary hypotheses which undermine their explanatory power.

15. An anonymous referee for this book made the point. In personal communication, Fodor himself also made this observation in response to the application of our current explanatory standard to the compositionality argument.

16. In truth, given our proposal to include in our definition of "Classicism" whatever is needed to account for the various systematic and productive features of thought, we should include some hypothesis concerning the computer program of the mind. Unfortunately, exactly what this hypothesis is remains unclear. Moreover, as we are about to see, the inclusion is immaterial. This gives us a way to rationalize an inconsistency here.

17. This point has been urged independently by Georges Rey and Victor Velarde in personal communication.

18. This possibility was suggested by Georges Rey.

CHAPTER 5

THE SYSTEMATICITY OF COGNITIVE REPRESENTATIONS

The structure of our discussion of the systematicity of cognitive representations argument will mirror the structure of our previous discussion of the systematicity of inference argument in Chapter 4. We will begin by describing, clarifying, and defending the putative explanandum, then review the Pure Atomist and Classical accounts of it indicating how neither Classicism nor Pure Atomism will explain the systematicity of cognitive representations up to the standard Fodor and Pylyshyn have in mind. The central problem for both theories will be their reliance upon hypotheses that are *ad hoc* in the sense we have seen in Chapters 2 and 4.

1   WHAT IS THE SYSTEMATICITY OF COGNITIVE REPRESENTATIONS?

At the heart of the systematicity of cognitive representations argument are a number of well-worn phrases used to introduce a putative explanandum. According to Fodor and Pylyshyn, the systematicity of cognitive representations consists of an "intrinsic connection" between the ability to have some thoughts and the ability to have others. The capacity for having certain thoughts is "intrinsically connected" to the capacity for having certain other thoughts. You don't find human beings who have the capacity to have the thought that John loves Mary, but lack the capacity to have the thought that Mary loves John.[1]

While both supporters and critics of this argument have paid a fair amount of attention to the clarification of this explanandum, or at least to some concept of systematicity of cognitive representations, there appears to have been less progress in this area than one might have liked. Critics have complained that Fodor and Pylyshyn rely too heavily on mere illustrative examples without providing a clear and precise definition.[2] In pressing this point, however, the critics are less than maximally helpful insofar as they do not explain what they take to be problematic. What, specifically, is wrong with saying only that the systematicity of cognitive representations is a matter of there existing intrinsic connections between thoughts? Were they more forthcoming in this regard, it might be easier to try to offer them the clarifications they believe are in order. As for the supporters of the argument, while McLaughlin (1993a, 1993b) does a good job of explaining the "core" notion of systematicity, which is useful for many purposes, he does not do complete justice to the diversity of explananda brought forth in Fodor & Pylyshyn, (1988).[3] In particular, McLaughlin does not try to explain the difference between what Fodor and Pylyshyn refer to as the systematicity of cognitive representations and the semantic relatedness of thought capacities. McLaughlin appears to roll both of Fodor and Pylyshyn's concepts into a single concept of systematicity. So, it appears that there remains a bit of work that might be done with Fodor and Pylyshyn's concept of the systematicity of cognitive representations.

Here we will venture an unfamiliar gloss on what constitutes this kind of systematicity. In fact, we will introduce two different ways to interpret the notion of an "intrinsic connection", both of which are consistent with what Fodor and Pylyshyn have to say about systematicity. Unfortunately, the gloss we develop here may well give rise to concerns that this sense of "systematicity" is not what "systematicity" means in the literature. This is fair enough as a generalization about papers written *after* Fodor & Pylyshyn, (1988), where "systematicity" has often come to mean something like the content-relatedness of possible occurrent thoughts. The concern, however, is much less well-founded when attention is limited to Fodor and Pylyshyn's original exposition. Fodor and Pylyshyn do seem to mean by "systematicity" what we will here describe as the systematicity of cognitive representations. Unfortunately, some of the textual support for this analysis must await the discussion of the compositionality of representations in Chapter 6, as it will draw on material from the corresponding section of Fodor & Pylyshyn, (1988). Be the correct interpretation of "systematicity" in Fodor & Pylyshyn, (1988), as it may, the more significant point is that, by articulating the conceptions of systematicity that we do, we can more clearly formulate a more challenging systematicity argument in this chapter, and indeed a more challenging argument in the next chapter. In other words, quite apart from the issue of what Fodor and Pylyshyn really meant, the conceptions of systematicity to be explored in this chapter have merits in their own right. Unfortunately, it will take this chapter and the next to vindicate all the textual and theoretical claims about to be advanced.

So, what are we to say about Fodor and Pylyshyn's conception of the systematicity of cognitive representations? Our exposition will proceed in stages. To begin with, we may observe that the claim regarding intrinsic connections concerns cognitive capacities or competences.[4] In this regard, the systematicity of cognitive representations argument is like the productivity and systematicity of inference arguments. The claim is that, in normal humans, the ability to have a thought, such as that John loves Mary, is intrinsically connected to the ability to have some other thought, such as that Mary loves John. The claim is decidedly not that any normal person who thinks that John loves Mary thinks, or will think, or has thought, that Mary loves John. It is not a claim about the history of actual thought processes; it is a claim about possible occurrent thoughts. Although the dress version of the explanandum involves thought capacities, we may, from time to time, slip into talk of thoughts. This is only a stylistic variation.

So, the intrinsic connections obtain between thought capacities. But, what are we to make of the notion of an "intrinsic connection"? At first glance, this notion might appear to beg the question in favor of Classicism. One might think that the explanandum is that systematic cognitive capacities share some common constitutive elements–that they must have some shared underlying bases–such as common representational atoms.[5] That is, one might think that what is to be explained is why distinct thought capacities have common representational elements. Such a take on the explanandum would indeed beg the question against Pure Atomism, since Pure Atomism denies *ex hypothesi* that there are common representational atoms to diverse cognitive representations. So, Classicism must appeal to some other non-question-begging gloss on the notion of an intrinsic connection.

An idea worth exploring, one that has not been explicitly endorsed by Fodor and Pylyshyn, is that intrinsic connections can be cashed out in terms of counterfactual dependencies.[6] In other words, we may say that the systematicity of cognitive representations is supposed to refer to the fact that there exist thought capacities that are counterfactually dependent upon each other. Thus, were one to lack the capacity for certain thoughts one would thereby lack the capacity for certain other thoughts. Further, were one to have the capacity for certain thoughts, one would thereby also have the capacity for certain other thoughts. In paradigmatic cases, the capacity to have the thought that A is nomologically necessary and sufficient for the capacity to have the thought that B.[7] This understanding of what is involved in paradigmatic cases perhaps captures the sense behind Fodor and McLaughlin saying that "if you meet the conditions for being able to represent aRb, YOU CANNOT BUT MEET THE CONDITIONS FOR BEING ABLE TO REPRESENT bRa" (Fodor & McLaughlin, 1990, p. 202, emphasis in the original). Yet, over and above the paradigmatic cases, Classicists are also committed to the existence of related cases. That is, we might distinguish three dependency relations among thought capacities:

1) The capacity to have the thought that A is nomologically necessary and sufficient for the capacity to have the thought that B.

2) The capacity to have the thought that A is nomologically necessary for the capacity to have the thought that B.

3) The capacity to have the thought that A is nomologically sufficient for the capacity to have the thought that B.

So, we now have a somewhat more refined explanandum. To a first approximation, what needs to be explained in the systematicity of cognitive representations argument is why the mind is such that there exist counterfactual dependencies among some thought capacities, rather than no counterfactual dependencies at all between any thought capacities.[8]

To further refine the explanandum, we should add that the counterfactual dependencies to which the Classicist is drawing attention are thought capacities in a single attitude, such as believing, hoping, and fearing. The explanandum we will entertain here is that the capacity to have one attitude toward some proposition is nomologically necessary and sufficient for having the capacity to have that attitude toward some other proposition. For the concept of systematicity being developed here, the attitude must be the same, even though the content toward which one has the attitude need not be. The rationale for this is simple: for purposes of running the systematicity of cognitive representations argument, the Classicist need not presuppose that the capacity to, say, believe something is nomologically necessary or sufficient for the capacity to, say, fear something. The capacities for believing and fearing may well be distinct capacities, so that one can believe without fearing and fear without believing. Although for the purposes of the systematicity of cognitive representations argument, the Classicist does not presuppose that capacities to have thoughts in one cognitive modality have any connection with capacities to have thoughts in other cognitive modalities, the Classicist also does not rule out this possibility. That is, for the present, the Classicist leaves open the possibility that there are other important relations among cognitive state capacities that cross attitude boundaries. Thus, it may be a psychological law that a normal human being can have attitude A_1 toward some content, if, and only if, she can have attitude A_2 toward some content. It may also be a psychological law that a normal human being has the capacity to have attitude A_1 toward P, if, and only if, she has the capacity to have the attitude A_2 toward P. There might even be some "conceptual" connection between the capacity to have attitude A_1 toward P and the capacity to have the attitude A_2 toward P. Be these matters as they may, Classicists are here concerned only to assert that there is some counterfactual dependency between the capacity to have some thoughts in attitude A and other thoughts in attitude A.

We are still not at the end of the refinements of the explanandum. When the Classicist envisions counterfactual dependencies, the ones she has in mind are *psychological-level* counterfactual dependencies. Were it not for such a restriction, both Classicism and Pure Atomism would have easy access to essentially the same implementation-level explanation of the dependence of one thought capacity upon another. Both could say that the capacity for the thought that John loves Mary is counterfactually dependent on the capacity for the thought that Mary loves John, because these thought capacities are implemented in the same region of the brain and that any bit of brain damage that prevents the tokening of a representation with the meaning that John loves Mary will of necessity prevent the tokening of a representation with the meaning that Mary loves John.   Given such an account, the theoretical difference between Classicism and Pure Atomism will be explanatorily idle.   Classicism will say that a representation with combinatorial structure appears in the damaged region of the brain, where Pure Atomism will say that a representation lacking combinatorial structure appears in the damaged region of the brain, but these additional hypotheses do no explanatory work.   So, if the systematicity of cognitive representations argument is to get off the ground, it must be presupposed that the dependence to be explained is an essentially psychological, rather than implementational, fact. To mark this supposition, we shall frequently note that the counterfactual dependencies are manifest via "cognitive causes."

Because the counterfactual dependence among thoughts at issue here is not supposed to be an implementational fact, one cannot detect the supposed counterfactual dependence by recourse to such things as brain lesion studies or organic psychopathology.   Such empirical studies will only find counterfactual dependencies among thoughts that derive from contingent facts about the way human psychology happens to be implemented in the brain. The question then arises as to what empirical evidence there could possibly be for psychological-level counterfactual dependencies. One might find such evidence unimaginable, but in truth one natural place to look for such dependencies is in learning and memory tests. The idea is this. If the capacity for one thought depends on the capacity for another thought, then one would expect to find patterns in the ways in which new thought capacities are formed and in the way in which thought capacities are lost or fail to be formed. So, consider test subjects who are read a long narrative that introduces the relation R and the terms a and b. One might then test whether having the capacity to entertain the thought that aRb is necessary and sufficient for having the capacity to entertain the thought that bRa.[9] One can check to see whether all and only the subjects having the capacity to think that aRb can also think that bRa. One can also see how these sorts of tests might be used to determine that one thought capacity is necessary for another. If one finds that the only subjects who can think "if aRb, then Qc" are those who can think "aRb", then one has reason to think that the capacity for the thought that aRb is necessary for the capacity for the thought "if aRb, then Qc". One might also conclude that the capacity for the thought that aRb is not sufficient for the capacity for the thought "if aRb, then Qc", if there are subjects who can think "aRb", but cannot think "if aRb, then Qc". Similarly, one can see how these sorts of tests might be used to determine that one thought capacity is sufficient for another thought capacity. One might find that, any subject who can think "if aRb, then Qc" can think "aRb". Here one might also find that the capacity to think "if aRb, then Qc" is not necessary for the capacity to think "aRb". This conclusion might be warranted by the discovery of subjects who can think "aRb" but cannot think "if aRb, then Qc". All of this is far short of providing a rigorously specified experimental protocol, since it fails to specify any sort of factors that must be controlled and how they will be controlled. Nevertheless, the central idea should be clear. The sort of experiments sketched here should conjure up visions of college-level multiple-choice tests on lengthy plays, novels, and historical periods. Presumably there will be patterns among the answers subjects will be able to provide about the characters and events in *A Midsummer's Night Dream*, *Anna Karenina*, Hitler's invasion of Russia, or the evolution of jazz. Why there are such patterns merits an explanation.

It should be emphasized that learning and memory tests are not to be taken to provide operational definitions of counterfactual dependencies. It is not that whatever counterfactual dependencies are found in learning and memory tests of the sort just vaguely described are simply defined to be the counterfactual dependencies that are in play in the systematicity of cognitive representations argument. Instead, memory tests are one possible way of detecting counterfactual dependencies among thoughts. Clever experimentalists are free to find other means of detecting these cognitive dependencies. The primary point of describing such tests is simply to move the explanandum from the realm of what cannot conceivably be confirmed to the realm of what is plausible.

In light of the foregoing emphasis on the counterfactual dependency of thought as a non-implementational fact, one might wonder whether this argument, and perhaps all of the systematicity arguments, presuppose that non-implementational explanations are always superior to implementational explanations. Do the systematicity arguments presuppose that, in these inference to the best explanation arguments, the best explanation must always be a non-implementational explanation? And if they do, why are non-implementational explanations always better?[10] To put a sharper point on these questions, we might observe that there are plenty of cases in which the best explanation appears to be an implementation explanation, rather than a cognitive explanation. So, for example, it appears that humans perform certain cognitive tasks more slowly at low oxygen levels. That is, if subjects perform a certain test at sea-level and at high altitudes, say, on the upper slopes of Mt. Everest, one finds that at high altitudes the time to completion of the test is increased. Here the explanation appears to be an implementational fact having to do with the role of oxygen in the metabolic processes of the brain. The relevant cognitive tasks presumably do not involve subjects measuring the level of ambient oxygen, then adjusting the number or rate of cognitive steps accordingly. Subjects do not in any sense decide to act more slowly because of the low ambient oxygen concentration. Similar considerations apply to the effects of substances, such as caffeine, nicotine, and codeine, on cognitive activity. So, were Classicists to suppose, for whatever reason, that all explanations of behavioral regularities must be non-implementational, then Classicism would be in a problematic situation.

But, of course, Classicists do not presuppose any principle according to which cognitive explanations are always better than non-cognitive explanations. They do, however, suppose that, in the case of the sundry systematicity explananda, the best explanation will be cognitive rather than non-cognitive. In finding the factors that explain some regularity, an experimental scientist holds certain factors constant and varies others. So, an experimentalist might vary the amount of oxygen a test subject receives in order to determine what cognitive effects, if any, this might have. Insofar as there are reproducible effects of oxygen concentration on subject performance, it is reasonable to explain the subject's performance in terms of oxygen concentration, an implementational feature. Similarly, an experimentalist might vary the information a subject is given about a particular domain, while holding various implementational features, such as oxygen levels, constant. So, when an experimentalist reads a story to a subject in anticipation of subsequently querying the subject about the story, the experimentalist will control for implementational factors, such as oxygen levels. Insofar as there are reproducible effects of the information a subject is given, it is reasonable to explain the subject's performance in terms of cognitive factors.[11] It, therefore, appears that the supposition that the explanation of the counterfactual dependencies among thought capacities should be cognitive is no more problematic than the supposition that there is in fact a reproducible cognitive explanandum. The evidence that there must be a cognitive explanation of the counterfactual dependence of thought is simply the evidence that there is a cognitive, rather than implementational, regularity to be explained.

To return to an earlier topic of concern, one might wonder whether the demand for an explanation of counterfactual dependencies among thought capacities begs any questions in favor of Classicism.[12] We have already encountered this kind of worry in our discussion of the productivity argument in Chapter 3, in our discussion of the systematicity of inference argument in Chapter 4, and in the opening pages of this chapter. The answer is that, in general, the kind of explanation we are seeking here is non-question begging. Stating or describing or asking for explanations of counterfactual dependencies seems to be a theoretically unproblematic task. In particular, it begs no questions in favor of any specific mechanisms that might give rise to those dependencies. To take a humdrum illustration of the idea, one can ask for an explanation of the counterfactual dependence between the amount of gasoline in an automobile's gas tank and the position of the needle on the gas gauge. One can know of this counterfactual dependence and ask for an explanation of it without making any particular presuppositions about the nature of the mechanism that effects the dependence. Or, take a scientific example to make the same point. One can know that, if one were to heat a sample of gas constrained to a fixed volume, the pressure of the gas would increase. Here is a fact of which one might want an explanation. Neither the explanandum nor the request for an explanation begs any questions in favor of a particular kind of underlying mechanism. In a similar fashion, there is no logical sleight of hand that brings in a Classical system of combinatorial representations with the supposition that there are counterfactual dependencies among thoughts.

As a final expository angle on the explanandum of systematicity of cognitive representations, we might compare it with the explananda in the systematicity of inference arguments. In particular, we might ask whether having systematic thought capacities logically implies having a systematic inferential capacity and whether having a systematic inferential capacity logically implies having systematic thought capacities.

Clearly, the fact that an agent Σ displays counterfactual dependencies among its thought capacities in a given attitude (e.g., believing, hoping, fearing) does not logically imply that Σ has systematic inferential capacities in that attitude. Two considerations bear this out. First, recall from Chapter 4 that inferential systematicity involves conditions on both possible occurrent cognitive states and possible transitions among those possible occurrent cognitive states. The counterfactual dependencies among possible occurrent cognitive states, however, do not place restrictions on the patterns of possible state transitions in the way that the systematicity of inference does. Second, it is logically possible for Σ to have the capacities for the thoughts P and Q be counterfactually dependent upon each other, but contentfully unrelated. In such a case, there is no pattern of inference that licences a move from P to Q, or *vice versa*. Recall that, as we are here understanding systematicity, it involves no principles concerning the content relations among thoughts, but simply a counterfactual dependency. So, we would have a case of systematicity of cognitive representations without inferential systematicity.

The implications of systematic inferential capacities for counterfactual dependencies among thought capacities in a given attitude is perhaps less clear. Return to our case of limited systematicity of conjunction elimination from Chapter 4, i.e., the capacity to infer John loves Mary both from John loves Mary and Mary loves John and from John loves Mary and Mary loves John and John is married to Mary. This degree of systematicity of inference requires that Σ have the capacities to think that John loves Mary, to think that John loves Mary and Mary loves John, and to think that John loves Mary and Mary loves John and John is married to Mary. It does not, however, require that there be a counterfactual dependence among these thoughts. What clouds matters is the fact that the representational capacities that constitute a systematic inferential capacity are logically necessary for the systematic inferential capacity. Were Σ to lose the capacity to represent John loves Mary, then Σ would lose the capacity to infer John loves Mary from John loves Mary and Mary loves John and from John loves Mary and Mary loves John and John is married to Mary. Further, were Σ to lose the capacity to represent John loves Mary and Mary loves John, then again Σ would lose the capacity to infer John loves Mary from John loves Mary and Mary loves John and from John loves Mary and Mary loves John and John is married to Mary. The same holds were Σ to lose the capacity to represent John loves Mary and Mary loves John and John is married to Mary. The dependence of the inferential capacity on its constituent representational capacities, however, should not be conflated with one representational capacity being either nomologically necessary or sufficient for another representational capacity.

To conclude this section, we succinctly restate the explanandum: the Classicist proposes that there must be an explanation of why there is a cognitive counterfactual dependence between the capacities for various thoughts under a single attitude A. In other words, why is it that the capacity for some thoughts under attitude A are nomologically necessary and sufficient for other thoughts under attitude A. Although this is our canonical formulation of the explanandum, we will from time to time abbreviate our description of it for stylistic reasons.

2 PURE ATOMISTIC ACCOUNTS OF THE SYSTEMATICITY OF COGNITIVE REPRESENTATIONS

Let us now proceed on the premise that there are counterfactual dependencies among thought capacities that require an explanation. How, then, might Pure Atomism attempt to explain why one thought capacity in a given attitude is nomologically necessary and sufficient for another thought capacity in that attitude? In their first pass through this argument, Fodor and Pylyshyn suggest that there is no account one can give of this other than the combinatorial story the Classicist has on offer.[13] In a later summary discussion, however, they suggest that even if Pure Atomism were to offer *some* account of this kind of systematicity, such an account would be lacking in some sense.[14] This second line of argumentation is the one to be pursued here.

As we know, Pure Atomism adopts the Computational Theory of the Attitudes and Representationalism. PA will also conjecture that the reason a person's thought is systematic is that the person's cognitive economy involves the syntactic atoms $\{\alpha, \beta\}$ such that α means, say, John loves Mary and β means, say, Mary loves John.[15] Finally, the Pure Atomist might account for the counterfactual dependence between these thoughts by appeal to the structure of the computer program of the mind realizing the computational relations toward representations. In the case of Turing machines, it might go like this. Pure Atomism might conjecture that the program of the mind is such that the ability to token α (meaning John loves Mary) is nomologically necessary and sufficient for the ability to token β (meaning Mary loves John), because tokening both α and β involves passing through a particular Turing machine state, say, s_{184}. Given the overall structure of the computer program of the mind, the ability to enter the state s_{184} is both necessary and sufficient to enable the system to token both α and β. That is, the capacity to token α is necessary to the capacity for tokening β, since unless one has the state that enables α to be tokened one will not have the state that enables β to be tokened. Further, given the structure of the Pure Atomist's hypothetical computer program, having the capacity to token α is sufficient unto having the capacity to token β. Thus, insofar as program instructions constitute cognitive-level features of a system, we have, at least in outline, a possible basis for a Pure Atomistic architecture giving rise to counterfactual dependencies among thoughts.

Classicists might here object that the appeal to a common machine state on which both α and β depend does not really capture what is meant by an "intrinsic connection." The connection between α and β is not intrinsic to the representations α and β, but is a feature of the computer program in which they figure. Further, Classicists might ask if the capacity to enter a particular computational state, such as s_{184}, is really sufficient for the capacity to token a particular representation, given the capacity to token another. Further still, Classicists might ask whether having certain instructions in the PA computer program of the mind is really sufficient for tokening one representation, given the capacity to token another. Whatever the merits of these worries and objections, they do not seem to pose the same depth of problem as does the line Fodor and Pylyshyn take up. To this end, we begin with what Fodor and Pylyshyn have to say in response to an unspecified (Connectionist) proposal for explaining the systematicity of cognitive representations, then show how the analysis we developed in Chapter 2 applies. The following passage from Fodor and Pylyshyn's critique is reworded for the present context of Pure Atomism.

It's possible to imagine a [Pure Atomist] being prepared to admit that while systematicity doesn't *follow from*--and hence is not explained by--[a Pure Atomist Architecture], it is nonetheless *compatible* with that architecture. It is, after all, perfectly possible to follow a policy of [writing programs] that have aRb [representational atoms] only if they have bRa [representational atoms] ... etc. There is therefore nothing to stop a [Pure Atomist] from stipulating--as an independent postulate of mind--that all biologically instantiated [programs of the mind] are, de facto, systematic.

But this misses a crucial point: It's not enough just to stipulate systematicity; one is also required to specify a mechanism that is able to enforce the stipulation. To put it another way, it's not enough for a [Pure Atomist] to agree that all minds are systematic; he must also explain *how nature contrives to produce only systematic minds.* Presumably there would have to be some sort of mechanism, over and above the ones that [Pure Atomism] per se posits, the functioning of which insures the systematicity of biologically instantiated networks; a mechanism such that, in virtue of its operation, every [program] that has an aRb [representational atom] also has a bRa [representational atom] ... and so forth (cf., Fodor & Pylyshyn, 1988, p. 50, italics in original).

Here Fodor and Pylyshyn are receptive to the possibility of a PA story about the systematicity of cognitive representations and suggest that not just any sort of story will do. The idea is that it is not enough just to stipulate a species of systematicity, there must be something more. So far, so good for the idea of viewing the systematicity of cognitive representations argument as requiring more than just some account or other that fits the data. It is, however, *not* clear from the foregoing passage that the weakness Fodor and Pylyshyn see in a Pure Atomist story about the systematicity of cognitive representations is the same weakness that we have found in the historical cases in Chapter 2. Nor is it clear from this passage that the weakness is the same one that we found in dealing with the systematicity of inference argument. All that the foregoing passage requires is that there be some mechanism that gives rise to the systematicity of cognitive representations and PA has given that.

To more closely relate Fodor and Pylyshyn's comments above to our discussion of the historical cases in Chapter 2 and to our discussion of the systematicity of inference in Chapter 4, we need to consider a passage from Fodor & McLaughlin, (1990). This passage is similar to the one just cited above, but presents a slightly different account of what they might take to be the inadequacy of the Pure Atomist account of the systematicity of cognitive representations. As the later of the two arguments, this one has some claim to being the more considered position. Here is the passage, originally worded for Connectionism, but now reworded to address Pure Atomism:

The point of the problem that systematicity poses for [a Pure Atomist account] . . . is not to show that systematic cognitive processes are *possible* given the assumptions of a [Pure Atomist] architecture, but to explain how systematicity could be *necessary*--how it could be a *law* that cognitive capacities are systematic--given those assumptions.

No doubt it is possible for [the Pure Atomist] to [program a computer] so that it supports a [symbol] that represents aRb if and only if it supports a [symbol] that represents bRa. . . . The trouble is that, although the architecture permits this, it equally permits [the Pure Atomist] to [program] a [computer] so that is supports a [symbol] that represents aRb if and only if it supports a [symbol] that represents zSq; or, for that matter, if and only if it supports a [symbol] that represents The Last of The Mohicans.   The architecture would appear to be absolutely indifferent as among these options (cf. Fodor & McLaughlin, 1990, p. 202).

Here it seems that Fodor and McLaughlin do have in mind exactly the sorts of considerations we touched on in Chapters 2 and 4.   To return to our Pure Atomist's Turing machine, while the program of the mind might allow the capacity to process α (meaning John loves Mary) to be linked to the capacity to process β (meaning Mary loves John), it is also possible to write a Turing machine program in which possession of the α capacity has no implications for the possession of the β capacity. The problem with this putative explanation of the systematicity of cognitive representations lies in the fact that the appeal to the structure of the computer program of the mind appears to be arbitrary within the context of Pure Atomism. It would appear that one can as easily have a computer program that respects the systematicity of cognitive representations as not.

One can readily imagine this passage reworded (yet again) to describe the problem that the motions of Mercury and Venus pose for Ptolemaic astronomy. The Copernican astronomer might say that the problem that the motions of Mercury and Venus pose for Ptolemaic astronomy is not to show that these motions are *possible* given the basic assumptions of Ptolemaic astronomy, but to explain how they could be *necessary* given those assumptions. No doubt it is possible for a Ptolemaic astronomer to rig the deferents of Mercury, Venus, and the Sun so that they make the motions of the planets come out right. The trouble is that, although the basic Ptolemaic assumptions permit this, they equally permit the Ptolemaic astronomer to rig the deferents of Mercury and Venus so that they wander arbitrarily far from the Sun or that they never wander far from Jupiter for that matter. The basic Ptolemaic architecture would appear to be absolutely indifferent as among these options. Recognizing that Fodor and Pylyshyn's locutions apply equally well to our example from the history of positional astronomy supports the analogy between the astronomical cases and our cognitive science cases.   The same point could be made equally well, however, with our example from biogeography.

Recall that, in Chapter 2, we saw that there is some measure of plausibility to the Fodor and Pylyshyn analysis applied to the Copernican versus the Ptolemaic account and the Darwinian versus the Creationist account. Yet, in Chapter 2, we also saw some reason to think that a better analysis is that one account, but not the other, relies on an arbitrary auxiliary hypothesis and that the relevant notion of arbitrariness is based on the ability to confirm the auxiliary hypothesis short of establishing the truth of the scientific theory that has explanatory recourse to it. This analysis applies very well to the case of Pure Atomism explaining the counterfactual dependency among thoughts. In the terms of this analysis, we should say that Pure Atomism must rely on some assumption about the nature of the computer program of the mind in order to have it be the case that Pure Atomism generates counterfactual dependencies among thoughts, rather than not. This hypothesis, one that ensures that one type of Pure Atomist computer program of the mind, rather than another, is implicated in cognition, appears to be inaccessible to confirmation short of establishing the truth of Pure Atomism. How could one know that the computer program of the mind manipulates Pure Atomist representations one way, rather than another, short of knowing that the computer program of the mind uses Pure Atomist representations? All of this is consistent with the view that we are presently on the right track in interpreting what Fodor and Pylyshyn have to say about the systematicity of cognitive representations and why Pure Atomism does not explain it.

3 CLASSICAL ACCOUNTS OF THE SYSTEMATICITY OF COGNITIVE REPRESENTATIONS

So, Pure Atomism does not provide the desired sort of explanation of the counterfactual dependencies among thoughts. What should be considered now is whether Classicism can pass muster by the same explanatory standard to which Pure Atomism was just held.[16] As we know, Classicism presupposes the Computational Theory of the Attitudes and Representationalism. Classicism further hypothesizes that cognitive representations have syntactically and semantically concatenative combinatorial structure, that there are some representations that have the meanings they do in virtue of the meanings of their parts and the way in which those parts are put together. This last is the Principle of Semantic Compositionality. Classicism is also committed to the hypothesis that syntactic items have contents that are context independent, that is, that syntactic items make the same semantic contribution to each context in which they occur. This is the Principle of Context Independence. This configuration of hypotheses generates an intrinsic connection or counterfactual dependency between the capacity for the thought that John loves Mary and the capacity for the thought that Mary loves John insofar as it invokes a common stock of capacities, namely, the representations of John, Mary, and loving, along with the capacity to form a single cognitive grammatical construction with them in a single cognitive attitude. In like manner, the Classicist will claim that the capacities for the thoughts that

> John talked to Mary about Alice,
> John talked to Alice about Mary,
> Mary talked to Alice about John,
> Mary talked to John about Alice,
> Alice talked to Mary about John,
> Alice talked to John about Mary,

form a cluster of thought capacities that are mutually nomologically necessary and sufficient, since they all involve the joint exercise of a capacity for a single cognitive attitude, a single grammatical construction, and the capacities for the concepts of John, Mary, Alice, and talking to about. In short, the Classicist maintains that the capacity to think one thought is nomologically necessary and sufficient for the capacity to think another thought because the one thought involves all and only the capacities that are involved in the other thought.

Once we see how Classicism plans to handle the paradigmatic cases of systematicity, where the capacity for thought A is nomologically necessary and sufficient for the capacity for thought B, it is obvious how Classicism attempts to explain the existence of cases in which the capacity for thought A is only nomologically necessary, or only nomologically sufficient, for the capacity for thought B. The capacity to have the thought that A is one of the subcapacities for the capacity to have the thought that B. Let the capacity for thought A be the capacity for the thought that John loves Mary and let the capacity for thought B be the capacity for the thought that if John loves Mary, then there is no present king of France. The A capacity is supposed to be nomologically necessary for the B capacity, since, the Classicist supposes, the A capacity is one of the sub-capacities that constitutes the B capacity and without A, there can be no B. To see the Classicist strategy for handling the sufficiency-only cases, switch A and B. Here, the capacity to think that if John loves Mary, then there is no present king of France is supposed to be nomologically sufficient for the capacity to think that John loves Mary, since, the Classicist supposes, once a system has the capacity for thinking that if John loves Mary, then there is no present king of France, then it must have the capacity to think that John loves Mary.

In addition, once we see how Classicism plans to handle the existence of thoughts that are only nomologically necessary or only nomologically sufficient for other thoughts, one can see that Classicism predicts that–under conditions that control for such things as content and implementation effects and other implementation effects per the discussion in Chapter 3–there are other dependencies or "intrinsic connections" among thoughts that are not covered by our notions of counterfactual dependency and thought capacities being nomologically necessary and/or sufficient. Take a pair of thoughts, such as John loves Mary and John loves Mark. According to Classicism, these thoughts will share common representational capacities, namely, the capacity for representing

John, the capacity for representing loving, and the capacity for using these representations in a common grammatical construction. Thus, we have what is arguably a species of "weak intrinsic connection" between the capacity to have the thought that John loves Mary and the capacity to have the thought that John loves Mark. Still, this kind of weak intrinsic connection is not captured by our notion of counterfactual dependencies and nomologically necessary and sufficient conditions. The Classicist does not maintain that, were one to lose by cognitive cause the capacity to have the thought that John loves Mary one would thereby lose the capacity to have the thought that John loves Mark. Maybe one thought would be lost with the other; maybe not. In the event that an agent loses the capacity to token the concept of John or the capacity to from the relevant grammatical structure, then indeed both cognitive capacities will simultaneously disappear. In the event, however, that an agent loses the capacity to think that John loves Mary in virtue of losing just the capacity to represent Mary, that agent might still retain the capacity to represent Mark, hence retain the capacity to think that John loves Mark.   This can be restated in terms of the nomologically necessary. The capacity for the thought that John loves Mary is not nomologically necessary for the thought that John loves Mark, since the agent need not have the capacity to represent Mary in order to have a set of capacities adequate unto the capacity to think that John loves Mark.

Our principal way of understanding the systematicity of cognitive representations has been in terms of counterfactual dependencies, which are, in turn, understood in terms of one thought capacity being nomologically necessary and sufficient for another. We also recognized that Classicists predict that some thought capacities might be nomologically necessary, but not sufficient for other thought capacities, and that some thought capacities might be nomologically sufficient for other thought capacities, even though not nomologically necessary. Maybe we could describe the nomologically necessary and sufficient connection as a "strong intrinsic connection" in order to contrast it with the "weak intrinsic connection" described in the last paragraph. In drawing these distinctions, and in selecting one way of developing the systematicity of cognitive representations argument, we are not driven primarily by the texts of Classicists's discussions. What Fodor, Pylyshyn, and McLaughlin have to say is consistent with interpreting systematicity in terms of nomologically necessary and sufficient conditions, but that is not the principal motivation for doing this. Instead, the possibility of drawing these distinctions is based on an understanding of Classical commitments and the consequences of these commitments. Further, the motivation for developing the systematicity arguments in terms of nomologically necessary and sufficient conditions, or strong intrinsic connections, is driven by the fact that, in the end, this choice makes for the most challenging explanandum in the systematicity of cognitive representations argument. In fact, it paves the way for the most forceful argument to be found in Fodor and Pylyshyn's discussion of the compositionality of representations. Unfortunately, the whole of the justification for this assertion will have to wait until chapters 6 through 8.

So, to take a critical look at the Classical account of the systematicity of cognitive representations, we may ask once again whether or not it passes muster by the standard to which we held Pure Atomism. In brief, the problem begins when we observe that, while there is no doubt that there are Classical computer programs of the mind that give rise to counterfactual dependencies among thoughts, it is also clear that there exist Classical computer programs that do not. In other words, there are computer programs that meet all the Classical conditions specified in Chapter 1 and do give rise to nomologically necessary and sufficient connections between thought capacities and there are other computer programs still meeting all the Classical conditions specified in Chapter 1, but which do not give rise to nomologically necessary and sufficient connections between thought capacities. This means that Classicism must rely on some further hypothesis that makes it the case that Classical computer programs of the mind generate counterfactual dependencies in thought. Further, this hypothesis will evidently not admit of confirmation short of securing the truth of Classicism. This is essentially the problem that beset Pure Atomism. It is the problem that kept Pure Atomism from having a *bona fide* explanation of the relevant kind of systematicity. Let's look at this in more detail.

Suppose that there is a set of syntactically atomic representations, Θ = {John, Mary, loves} with the obvious semantic interpretation. There, of course, exists a computer program such that the atoms in Θ combine to form the representations Θ^*_1 = {John loves Mary, Mary loves John}, where these representations have the obvious semantic interpretation. Yet, there is also another computer program that combines the atoms in Θ to form only Θ^*_2 = {John loves Mary}, which has the obvious semantic interpretation, and yet another computer program that combines the atoms in Θ to form only Θ^*_3 = {Mary loves John}, which also has the obvious semantic interpretation. In Θ^*_1, one syntactically molecular representation can be nomologically necessary and sufficient for the other, whereas in Θ^*_2 and Θ^*_3 this is not true.[17] So, given the set of Classical hypotheses introduced in Chapter 1, one can as easily have a systematic set of representations, as not. This means that, in order to generate a systematic set of representations, Classicism must be augmented or enriched with some hypothesis specifying what representations the computer program of the mind will generate. Yet, if we were to have empirical confirmation that the Classicist's hypothetical computer program of the mind generates one set of representations, rather than another, we would already have secured the Classical theory that there exists a syntactically and semantically combinatorial system of representation. So, it would appear that Classicism falters on the systematicity of cognitive representations in just the way Pure Atomism did.

Moreover, it would appear to falter on the systematicity of cognitive representations in just the way it did on the systematicity of inference.

Nothing is essentially changed for Classicism if we use the weaker notion of intrinsic connections among thoughts.[18] The argument goes through as before. Take a set of syntactic atoms Γ = {John, Jane, Mary, Lisa, loves, hates}, with the obvious semantic interpretation. It is, of course, possible that the computer program of the mind allows the atoms in Γ to be combined so as to yield the set $\Gamma^*_1 =$

{John loves John	John loves Jane	John loves Mary
Jane loves John	Jane loves Jane	Jane loves Mary
Mary loves John	Mary loves Jane	Mary loves Mary
John hates John	John hates Jane	John hates Mary
Jane hates John	Jane hates Jane	Jane hates Mary
Mary hates John	Mary hates Jane	Mary hates Mary},

with the obvious semantics. Still, the atoms of Γ might also be combined to form the set Γ^*_2 = {John loves Mary, Jane hates}, where these have the obvious semantic interpretation. There will be counterfactual dependencies among some of the elements of Γ^*_1, but not among the elements of Γ^*_2. In Γ^*_1 there are representations that have common lexical items in a common grammatical construction, whereas in Γ^*_2 there are no representations sharing common lexical items and no common grammatical constructions. As with the set Θ, the hypothesis about the nature of the hypothetical computer program of the mind is the undoing of Classicism.

Here is another way of thinking about the problem that the systematicity of cognitive representations poses for Classicism. Classicism does not merely invoke a grammar of cognitive representations, it must invoke *a particular (kind of)* grammar. A Classical grammar must lead to sets of sentences with common parts, rather than sets of sentences lacking common parts; a Classical grammar must lead to thoughts with common cognitive capacities, rather that thoughts lacking common capacities. The problem with this stronger auxiliary hypothesis, the one that specifies the *(kind of)* grammar, rather than the mere existence of *some* grammar, is the familiar one: it lacks the kind of independent confirmation that seems to be required for valid explanations of the desired sort. Short of such confirmation, the auxiliary appears to be a mere stipulation that gets the theory to fit the data.[19] Put in other familiar words, how could one have confirmation of the existence of a particular (kind of) grammar that constructs sentences from syntactic and semantic atoms without knowing as well that there exists syntactic and semantic atoms? One evidently could not.

A common reaction to the contrast between Θ^*_1 and Θ^*_2/Θ^*_3, or the contrast between Γ^*_1 and Γ^*_2, is to think that Θ^*_1 and Γ^*_1 constitute the "natural" way to combine the elements of Θ and Γ, where Θ^*_2/Θ^*_3 and Γ^*_2 are somehow "unnatural" or "less natural." Maybe, then, this "naturalness" justifies or confirms the hypothesis that the grammar of the mind is like that found in $\Theta*_1$ or $\Gamma*_1$, rather than that found in $\Theta*_2/\Theta*_3$ or $\Gamma*_2$. This is a powerful intuition that needs to be addressed. What appears to drive the intuition that $\Theta*_1$ and $\Gamma*_1$ are more "natural" than $\Theta*_2/\Theta*_3$ and $\Gamma*_2$ has to do with the assumptions one makes about the typing of the elements of Θ and Γ into terms and relations. By the looks of things, one might suppose that "John," "Mary," and "Jane" are terms, where "loves" and "hates" are two-place relations among terms. Given this supposition, it is pretty hard to resist saying that Θ and Γ "naturally" generate $\Theta*_1$ and $\Gamma*_1$, rather than $\Theta*_2/\Theta*_3$ and $\Gamma*_2$. The thing to observe, however, is that alternative "unnatural" typings of the elements of Θ and Γ are available. To see this for the set Θ, we might note that, while it is possible to classify "John" and "Mary" as terms of type T_1 and "loves" as a two-place relation of type R_1 that takes arguments for type T_1 as both of its relata, it is also possible to classify "John" as a term of type T_1, "Mary" as a term of type T_2, and "loves" as a relation of type R_1 that only takes representations of type T_1 as its first relatum and representations of type T_2 as its second relatum. While the former option generates $\Theta*_1$, the latter generates $\Theta*_2$. Similarly for the set Γ. While one can type the members of the set Γ in the familiar way so as to get $\Gamma*_1$, there is also an alternative that generates $\Gamma*_2$. Classify "John" as a term of type T_1, "Mary" as a term of type T_2, "Jane" as a term of type T_3, "loves" as a two-place relation of type R_1, and "hates" as a one-place relation of type R_2. If, in addition, R_1 takes only arguments of type T_1 as its first relatum, arguments of type T_2 as its second relatum, and R_2 only takes arguments of type T_3 as its relatum, then Γ generates $\Gamma*_2$ rather than $\Gamma*_1$. So, it looks as though the sense that $\Theta*_1$ and $\Gamma*_1$ are more "natural" than $\Theta*_2/\Theta*_3$ and $\Gamma*_2$ comes down to the sense that one way of typing the syntactic items is more "natural" than the other way of typing the syntactic items. Yet, the "naturalness" of one way of typing over another is illusory. It is merely a product of our conventional understanding of the orthography of English. Suppose that we presented our syntactic atoms as the set $\Delta = \{\delta_1, \delta_2, \delta_3\}$. What basis can there be for saying that one way of typing the elements of Δ is more "natural" than another? Presumably none.

To drive home this point, run through the systematicity of cognitive representations argument for Classicism one more time in terms of Δ and $\Delta*$. The Classical idea is that there exists a set of syntactic atoms Δ that are to be combined into syntactic molecules. In order for Δ to generate a set $\Delta*$ containing a nomologically necessary and sufficient connection between its members, one must have an auxiliary hypothesis as to how these atoms are to be typed and combined. This auxiliary hypothesis is over and above the hypotheses we introduced into our version of Classicism in Chapter 1. Let us hypothesize that $\{\delta_1, \delta_2\}$ are terms, where $\{\delta_3\}$ is a two-place relation that take all the terms in both of the argument positions. This auxiliary hypothesis is one that can be as easily adopted as not. It is one for which there is no independent confirmation. After all, were we to have evidence that the mind contains the syntactic atoms in Δ typed in a particular way, we would already have independent evidence for Classicism. In other words, we really wouldn't need the systematicity of cognitive representations argument, if we already had the well-confirmed auxiliary hypothesis.

In order to forestall another response to our present argument, it is important to note that the problem being raised here has nothing to do with what counts as being "Classical". It doesn't matter whether we define Classicism as the set of hypotheses introduced in Chapter 1, or as some richer set of hypotheses. We are not challenging the use of auxiliary hypotheses *qua* auxiliary hypotheses. The problem is that Classicism must rely upon some hypothesis that specifies one type of computer program for the mind, rather than another, or what amounts to the same thing, one grammar for cognitive representations, rather than another. Whether or not this hypothesis is part of the definition or essence of Classicism, there is still no independent confirmation of this hypothesis short of having Classicism already established. To think otherwise is evidently to think that changing the name of a set of hypotheses can change its explanatory power.

What we have just said might be further illuminated by reference to Ptolemaic astronomy. Suppose that a Ptolemaic astronomer were to claim that the hypothesis of the colinearity of the deferents of Mercury, Venus, and the sun is among the defining characteristics of Ptolemaic astronomy. Suppose the Ptolemaic astronomer were to claim that the hypothesis is of the essence of the Ptolemaic approach. We cannot accept this response from the Ptolemaic astronomer, since it would save Ptolemaic astronomy from the Copernican challenge. The superiority of the Copernican account, however, is essentially non-negotiable. We can even provide some further rationale for rejecting the Ptolemaic argument. What the Ptolemaic astronomer is trying to do is take a non-explanatory set of hypotheses (geocentrism plus a range of auxiliary hypotheses) and render them explanatory simply by changing the name of the set. What was previously thought of as Ptolemaic astronomy plus some auxiliary hypotheses is now to be thought of as simply Ptolemaic astronomy. Such a change clearly cannot change explanatory power. Explanatory power has something to do with the structure of the explanation and the place of the hypotheses within a broader empirical context. Here, again, the history of science provides some constraint on what cognitive scientists might argue regarding combinatorial representations.

Turn now to a relatively promising, but ultimately unsuccessful, strategy for defending Classicism. Suppose that the hypothetical system of cognitive representation is not merely combinatorial, but also recursive in the sense introduced in Chapter 3.[20] That is, suppose that the syntactic and semantic combinatorial apparatus contains one or more mechanisms for the recursive generation of syntactic and semantic molecules. This additional hypothesis might be confirmed by its ability to explain the productivity of thought. Given that the system is recursive, it appears that there must be *some* systematic relations among a person's set of possible thoughts. Thus, with mechanisms for the recursive application of negation, a human being who has the capacity to think not-S will *ipso facto* have the capacity to think not-not-S, not-not-not-S, and so on. Such a person will have a set of thought capacities in a given modality such that there exists a nomologically necessary and sufficient connection among all its members. This is because all of the members of the set will share all and only the same cognitive capacities. Alternatively, with mechanisms for the recursive application of "believes", a person who has the capacity to think that John believes that S will also have the capacity to think that Mary believes that John believes that S, Jane believes that Mary believes that John believes that S, and so forth. Again, there will exist nomologically necessary and sufficient connections among some of the agent's thought capacities, since some of the thought capacities will involve the joint exercise of all the same cognitive subcapacities. It is worth emphasizing that the putative recursivity of cognitive representations does not entail that if a person can think that not-S, then the person can think not-not-S, not-not-not-S and so forth. There are perfectly good recursive languages that do not have the recursive application of negation. Nor does the putative recursivity of cognitive representations entail that if a person can think that John believes that S, then she will have the capacity to think that Mary believes that John believes that S, or Jane believes that Mary believes that John believes that S. Again, there are perfectly good recursive languages that do not have the recursive application of belief contexts. All that follows from the recursivity of cognitive representations (against the backdrop of the other tenets of Classicism) is that there will be *some* counterfactual dependencies among the members of a set of possible thoughts.

This is a significant line of reasoning. It has a fair degree of *prima facie* plausibility, while at the same time gives some insight into the inter-relations among possible Classical hypotheses. Yet, it does not solve Classicism's difficulties. Let's begin with the obvious. The foregoing strategy relies on the productivity argument, which in turn relies upon an extrapolation to an unbounded cognitive capacity. Insofar, however, as the move from the productivity argument to the systematicity arguments was supposed to dispense with a reliance on the theory that human cognitive competence was unbounded in scope, the present move to use the productivity argument to defend an hypothesis for use in the systematicity arguments is a considerable disappointment. The primary motivation for the systematicity arguments has been undercut. The Classicist is no longer able to avoid recourse to the theory that cognitive competence is unbounded.

Now for the subtle: a recursive language of thought does not imply that there will be counterfactual dependencies among the members of a finite set of representations.[21] So, consider the following set of thought capacities:

{¬John loves Mary,

¬¬John loves Mary,

¬¬¬John loves Mary}.

One thought in this cluster might be nomologically necessary and sufficient for all the other members of this set, hence the members of the set are intrinsically connected or systematically related. Classicism might propose that underlying these possible thoughts is a grammar, G_1, with the following rewrite rules

S → ¬John loves Mary

S → ¬S.[22]

Even though there are recursive languages that generate counterfactual dependencies among thoughts, there are also recursive languages that do *not* generate the set of systematic representations. Consider G_2:

S → ¬John loves Mary

S → ¬¬¬S.

G_2 is a recursive language in the sense defined above, but it does not generate the systematic relations found in our language above. G_2 generates

{¬John loves Mary,

¬¬¬¬John loves Mary,

¬¬¬¬¬¬¬John loves Mary,

...}

The point here is not that the recursivity of a language does not guarantee systematic relations *involving negation*. That's true, but it is not the point being made here. The point being made here is that a recursive grammar need not give rise to *any* systematic relations within any *finite* set of sentences. So, if the appeal to a recursive grammar is to generate the nomologically necessary and sufficient connections among thought capacities, Classicism must invoke yet another hypothesis that insures that the recursive grammar is like G_1, rather than like G_2. But, this brings us back to our familiar kind of problem. Evidently anything that confirms that the grammar is like G_1, rather than G_2, will have to be sufficiently robust as to have already secured Classicism. So, again, it appears that even with more complex reasoning, Classicism falters in just the way that did Pure Atomism.

In Chapter 4, we saw that Classicism ran afoul of Fodor and Pylyshyn's explanatory standard for explaining the systematicity of inference in two ways, by relying on some hypothesis about the computer program of the mind and by relying on the Principle of Compositionality and the Principle of Context Independence. How does this bear on the systematicity of cognitive representations? Much the same analysis as applied there applies here. In the current systematicity argument, the Principles of Compositionality and Context Independence are essential, yet inaccessible to the kind of independent confirmation that appears to be required. The systematicity of cognitive representations requires that two separate thoughts be counterfactually dependent upon each other. The Principle of Context Independence is Classicism's mechanism for insuring this. The fact that the string of symbols, "John loves Mary" has one and the same meaning when it occurs in "John loves Mary and Mary loves John" and "Mary loves John and John loves Mary" means that they will give rise to two distinct thoughts, hence that there can be counterfactual dependencies between two distinct thoughts. As in Chapter 4, this suggests that Classicism may, in fact, be in deeper trouble than Pure Atomism when it comes to meeting the explanatory challenges of systematicity.

4 TAKING STOCK

Suppose that some sense can be made of the notion of intrinsic connections between thoughts in terms of counterfactual dependencies among thoughts and that empirical evidence can be given for thinking that there are such counterfactual dependencies. There, therefore, arises the need for an explanation: Why are there counterfactual dependencies among thoughts? Why are the capacities for some thoughts nomologically necessary and sufficient for the capacities for other thoughts? We have seen that, while Pure Atomism might be able to develop some cluster of hypotheses that might give rise to counterfactual dependencies in thought, there is the more difficult problem of providing a kind of principled explanation. More is needed than a system that exhibits counterfactual dependencies among thoughts; one needs a system that genuinely explains those dependencies. Pure Atomism is unable to provide such an explanation. The reason is that Pure Atomism must rely on arbitrary hypotheses, hypotheses that seem to admit of no confirmation, short of confirmation of Pure Atomism itself. To this extent, the present chapter has been a vindication of the Fodor and Pylyshyn analysis.

Unfortunately for Classicism, the very same charge that has been brought against Pure Atomism can be extended to Classicism. In order for a computational system using a syntactically and semantically concatenative combinatorial system of representation to have intrinsic connections between its representations, one must add certain auxiliary hypotheses. The hypotheses that Classicism needs in order to generate an account of intrinsic connections among thoughts have the same weakness as do any Pure Atomistic hypotheses that might also be pressed to generate an account of intrinsic connections among thoughts. They cannot be confirmed short of the confirmation of the approach used in giving the account. This is a problem for a set of hypotheses regardless of the name of the set.

A number of cognitive scientists have independently come to much the same conclusion we have just reached, namely, that a Classical system of cognitive representation does not explain the systematicity of cognitive representations in the sense Fodor and Pylyshyn have in mind (cf., e.g., Smolensky, (1997), Hadley, (1997), Matthews, (1997)). Their argument, however, differs from that presented here. One might say it stops one move short of what has been covered here. These other arguments observe that, since the set of hypotheses in the version of Classicism set out in Chapter 1 does not entail that thought will have the requisite systematic capacities, Classicism does not explain the systematicity of thought.[23]   In response to this, the Classicist will surely claim that the Classicism of Chapter 1 must be augmented by some hypothesis about the particular grammar of the mind. Critics, then, will claim that the appeal to a specific grammar of the mind is merely stipulative or *ad hoc*. The step that we take in this book is to provide a much more substantial accounting of what is wrong with this appeal to a particular (kind of) grammar of cognitive representations. This is the explanatory principle we have been working with for several chapters.

What we have seen, so far, is that there is an explanatory principle that proves to be just as challenging for Classicism as it is for Pure Atomism. Only in the next chapter do we find a case in which the principle genuinely favors Classicism over Pure Atomism.

NOTES

1. Cf. Fodor & Pylyshyn, (1988), p. 37, p. 39, cf. Fodor, (1987), p. 149. Just for the record, we may note that, McLaughlin (1993b), p. 221, uses the notion of an intrinsic connection as part of the explanans for systematicity, rather than the explanandum.

2. Cf., e.g., Matthews, (1994), Niklasson and van Gelder, (1994), van Gelder and Niklasson, (1994), and Hadley, (1997).

3. Cf., McLaughlin, (1993a, 1993b).

4. McLaughlin, (1993a, 1993b), is quite explicit about this.

5. Recall our discussion in Chapter 4 of Rowlands's observation that "The demand that connectionism postulate and account for logically or sententially structured representations is simply not a legitimate demand" (Rowlands, 1994, p. 495).

6. McLaughlin, however, does use some counterfactual language in his explication of systematicity. He writes, "two capacities are systematically related if and only if they have constitutive bases such that a typical possessor of the one capacity would possess the other" (McLaughlin, 1993a, p. 220).

7. There is, perhaps, an understanding of one thing being counterfactually dependent on another which is not equivalent to the one thing's being nomologically necessary and sufficient for the other. What will banked upon here, however, is that there is (also) an understanding of one thing being counterfactually dependent on another which *is* equivalent to the one thing's being nomologically necessary and sufficient for the other. The significance of this assumption will become clearer in our discussion of the Classical account of the systematicity of cognitive representations.

8. McLaughlin, (1993a, 1993b), explicates systematicity in terms of pairs of thought capacities. Presumably, he does this merely for the sake of expository convenience, since, as we shall see, there is no need to limit the counterfactual dependence to pairs of cognitive capacities, rather than to clusters of cognitive capacities.

9. In the concept of systematicity being developed here, all that really matters is that some thought capacities are counterfactually dependent upon each other. The content of the capacities that are so dependent is not at issue. The content relations are only introduced for expository simplicity.

10. These questions were posed by Chris Hill, personal communication.

11. In truth, an experimentalist will partition performance variables more finely than simply implementational versus cognitive. An experimentalist will want to know about a range of implementational factors, such as oxygen, caffeine, and nicotine, as well as a range of cognitive factors, such as memory, attention, comprehension, and motivation. Each of these parameters of performance will be studied with the use of appropriate controls.

12. Cf., Cummins, (1996b), where it is urged that the very statement of another of some of the various systematicity explananda begs questions in favor of Classicism.

13. More precisely, in discussing the systematicity of sentences in natural language, Fodor and Pylyshyn write, "On the view that the sentences [of natural language] are atomic, the systematicity of linguistic capacities is a mystery" (Fodor & Pylyshyn, 1988, p. 38).

14. Fodor & Pylyshyn, (1988), p. 50.

15. Although the syntactic atoms α and β must have some semantic content, the specific content does not matter for the present. The current meanings are retained only out of tradition.

16. It is common enough to suggest that the systematicity arguments involve some sort of trickery or sleight of hand (Matthews, 1994, Cummins, 1996b). While such analyses are largely erroneous, Fodor, et al., may have introduced some (unintended?) misdirection at this point in the arguments. While one's attention is focused on how poorly the Pure Atomist account fares, the Classical account is not similarly scrutinized.

17. The hedge about what is possible, rather than what is, is based on the epistemic possibility that a program might form the representations in Θ^*_1, but that these representations lack a common grammatical structure. If this epistemic possibility is a genuine logical possibility, then perhaps some auxiliary hypothesis is required to have both "John loves Mary" and "Mary loves John" possess the same grammatical structure. Then, there is an opening for a further arbitrariness problem for Classicism. Once you see how these arguments work, they threaten to get all out of control!

18. Actually, the result is unchanged for Pure Atomism as well. Pure Atomism can no better explain the weak intrinsic connections than it can the strong intrinsic connections.

19. This is how Matthews, (1997), puts the point.

20. This line of response was provided by Kevin Falvey.

21. This objection was brought to my attention by Cory Juhl.

22. G_1, of course, generates sentences other than those in our language, but that is beside the present point.

23. Actually, these arguments do not use the same explanandum that we have considered here, but the logic remains the same.

CHAPTER 6

THE COMPOSITIONALITY OF REPRESENTATIONS

The preceding discussions of the systematicity of inference and systematicity of cognitive representations argument have followed a pattern. The putative explananda were introduced along with clarifications and sundry friendly revisions. It was then argued that a Pure Atomist theory of cognitive representation, while able to accommodate the data, could not explain it to the standard implicit in Fodor and Pylyshyn's critique. The most surprising finding was that, when this standard was made explicit and prominent, one can see that Classicism fails to explain the systematic relations in thought for essentially the same reasons as does Pure Atomism.

The discussion of this chapter will deviate from this pattern to some degree. In the previously discussed sections of Fodor & Pylyshyn, (1988), we found essentially one argument for Classicism, albeit with more than one way in which it might be developed. By contrast, Fodor and Pylyshyn's discussion of the compositionality of representations has at least two distinguishable arguments, both of which have some claim to being reasonable arguments Fodor and Pylyshyn might give for believing in a Classical theory of cognitive representations. The first of these, perhaps the only one fully appreciated in the literature, is based on the supposition that possible occurrent thoughts are contentfully related. The second of these, one that seems not to be widely discussed in the cognitive science literature, is based on the putative fact that the thoughts that are counterfactually dependent upon one another are at the same time semantically related. Although we shall argue that neither Pure Atomism nor Classicism has the desired sort of explanation of the content relatedness of possible thoughts, we shall go on to claim that the less familiar explanandum introduced in the second argument is not explained by a Pure Atomistic theory, but is explained by Classicism. Thus, this last explanatory success gives us some defeasible reason to think that Classicism might be right about the architecture of cognition.

Another deviation from the pattern established in the preceding chapters will involve a digression that examines some additional empirical arguments for Classicism, namely, Terry Horgan and John Tienson's (1996) "tracking argument" and two of Fodor's (1985, 1987) "arguments from psychological processes." These arguments merit a consideration here for what they illuminate about the systematicity arguments and for what the systematicity arguments illuminate about them.

1 WHAT IS THE SEMANTIC RELATEDNESS OF THOUGHT?

The systematicity of cognitive representations is the idea that there are intrinsic connections between possible thought capacities. This we have glossed in terms of counterfactual dependencies among thoughts. The semantic relatedness of thought, however, is a distinct property of thoughts. It is the idea that the set of possible occurrent thoughts is semantically related: "the ability to be in some representational states must imply the ability to be in certain other semantically related representational states" (Fodor & Pylyshyn, 1988, p. 44).[1] Roughly speaking, the systematicity of thought is a syntactic feature of thought, where the semantic relatedness of thought is, obviously, a semantic matter.[2] So, for example, a normal human being will have the cognitive capacity to think a set of occurrent thoughts, such as,

John loves John	Mary loves John	Jane loves John
John loves Mary	Mary loves Mary	Jane loves Mary
John loves Jane	Mary loves Jane	Jane loves Jane

or

John loves John	John hates John	John fears John
John loves Mary	John hates Mary	John fears Mary
John loves Jane	John hates Jane	John fears Jane
Mary loves John	Mary hates John	Mary fears John
Mary loves Mary	Mary hates Mary	Mary fears Mary
Mary loves Jane	Mary hates Jane	Mary fears Jane
Jane loves John	Jane hates John	Jane fears John
Jane loves Mary	Jane hates Mary	Jane fears Mary
Jane loves Jane	Jane hates Jane	Jane fears Jane,

but one does not find normal human beings who can think all and only the occurrent thoughts

John loves Mary
Einstein studied physics
Bears hibernate
Cats chase mice and other rodents.

There are semantic relations among the items in the first two sets, but not among items in the third. In the first two sets, there are common properties and relations that hold between a common stock of individuals; in the third set, there are neither common properties, relations, nor individuals. This is evidently what Fodor and Pylyshyn had in mind when they wrote, "Just as you don't find linguistic capacities that consist of the ability to understand sixty-seven unrelated sentences, so too you don't find cognitive capacities that consist of the ability to think seventy-four unrelated thoughts" (Fodor & Pylyshyn, 1988, p. 40). Although this feature of thought has often come to assume the name of systematicity or compositionality, a more apt description of the regularity is surely the "content relatedness of thought."[3]

Back in Chapter 5, we promised to provide some textual evidence for thinking that Fodor and Pylyshyn think of systematicity in terms of counterfactual dependencies among thoughts, rather than in terms of, say, the content relatedness of thought. Now it is time to make good on that promise. Consider the following, formulated with regard to linguistic capacities, rather than thought, but not, for that reason, irrelevant:

We said that the systematicity of linguistic competence consists in the fact that 'the ability to produce/understand some of the sentences is intrinsically connected to the ability to produce/understand certain of the others'. We now add that which sentences are systematically related is not arbitrary from a semantic point of view. For example being able to understand 'John loves the girl' goes along with being able to understand 'the girl loves John', and there are correspondingly close semantic relations between these sentences: in order for the first to be true, John must bear to the girl the very same relation that the truth of the second requires the girl to bear to John. By contrast, there is no intrinsic connection between understanding either of the John/girl sentences and understanding semantically unrelated formulas like 'quarks are made of gluons' or 'the cat is on the mat' or '2 + 2 = 4'; it looks as though semantic relatedness and systematicity keep quite close company (Fodor & Pylyshyn, 1988, pp. 41-42).

From the foregoing, it should be clear that systematicity of thought is one thing, but semantic relatedness is another. The contrast pops up at other points as well,

> you need to assume some degree of compositionality of English sentences to account for the fact that systematically related sentences are always semantically related (Fodor & Pylyshyn, 1988, p. 43),

and

> if . . . we make the usual Classicist assumptions (vis., that systematically related thoughts share constituents and that the semantic values of these shared constituents are context independent) the correlation between systematicity and semantic relatedness follows immediately (Fodor & Pylyshyn, 1988, p. 45).

So, at least in Fodor & Pylyshyn, (1988), there is strong textual evidence indicating that we should not equate systematicity with semantic relatedness. Moreover, anyone wishing to offer an alternative interpretation of what systematicity and semantic relatedness "really are," or what Fodor and Pylyshyn "really mean," will have to make sense of these passages. In addition to the textual evidence for the present understanding of semantic relatedness and systematicity, we shall presently find equally strong theoretical reasons for making out this contrast, namely, that is provides the groundwork for a new argument that makes a stronger case for Classicism over Pure Atomism.

So, what is to explained regarding the semantic relatedness of thought? As is usual, the putative regularity to be explained has to do with a finite set of cognitive capacities, rather than actual performance. It is not that any normal human being who thinks that John loves Mary will also think that Mary loves John. The semantic relatedness of thought capacities also does not place any requirements on the nature of thought, the existence of mental representations, or the structure of propositions. As was hinted in Chapter 4, it is perfectly consistent with thought capacities being contentfully related to have it that thoughts are mere instrumental stance-takings. So, the fact that a normal human being can think that John loves Mary just in case she can think that Mary loves John might simply be a matter of there being certain patterns in the way in which we attribute capacities for thoughts to physical objects. Such a fact about these patterns would, of course, demand an explanation, but again the explanandum makes no presuppositions about the nature of thought or mental representations or propositions.

The content relatedness of thought, like productivity and the systematicity of inference, has been met with scepticism in some quarters. Cummins, (1996b), for example, suggests that the very way in which we formulate the explanandum regarding the content relatedness of thought begs the question in favor of a Classical account. Cummins claims that the intuitive appeal of the claim that possible occurrent thoughts are contentfully related depends on properties of the natural language we use to describe the regularity. Thus, he observes that it is intuitively plausible to say that

(1) Anyone who can think that *John loves Mary* can think that Mary loves John,

whereas it is much less plausible to claim that

(1') Anyone who can think *Mary's favorite proposition* can think that Mary loves John.

As Cummins puts it,

(1) gets all of its appeal from the fact that it incorporates linguistic expressions for the propositions that are interderivable by permutation. . . . The apparent obviousness of the [semantic relatedness of thought] looks to be an illusion created by reading the structure of contents off the structure of their representations (ibid., pp. 596-7).[4]

Cummins concludes from this that

You can make things look hard for (some) connectionists by (a) covertly relativizing [content relations] to a natural language, and (b) reminding them that they favor a nonclassical scheme of mental representation. If you can get them to accept this "challenge," they will then labor away trying to show that a user of a nonclassical scheme might still exhibit the [content relations] visible from a classical perspective. Getting connectionists to accept this challenge is nice work if you can get it, and apparently you can. There may still be job openings in this area if you want employment in the confidence business (ibid., pp. 597-8).[5]

So, just as Cummins tried to offer some reason for thinking that there is nothing to the systematicity of inference, hence that there is nothing to be explained, so again in the semantic relatedness of thought argument, Cummins contends that there is nothing to the content relatedness of thought–save for an illusion created by natural language–hence that there is nothing to be explained here either.[6]

Cummins's argumentation here is far from compelling on a number of counts. To begin with, it is not really clear why the combinatorial syntax and semantics of *natural language* should lead us to believe in the semantic relatedness of thought.[7] Why should a combinatorial natural language leads us to believe that one's possible occurrent thoughts are content related? How does this work? Why, exactly, does the combinatorialism of natural language make

(1) seem more plausible than (1')?   Cummins's argument fails to carry conviction here for lack of clarity.

The lack of clarity is, however, the least of the problems here. Cummins thinks that an examination of (1) and (1') reveals that the permutations of representations that are possible with the combinatorial structure of natural language beguiles us into attributing to people capacities for content related thoughts. But the comparison between (1) and (1') involves a confound. (1) uses a permutation of representations in a natural language in a way that (1') does not, but, in addition, there are epistemic differences between (1) and (1'). Whereas we know the contents picked out by the English language expressions "John loves Mary" and "Mary loves John," we do not know the content of Mary's favorite proposition.[8] This is, in part, why we can be more confident of what is asserted in (1) than what is asserted in (1'). To put matters in another way, where Cummins proposes that the difference in plausibility between (1) and (1') is due to the differing roles of combinatorial representations in (1) and (1'), the Classicist is free to maintain that the difference in plausibility is due to the difference in what we know about the content of the expression "John loves Mary" versus the content of the proposition picked out by the expression "Mary's favorite proposition." In a more compelling thought experiment, (1) would be compared to a sentence that differs from (1) only in lacking the permutation of representations.   If there were a difference in intuitive plausibility between (1) and this new alternative, then Cummins's case would be much strengthened.

Be the foregoing as it may, Cummins still lacks a compelling case for yet another reason. Concede, if only for the sake of argument, that Cummins is right that our intuitions about the content relatedness of possible occurrent thoughts are colored by our use of a natural language to describe the explanandum of the argument. In fact, our intuitions may be colored by our theories concerning the existence and nature of mental representation. The more confident we are that the mind uses a Classical system of representations, the more plausible it may seem that thought capacities have related contents and that there is some psychological regularity to be explained.   This, however, is obviously not sufficient grounds for saying that there is nothing to be explained regarding possible content relations in thought. Not-p obviously does not follow from the premise that we have a bias in favor of p. Nor does not-p follow from the premise that all the appeal of p comes from some non-evidential source. Our fear of theoretical bias should not be an insuperable barrier to accepting that thought capacities are contentfully related, *provided* we have some independent means of verifying that the putative regularity is a genuine regularity. *If* we have independent reason to think we have a *bona fide* explanandum, we can set aside the worries about the legitimacy of our intuitions. Once again, a bit of history of science can bring out this point. If we believe in evolution, then the following putative regularities seem plausible:

I. There are no batrachians on remote oceanic islands.

II. Endemic plants on oceanic islands tend to resemble forms on the nearest mainland.

III. Bats are the only mammals on remote oceanic islands.

By contrast, we may doubt the hypothesis that

IV. The temporal order of creation in Genesis I is the same as the temporal order of creation revealed by the paleontological record.

No matter what our beliefs concerning the plausibility of evolution may be, we have some independent access to the truth of these regularities. In the case of the first three hypotheses, we dispatch expeditions to survey the flora and fauna of oceanic islands. In the case of the last hypothesis, we review Genesis I, then review the paleontological record. So, while Cummins points out a potential source of bias, he makes no case against the view that there are content relations among possible occurrent thoughts.

So, Cummins has given no reason to doubt the existence of the content relatedness of thought. On the other hand, what reason is there to believe that the set of a person's possible occurrent thoughts is contentfully related? Is there any positive reason to think that possible occurrent thoughts are contentfully related? Yes. Fodor and Pylyshyn argue along the following lines.[9] For a wide range of propositions p, if a person hears a sentence that means that p in a natural language she understands, then, lacking evidence to the contrary, the person will believe that p. So, if you are an English speaker and a friend utters, "Mary forgot her umbrella" loudly and clearly, then, *ceteris paribus*, you will think that Mary forgot her umbrella. Further, there will be patterns in the set of beliefs you can come to entertain in this way. If you can be brought to believe that Mary forgot her umbrella in this way and to believe that John brought his book in this way, then you can be brought to believe that John forgot his umbrella and Mary brought her book in this way. In brief, the argument is that contentfully related sentences cause contentfully related thoughts. We can, however, also have cases where apparently contentfully related thoughts can cause contentfully related sentences. We can have subjects view cartoon images on a computer monitor and describe what they see. So, when shown an image of a man laughing at a dog, subjects will say something like "A man is laughing at a dog" or "The man is laughing at the dog," and when shown an image of a dog laughing at a man, subjects will say something like "A dog is laughing at a man" or "The dog is laughing at the man." Here, the sentences the subject utters are contentfully related. If, however, we postulate that a subject's thinking that the man is laughing at the dog or that the dog is laughing at the man is (part of) the cause of the subject uttering 'the man is laughing at the dog" or "the dog is laughing at the man," then there is reason to think that among normal humans there are content relations among the set of possible thoughts.

For those who worry that the apparent content relations among possible thoughts are the product of current uses of natural language, we can envision other experimental paradigms. Take the following task. Subjects are shown images of two regular solids, such as cubes, tetrahedrons, and dodecahedrons, side by side. One of these solids will be large and the other small. Subjects must push a button beneath the one they think is large. Human subjects can easily perform this task. If the large object is on the right, they push the right button; if the large object is on the left, they push the left button. If we suppose that before pushing the button for a given side, the person thinks that there is a large object on that side, then we have evidence that subjects are capable of thinking that large objects are on the left and that large objects are on the right. These thoughts are contentfully related. Further, there is nothing special about large and small. Normal human subjects could do just as well with red/blue, red/green, animate/inanimate, and so forth. The sort of account we have just provided, of course, falls far short of the provision of an experimental protocol, but genuine experimental psychologists can easily see how one might go about to constituting the appropriate kinds of protocols. These sorts of experimental paradigms have never been addressed by critics of the content relatedness of thought, but they, and many others like them, give us reason to think that there are semantic relations among the possible thoughts.

2 ACCOUNTS OF THE SEMANTIC RELATEDNESS OF THOUGHT

How then might Pure Atomism explain the putative fact that the possible occurrent thoughts for a normal human being are contentfully related–that a normal human being who can have the occurrent thought that John loves Mary can also have the occurrent thought that Mary loves John? In addition to invoking Representationalism and the Computational Theory of the Attitudes, Pure Atomism will also say that the thought that John loves Mary involves a representation α that means that John loves Mary and that the thought that Mary loves John involves a representation β that means that Mary loves John. As before, the problem for the Pure Atomistic account lies in its reliance on a problematic auxiliary hypothesis about the nature of the computer program of the mind. Although there exist Pure Atomistic computer programs of the mind in which possible occurrent thoughts are contentfully related, this is not a necessary feature of a Pure Atomist architecture. So, some additional hypothesis must be added to insure that the Pure Atomist architecture generates contentfully related cognitive states. Yet, an hypothesis that guarantees that Pure Atomism will have representations for both John's loving Mary and Mary's loving John would appear to require enough information about the computer program of the mind to have vindicated Pure Atomism without recourse to the semantic relatedness of thought capacities argument.

Now take up the Classical approach. The Classical account of the content relations in thought invokes the Computational Theory of the Attitudes, Representationalism, the hypothesis that thoughts involve a set of syntactic atoms, the hypothesis that there is some way of concatenatively composing the syntactic atoms into syntactic molecules, the hypothesis that these syntactic molecules have a combinatorial semantics that respects the Principle of Context Independence, and the hypothesis that the computer program of the mind is causally sensitive to the combinatorial structure of the cognitive representations. This much in place, we have seen that there are ways of building molecules and there are ways of building molecules. A set of syntactic atoms $\Sigma = \{$John, Jane, loves, hates$\}$ can be combined to form the set of syntactic items

$$\Sigma^*_1 = \quad \{\text{John loves John} \quad \text{John loves Jane}$$
$$\text{Jane loves John} \quad \text{Jane loves Jane}$$
$$\text{John hates John} \quad \text{John hates Jane}$$
$$\text{Jane hates John} \quad \text{Jane hates Jane}\},$$

or it can be combined to form the set of strings

$$\Sigma^*_2 = \quad \{\text{John loves John, Jane hates}\}.$$

Yet, the well-known Classical hypotheses do not guarantee that possible occurrent thoughts will be contentfully related. To get this, Classicism must, therefore, invoke an auxiliary hypothesis to the effect that Σ is combined to form syntactic items in a set like Σ^*_1, rather than a set like Σ^*_2. But such an auxiliary cannot be confirmed short of having previously secured the truth of Classicism. This means that leaving Classicism has no *bona fide* explanation of the content relations among possible occurrent thoughts.

We might also, once again, draw attention to the problem as it relates to the Principles of Semantic Compositionality and Context Independence. These principles are needed in order to generate semantically related contents in a set of Classical representations. Without Semantic Compositionality and Context Independence or some equivalent hypotheses, thoughts would not be contentfully related. Yet, insofar as they cannot be confirmed short of confirming Classicism, they are problematic.

3 A SECOND ARGUMENT

In Chapters 4 and 5, we considered a number of possible ways in which one might try to defend Classicism against the charge that it cannot explain the systematicity of cognitive representations. Here, therefore, we might try to defend Classicism against the charge that it cannot explain the compositionality of thought. Yet, as so much of this would be repetitive, it is probably more fruitful to consider another argument for Classicism that might be culled from Fodor and Pylyshyn's discussion of the compositionality of representations.

We begin by recalling that Fodor and Pylyshyn distinguish the systematicity of thought from the content relatedness of thought, then point out that these are logically distinct and separable properties. So, on the one hand, it is logically possible to have one thought be counterfactually dependent on another without those thoughts having related contents. That is, it is logically possible that were one, as a matter of psychological fact, to lose by cognitive cause the capacity to have the thought that John loves Mary one might thereby lose the capacity to have the thought that Aristotle was a shipping magnate. It is also logically possible that, as a matter of psychological fact, were one to have the capacity to have the thoughts that John loves Mary and that Charles loves China, one would also have the capacity to have the thought that Aristotle is a shipping magnate. The discovery that humans are systematic, but not content related might be puzzling in the extreme, but such a discovery is nonetheless a logical possibility. On the other hand, it is also logically possible to have thought capacities that are related by content, having common semantic contents, without their being counterfactually dependent. One could have a capacity for the thought that John loves Mary and a capacity for the thought that Mary loves John without the loss by cognitive cause of either capacity precipitating the loss of the other. A counterfactual dependence among thoughts does not logically imply contentful relations among those thoughts, nor do contentful relations among thoughts logically imply counterfactual dependence among those thoughts.

Given the logical separability of counterfactual dependence and content relatedness, we can ask why it is that these logically distinct properties in fact co-occur. If a normal human being has a systematic mind, then it also has a mind in which possible occurrent thoughts are contentfully related?. Why is this? We have noted before that neither Pure Atomism nor Classicism has an appropriate account of these independent regularities, but what about one following upon the other? While this is not the most familiar interpretation of what Fodor and Pylyshyn are about in their discussion of the compositionality of representations argument, they do appear to have something like this in mind at a number of points during their discussion. In particular, they appear to have this in mind when they write that, you need to assume some degree of compositionality of English sentences to account for the fact that systematically related sentences are always semantically related (Fodor & Pylyshyn, 1988, p. 43),

to the extent that the semantic value of these parts is context-independent, that would explain why these systematically related thoughts are also semantically related (ibid, italics in original).

if . . . we make the usual Classicist assumptions (viz., that systematically related thoughts share constituents and that the semantic values of these shared constituents are context independent) the correlation between systematicity and semantic relatedness follows immediately (ibid., p. 45).

All of these passages suggest that the co-occurrence of the systematicity of cognitive representations and the content relations in thought, i.e., the co-occurrence of the counterfactual dependence of one thought upon another and the semantic relatedness of possible thoughts, is something that Fodor and Pylyshyn want a theory of cognitive architecture to explain.

While Classicism does not have the desired sort of explanation of either regularity in isolation, it does appear to have the right sort of account of the co-occurrence. Given the apparatus Classicism needs to account for the nomologically necessary and sufficient connections among thought capacities, one has without further assumption the apparatus necessary to account for the semantic relations among possible thoughts. As always, the Classical account of the systematicity of thought begins with Representationalism, the Computational Theory of the Attitudes, the hypothesis that there exist syntactically and semantically atomic representations that combine to form syntactically and semantically molecular representations, and that these atomic representations have context independent content. We also suppose that cognitive representations involve grammatical structures that might be shared by more than one representation. The reason that some thought capacities are counterfactually dependent on others–the reason that some thought capacities are nomologically necessary and sufficient for other thought capacities–is that they share all the same cognitive capacities. They share atomic representations, the apparatus for forming a particular grammatical construction, and computational apparatus that is sensitive the combinatorial structure of the cognitive representation and that is able to support a propositional attitude under which these representations are cognized. Thus, the reason that the capacity for the hope that John loves Mary is nomologically necessary and sufficient for the capacity for the hope that Mary loves John is that both thoughts use the atomic representations "John," "loves," and "Mary" that have context independent content, that both involve a common grammatical construction, and both involve the computational apparatus that gives rise to the attitude of hoping. If, for some psychological reason, a normal human being could not hope that John loves Mary, then that human being would not have the ability to hope that Mary loves John because of having lost the atomic representation of John, or of loves, or of Mary, or the capacity for use a particular grammatical construction or the capacity to adopt the attitude of hoping. Given this sort of account of the systematicity of thought, the compositionality of thought, i.e., the content relatedness of possible occurrent thoughts, follows without additional assumption. The set of Classical assumptions that are minimally sufficient for accounting for counterfactual dependencies among thought capacities entails the content relations among thought capacities.[10]

At this point, we should recall that our notion of the counterfactual dependency between the capacity for thought A and the capacity for thought B is a matter of the capacity for thought A being nomologically necessary and sufficient for the capacity for thought B. There are, however, the weaker kinds of dependencies we discussed briefly in Chapter 5. The Classicist might think it is possible, for example, that a person could lose both the capacity to hope that Laurent wins the race and the capacity to hope that Greg will be a good sport, in virtue of losing the capacity for hoping. The Classicist might also think it is possible that a person could lose both the capacity to hope that John loves Mary and the capacity to fear that Mark likes Alice, because that person could lose the capacity for a particular grammatical structure these thoughts share. The Classicist might also think that it is possible that a person could lose the capacity to hope that Greg wins and the capacity to believe that Greg loves Mary by losing the capacity to token a concept of Greg. The Classicist is committed to there being these kinds of dependencies. Yet, the reason we should recall our specific version of the counterfactual dependency of thought at this point is that this version gets the co-occurrence argument to work properly. This version enables Classicism to explain why counterfactually dependent thoughts are contentfully related. If the Classicist were to use a weaker notion of dependency, where, say, one thought is dependent on another in virtue of a common grammatical construction, then the thoughts that are counterfactually dependent in this way need not be contentfully related. Similarly, if the Classicist were to use a notion of dependency in which one thought is dependent on another in virtue of using a common computational subroutine for realizing a propositional attitude, such as believing, hoping, or fearing, then, again, the thoughts that are counterfactually dependent in this way need not be contentfully related. By contrast, given that we conceive of counterfactual dependencies among thoughts as a matter of them being mutually nomologically necessary and sufficient, then content related thoughts follow of necessity.[11]

Just for the record, there might be some value in pointing out that there is reason to believe that Classicism can explain the co-occurrence of nomologically necessary and sufficient connection between thought capacities and the semantic relatedness of thought capacities in the desired way only by having semantic relatedness stem from nomologically necessary and sufficient connections. To approach this another way, there is reason to think that the minimal Classical account of the semantic relatedness of thought capacities does not lead automatically to nomologically necessary and sufficient connections between thought capacities. This has to do with the possibility of synonymous terms in the system of cognitive representations. Consider the set of syntactic atoms Γ = {John, John*, loves, loves*, Mary, Mary*}, where both "John" and "John*" mean John, both "loves" and "loves*" mean loves, and both "Mary" and "Mary*" mean Mary. The starred and un-starred terms are supposed to be synonymous. Further suppose that the formation rules involving these atoms counts as well-formed, just the following molecules, "John loves Mary" and "Mary* loves* John*". Supposing that the Principles of Semantic Compositionality and Context Independence are in force, "John loves Mary" will mean that John loves Mary and "Mary* loves* John*" will mean that Mary loves John. These two syntactic molecules will be semantically related, but neither thought capacity will be nomologically necessary or sufficient for the other. Presumably, one could lose, by cognitive cause, the capacity to token "John" without thereby losing the capacity to token "John*", so that one would lose the capacity to think that John loves Mary without thereby losing the capacity to think that Mary loves John. Similarly, one could lose, by cognitive cause, the capacities to token "loves" and "Mary" without thereby losing the capacities to token "loves*" or "Mary*". In such cases, one would again lose the capacity to think that John loves Mary without, thereby, losing the capacity to think that Mary loves John. Of course, insofar as "John loves Mary" and "Mary* loves* John*" rely on a common grammatical construction, there will be what we have called a weak intrinsic connection between these thought capacities, but still no nomologically necessary and sufficient connection. So, unless the possibility of synonymous terms in thought can be ruled out, it appears that semantic relatedness does not lead to nomologically necessary and sufficient connections, hence that the Classicist's only way of explaining the co-occurrence of these features of thought is via nomologically necessary and sufficient connections among capacities leading to semantically related thought capacities.

By contrast with Classicism, Pure Atomism has no satisfactory method for connecting the systematicity of cognitive representations with the semantic relatedness of thought capacities. This arises because the content of one representation is completely independent of the content of any other representation. Suppose, for the sake of argument, that Pure Atomism can generate an account of the nomologically necessary and sufficient connection between thought capacities. Given a minimal Pure Atomistic account of the counterfactual dependence of thoughts, there is no reason why, short of adding some arbitrary auxiliary hypothesis, counterfactually dependent thoughts should at the same time be semantically related. Even if, however, the Pure Atomist can make good on the hypothesis that the program of the mind is such that two syntactic items α and β, with their respective contents, are counterfactually dependent on each other, it would require an auxiliary hypothesis regarding the specific semantic content of α and β to have it work out that α and β are also contentfully related. Such an additional hypothesis, however, would be just the sort of hypothesis that could not be confirmed independent of the hypothesis of a Pure Atomistic system of mental representation. The point here is the familiar one. Explaining the co-occurrence of the relevant nomological connections and semantic relations requires more than simply developing a model that displays both features. One must, in addition, show a kind of necessary connection between the explanation of one regularity and the explanation of another regularity.

This argument invokes a notion of a set of hypotheses being minimally sufficient to account for some regularity. The notion is that an explanation only relies upon hypotheses that do genuine explanatory work; no extra non-working hypotheses should be built into a putative explanation. The notion prevents irrelevant hypotheses from becoming part of an explanation. While this is a relatively unproblematic, implicit feature of explanations, the assumption needs to be made explicit in order to block a possible Pure Atomist attempt to explain the co-occurrence of nomological connections and semantic relations. The basic worry is that one build in unnecessary structure in the "explanation" of the nomologically necessary and sufficient connections, then use that "surplus" structure to explain the semantic relatedness of thought capacities. Thus, a Pure Atomist might claim that α means that John loves Mary and that β means that Mary loves John, and that, in virtue of a computer program of the mind, the thought that John loves Mary is counterfactually dependent on the thought that Mary loves John. Furthermore, the computer program of the mind that enables one thought to be counterfactually dependent on another at the same time renders the counterfactually dependent thoughts semantically related.[12] The problem with this account is that while it is possible to have the counterfactually dependent thoughts be semantically related in a Pure Atomist computer program of the mind, the putative explanation of the nomological connections violates the metatheoretic minimal sufficiency condition on explanations. The putative explanation of the systematicity of cognitive representations invokes more than is necessary to account for the counterfactual dependence of one thought on another. The inessential part of the putative explanation of the systematicity of thought is the addition of the supposition that α and β are semantically related. In order for one thought to be dependent on another, the syntactic atoms α and β must, of course, have *some* semantic content, but they need not have related semantic contents. Thus, one might have a Pure Atomistic system where α means John loves Mary and β means bears hibernate in the woods. Such a system might be programmed such that the thought that John loves Mary is counterfactually dependent on the thought that bears hibernate in the woods. By contrast, this cannot be done with a Classical system. Thus, to repeat the main contention of this "new" argument, we have a defeasible reason to believe in a Classical cognitive architecture, rather than a Pure Atomist architecture, because the minimally sufficient Classical account of the systematicity of cognitive representations entails an account of the semantic relatedness of thought capacities, where the minimally sufficient Pure Atomist account cannot make the same boast. This gives us a powerful, though defeasible, reason to think that cognitive architecture is Classical.

The strength of this sort of explanatory argument is borne out in one of the examples from Chapter 2. Recall that ancient astronomers had observed that the usual motions of the superior planets (Mars, Jupiter, and Saturn) through the fixed stars from west to east is periodically interrupted by a period of retrograde motion which involved these planets slowing in their normal eastward motion, stopping, moving for a time in a westward retrograde manner, before again slowing, stopping, and finally resuming a normal eastward motion. Ptolemaic astronomers were aware of these irregularities and were able to provide a qualitatively correct model of them. The basic idea is to have a superior planet, such as Mars, orbiting on an epicycle. This epicycle then orbits at the end of a deferent. By careful adjustment of the relative sizes and relative rates of rotation of the epicycle and deferent, it is possible to generate, to a first approximation, the observed motions of the superior planets. The Copernican account of retrograde motions is fundamentally different. According to Copernicans, retrograde motions are merely apparent motions that arise from the Earth's overtaking a superior planet as both orbit the Sun. Where the Copernican account proved to be far superior to the Ptolemaic account was in its ability to account for a particular feature of retrograde motions: they always occur when the superior planet stands in opposition to the sun. Whenever a planet is in the very middle of its westward retrograde motion, it is found to be separated from the Sun by 180°. By clever manipulation of features of the epicycle on deferent system, Ptolemaic astronomy could provide an account of this feature of retrograde motion, but the Copernican system generated the further fact without any additional hypothesis. Simply given the proposed nature of retrograde motions on the Copernican system, it follows of nomological necessity that retrograde motions will occur at opposition. The minimally sufficient Copernican account of retrograde motions also accounts for retrograde motions occurring at opposition. The Ptolemaic account doesn't have this strength. The proposal here is that Classicism enjoys a similar advantage over Pure Atomism.

4 OTHER CO-OCCURRENCE EXPLANANDA?

The fact that Classicism can explain the co-occurrence of one regularity upon another suggests that this little twist on the familiar semantic relatedness argument might have fruitful extensions. Perhaps there is some comparable link to forge between, say, the systematicity of inference and the systematicity of cognitive representations. Recall that, in Chapter 5, we considered whether the state commitments of the systematicity of certain inferences implied that there would be some degree of systematicity of thought and whether the systematicity of thought has any implications for the systematicity of inference. There we concluded that the systematicity of thought does not logically entail the systematicity of inference, since the systematicity of inference requires certain sorts of state transitions that the systematicity of cognitive representations does not. Nor is there an obvious link between the state requirements of the systematic of inference and the systematicity of cognitive representations. So, the stage is set for the possibility of there being some connection between the systematicity of cognitive representations and the systematicity of inference. Yet, even if there were some connection between the two types of systematicity, there is no obvious way for Classicism to link them. This is a possibility that might repay further attention.

What, then, of the possibility of a co-occurrence type argument using the systematicity of inference and the semantic relatedness of thought capacities? Here, the systematicity of thought entails that there will be some degree of content relations among possible occurrent thoughts. This is because the premises of any argument must have some content that overlaps with the content of the conclusion. For example, with *modus ponens*, the "premise" state (or states) will share with the "conclusion" state, the content of the consequent of the conditional. In other words, the Q in the "conclusion" state will be contentfully related, to some limited degree, to the consequent in, say, P→Q. As another example, with disjunctive syllogism, the "premise" state (or states) will have contents we describe schematically as PvQ and ¬P which will share the content Q with the "conclusion" state. Thus, any system, either Pure Atomist or Classical, that is inferentially systematic will also have some degree of content relations among its states. Thus, asking why a system that is inferentially systematic also displays compositionality–if, in fact, this is the case–gives us an explanandum that will do no work for either Pure Atomism or Classicism.

There is, however, another possible explanandum that might be used in a co-occurrence type of argument. The systematicity of cognitive representations might be thought of as a synchronic psychological regularity. At any given time, there is an intrinsic connection between thoughts. In addition to this synchronic systematicity, we might recognize a diachronic phenomenon. Through the course of normal human development, the number of possible thoughts does not increase one by one. Rather the number increases by leaps and bounds. So, while it is, in point of logic, possible to have a person whose stock of possible occurrent thoughts increases one by one, say, from 4 to 5 to 6, in actual development, one's stock of thoughts increases by several at a time, say, from 4 to 9 to 18. Thus, during the interval t_0-t_1, a normal person might have the capacity to have the thoughts

John loves John	John loves Mary
Mary loves John	Mary loves Mary,

then, during the interval t_1-t_2, have the capacity to have the thoughts,

John loves John	John loves Mary	John loves Jane
Mary loves John	Mary loves Mary	Mary loves Jane
Jane loves John	Jane loves Mary	Jane loves Jane

then, during the interval t_2-t_3, have the capacity to have the thoughts,

John loves John	John loves Mary	John loves Jane
Mary loves John	Mary loves Mary	Mary loves Jane
Jane loves John	Jane loves Mary	Jane loves Jane
John hates John	John hates Mary	John hates Jane
Mary hates John	Mary hates Mary	Mary hates Jane
Jane hates John	Jane hates Mary	Jane hates Jane.

The idea behind developmental systematicity is here explained through an example in which the thoughts are contentfully related, but this is not essential. What is essential is the nature of the growth of one's stock of possible thoughts: growth is by leaps and bounds. It should be noted that the diachronic and synchronic systematicity of thought are logically separable. It is, in point of logic, possible that people could increase their stock of possible thoughts by leaps and bounds-hence be diachronically systematic- yet once that stock is obtained each thought is counterfactually independent of the others-hence not synchronically systematic.

Like the other lone systematic explananda we have surveyed, diachronic systematicity cannot be explained by either Classicism or Pure Atomism for just the sorts of reasons we have seen on many occasions. Given, however, that diachronic and synchronic systematicity are logically independent, we might do well to ask why it is that they co-occur. Why is it that normal people display both diachronic and synchronic systematicity? The problem for Pure Atomism is that even if it were able to generate a model that exhibits both forms of systematicity, a minimally sufficient account of one form would not be at the same time sufficient for the other. Even if a Pure Atomist model could be set up such that new meaningful syntactically atomic representations were added to a system in groups at a time, the members of these clusters of representations need in no way be synchronically counterfactually dependent upon each other.

Classicism, however, fares much better. According to Classicism, the diachronic systematicity of thought presumably arises in two ways. In the first, new atomic mental representations are fitted into existing mechanisms of complex representation formation.[13] Thus, during t_0-t_1, a cognitive system will have three syntactically atomic representations, {John, loves, Mary}, with the obvious meanings, along with the mechanisms to compose these into four distinct, syntactically molecular combinations whose semantics is context independent. At the transition from the period t_0-t_1 to the period t_1-t_2, the system acquires a new syntactic atom, "Jane," meaning Jane (hence not synonymous with existing representations), which is typed in the same category as is "John" and "Mary," and which has context independent content. Thought capacities so developing are, thus, diachronically systematic. According to the Classicist, a second reason thoughts increase in number by leaps and bounds is that, through the course of development, new syntactic and semantic combinatorial processes may emerge to be applied to the existing stock of atomic and molecular representations. Insofar as these new combinatorial processes respect the Principle of Context Independence, new thought capacities will emerge. So, the emergence of cognitive capacities to form relative clauses, unbounded conjunctions, unbounded disjunctions, etc., will lead to dramatic increases in the number of distinct thoughts which an agent is capable of entertaining.[14]

Another possible explanandum is that the thought capacities that are diachronically systematic are at the same time semantically related. In other words, the thought capacities that are acquired by leaps and bounds have related contents. This Classicism would explain in the obvious way, in terms of the increasing number of thought capacities being a product of the addition of new representations or new grammatical constructions. By contrast, Pure Atomism would appear to have no acceptable account on offer.

These Classical stories, of course, implicate a large number of auxiliary hypotheses over and above the central Classical hypothesis of a combinatorial system of cognitive representations. These stories invoke a more expansive version of Classicism than was set out in Chapter 1. Thus, we do not have an acceptable account of the diachronic systematicity of thought. Nonetheless, once all these hypotheses are in place, it is clear that thought must also be synchronically systematic. Thoughts are counterfactually dependent on each other in virtue of their shared components. The situation is, in relevant respects, like the Copernican account of retrograde motions at opposition.

The principal inspiration for these new systematicity arguments has been to avoid the troubles with auxiliary hypotheses that beset the older systematicity arguments. In addition, however, these new arguments provide a response to an argument in Matthews, (1997). Matthews's argument might be called the problem of incomplete systematicity. While one can think, for example, the thought that x is the sole member of the singleton set {x}, one may well be unable to think that the singleton set {x} is the sole member of x. In order to account for this incompleteness of systematicity, for the fact that there exists a thought of the form aRb without a corresponding thought of the form, bRa, Fodor, et al., must rely on some sort of arbitrary hypothesis to the effect that some thoughts are exceptions to the general rule that normal people who can think thoughts of the form aRb can also think thoughts of the form bRa. The principal co-occurrence arguments avoid this problem by building in the requisite auxiliary hypotheses into one of the lone explananda. In the case of the co-occurrence of the systematicity and the semantic relatedness of thought, the auxiliary hypothesis needed to account for the incompleteness of systematicity is built into the account of systematicity. In the case of the co-occurrence of diachronic and synchronic systematicity, the requisite auxiliary hypothesis is built into the account of diachronic systematicity. In the case of the semantic relatedness of diachronically systematic thoughts, the potentially problematic auxiliary hypothesis is again built into the account of diachronic systematicity. In all these cases, the sort of auxiliary hypothesis to which Matthews draws our attention is part of a minimal account of one of the lone explananda. As Matthews points out, the account is not qualitatively correct without such an auxiliary. Once the auxiliary hypothesis needed to meet Matthews's objection is (arbitrarily) included in the account of one of the lone explananda, however, the co-occurrence explananda of the new systematicity argument follows without additional hypothesis. So, the co-occurrence systematicity arguments sidestep Matthews's objection.

5 WHAT IS FODOR AND PYLYSHYN'S "REAL" ARGUMENT?

To this point in this chapter we have extracted two arguments from Fodor and Pylyshyn's discussion of the compositionality of representations. The first of these is the challenge to explain how it is that thought capacities are contentfully related. The explanandum in this argument is relatively familiar from the cognitive science literature and shares some important features with the systematicity of inference and systematicity of cognitive representations argument. This gave us some reason to examine this interpretation in the early part of this chapter. The second of these is the challenge to explain why counterfactually dependent thought capacities also share common contents. This argument appears to be the one that meets the explanatory standard we have been invoking since Chapter 2. This gives us some reason to examine this interpretation. Yet, there are passages in Fodor and Pylyshyn's discussion of compositionality that do not mesh neatly with either interpretation, perhaps suggesting that Fodor and Pylyshyn have been misinterpreted or misunderstood both in the present examination, and in the cognitive science literature generally. Here we wish to review the relevant text simply to keep the record straight. Readers who are not interested in the textual details can skip this section without loss.

Fodor and Pylyshyn begin their discussion of the compositionality of representations with an argument for the combinatorial structure of natural language. This is then supposed to be used to generate a parallel argument for the combinatorial structure of thought. Fodor and Pylyshyn begin by introducing what they call the "Principle of Compositionality," what we have here called the "Principle of Context Independence," namely, that "a lexical item must make approximately the same semantic contribution to each expression in which it occurs" (Fodor & Pylyshyn, 1988, p. 42). This leads to the following case for the combinatorial structure of natural language:

> So, here's the argument so far: you need to assume some degree of compositionality of English sentences to account for the fact that systematically related sentences are always semantically related; and to account for certain regular parallelisms between the syntactic structure of sentences and their entailments. So, beyond any serious doubt, the sentences of English must be compositional to some serious extent. But the principle of compositionality governs the semantic relations between words *and the expressions of which they are constituents.* So compositionality implies that (some) expressions have constituents. So compositionality argues for (specifically, presupposes) syntactic/semantic structure in sentences (Fodor & Pylyshyn, 1988, pp. 43-44, italics in original).

The argument appears to be that what Fodor and Pylyshyn call "compositionality" is part of what is required in order to explain a) the co-occurrence of systematicity and content-relatedness in natural language (roughly, the argument we have championed above) and b) "certain regular parallelisms" between the syntactic structure of sentences and their entailments. If, however, natural language is compositional, then *ipso facto* it must be combinatorial.

Yet, when the discussion moves from the case of natural language to the case of cognitive representations, talk of a parallelism between the syntactic structure of [mental] sentences and their entailments disappears. Further, the idea of compositionality bringing with it combinatorialism drops from sight as well. Instead, we only find the idea of explaining how systematically related thoughts can be contentfully related:

> So, if the ability to think certain thoughts is interconnected, then the corresponding representational capacities must be interconnected too; specifically, the ability to be in some representational states must imply the ability to be in certain other semantically related representational states.
> But then the question arises: *how could* the mind be so arranged that the ability to be in one representational state is connected with the ability to be in others that are semantically nearby? (ibid., p. 44, italics in original).

> That would explain why these thoughts are *systematically* related; *and, to the extent that the semantic value of these parts is context-independent, that would explain why these systematically related thoughts are also semantically related* (ibid., italics in original).

We now see some basis for the charge that Fodor and Pylyshyn's discussion is genuinely equivocal. We have noted where this problems lie. Yet, even though there is no single argument that has a lock on being *the* correct interpretation of what Fodor and Pylyshyn were up to, we do find that there continues to be some basis for tracing the various arguments we have explored to Fodor and Pylyshyn's discussion. In fact, given the ambiguities in Fodor and Pylyshyn's discussion, we seem to have taken the only reasonable course in exploring the merits of the two possible arguments that might trace their origins to this discussion.

6 THE TRACKING ARGUMENT AND THE ARGUMENTS FROM PSYCHOLOGICAL PROCESSES

In this section we digress from the main line of exposition and argumentation in order to consider some additional empirical arguments for Classicism. The first of these is Terry Horgan and John Tienson's "tracking argument," which urges that combinatorial representations are essential to explaining how people are able to handle the diverse cognitive tasks that they handle. The second of these arguments, found in Fodor, (1985), is what we will here call the "Argument from Psychological Processes I." This argument maintains that only Classicism can explain the parallelism between the logical and causal order in reasoning. Yet a third argument, the "Argument from Psychological Processes II," is found in the appendix to Fodor's *Psychosemantics*. This argument maintains that, since psycholinguists have a well-confirmed theory that speaks of processes involving combinatorial representations, we have some *prima facie* reason to suppose that cognitive processes involve combinatorial representations. The rationale for this digression is that these arguments and the systematicity arguments are mutually illuminating.

6.1 The Tracking Argument

According to Horgan and Tienson, (1996), people have to have Classical representations in order to keep track of the multitude of objects in their environments and the multitude of properties these objects might have. They consider, as two illustrative cases, the representational capacities we must suppose a person needs in order to entertain beliefs about her local environment and the capacities needed in order to play college-level basketball.

At any given moment, humans typically have beliefs about a multitude of objects in their immediate vicinity. The beliefs can be about the perceptual and the non-perceptual properties of seen and unseen objects. They may concern the functions or uses of objects, their dispositional properties, their ages, parts, contents, and so forth. Not all such beliefs are occurrent beliefs; they are not all beliefs to which one consciously attends at a particular time in a particular place. Nonetheless, they are potentially occurrent beliefs. As little as a comment or a question in one's natural language can be sufficient to elicit many such beliefs. Even though the vast majority of these beliefs are only tacit, they are beliefs that can be made explicit, hence there must be some representational capacity which makes this possibility a possibility. What is such a representational capacity like? According to Horgan and Tienson, the capacity must be Classical.

In the course of a college basketball game, many a player must make many a decision: to pass or shoot on a fast break, to pass inside or not, to switch on defense or stick with the current opponent, to try to intercept a pass or continue checking a player, and so forth. Consider the range of variables that must be taken into consideration in making a single decision, such as making a bounce pass to a team mate cutting between two defensive players. The passer must note her team mate's position and motion relative to the goal, the positions and motions of each of her other team mates, and the positions and motions of each of the opponents. There are the properties of the individual players: height, jumping ability, speed, shooting ability, etc. There are the transient properties, such as who is guarding whom, who is having a good game and who isn't, who is shooting well, who needs an easy basket to get in the game, and who is in foul trouble. Then there are global factors such as the time left on the game clock, the time left on the shot clock, the coach's game plan, and the defense. Horgan and Tienson contend that, in order to keep track of all these factors, one needs a combinatorial system of representation. Moreover, basketball play is not unique with regard to the representational demands it makes on people. Other sports and activities might serve as well to make the same point.

Were the tracking argument a kind of inference to the best explanation we might well wish to pursue what principle underlies its being the best explanation. This is, after all, what we have, in essence, done in the case of the systematicity arguments. The tracking argument is not, however, meant to be an inference to the best explanation. Horgan and Tienson tell us that it is meant to be an inference to the only possible explanation. This idea they explain by way of an analogy. Since Smith was in London yesterday and is in New York today, she must have taken an airplane. In such inferences, one is inferring not merely the best explanation, but the only explanation that is a real possibility. The reason is that, given the available technology, only a plane has the capability to get Smith from London to New York in one day. Now, just as we can pursue the principle underlying an inference to the best explanation, so too we can pursue the principle or cause which makes some account the only possible explanation. In particular, we can ask what makes a combinatorial system of representation the only possible explanation of tracking. While we understand the restrictions on the possible in the case of Smith's travels, we don't have a comparably clear understanding of why Classicism is the only real nomologically possible basis for so many of our cognitive capacities. Perhaps a Classical system of representation is the only real possibility, but it is not clear why it is. Horgan and Tienson do not elaborate on this point, so we must scout about for our own account of the source of the impossibility.

One might try to argue that Classicism is the only real possible basis of our cognitive capacities by a modification of an argument by Ray Jackendoff. Jackendoff, (1994), argues that natural language must involve a combinatorial apparatus. Suppose that there are 10,000 nouns in English. Each of these 10,000 nouns forms a sentence of the form, "An X is not a Y". Thus, we have

(2)   A numeral is not a numbskull.
       A numeral is not a nun.
       A numeral is not a nunnery.
       . . .
       A numbskull is not a numeral.
       A numbskull is not a nun.
       A numbskull is not a nunnery.
       . . .
       A nun is not a nursery.

. . .

An oboe is not an octopus.

. . .

There are 10^8 sentences of this form. Further sentences can be constructed from these using the schema "Since A, B":

(3)   Since a numeral is not a numbskull, a numbskull is not a nun.
       Since a numeral is not a numbskull, a numbskull is not a nunnery.
       Since a numeral is not a numbskull, a numbskull is not a nuptial.
       . . .
       Since a numeral is not a nursery, a numbskull is not a nun.
       . . .
       Since an oboe is not an octopus, a numeral is not a numbskull.
       . . .

These sentences number $10^8 \times 10^8 = 10^{16}$. Since there are only 10^{10} non-sensory neurons in the brain, Jackendoff infers that this means that each neuron in the brain would have to be responsible for processing something on the order of 10^6 sentences. This, however, he finds implausible, even for what he takes to be a small fragment of a natural language. So, natural language must be a syntactically and semantically combinatorial.

This is Jackendoff's argument for supposing that there must be a combinatorial representational system underlying language. It may, however, be pressed into service as an argument for a combinatorial representational system underlying cognition, if we further suppose that understanding one sentence requires one dedicated neuron.[15] So, perhaps the reason that we must postulate a combinatorial representational system as the only possible basis for the human tracking capacity is that there are not enough cells in the human brain to support a mental representation for each possible thought. Only a combinatorial representational system will allow the resources of the brain the capacity to have all the thoughts it does.

The weak point in this extension of Jackendoff's argument is the assumption that, given a non-combinatorial system of representation, each thought must be implemented in its own neuron. An alternative, equally viable, assumption is that each thought corresponds to the level of activity in a cluster of neurons. In fact, Paul Churchland, (1989), has offered a sketch of how this might go, intended to show that there are indeed enough brain states to code each of a very large number of possible cognitive states. Assuming that the brain contains on the order of 10^{11} non-sensory neurons, Churchland supposes that each of these may be parceled out among something on the order of a thousand more specialized brain regions, each of which may contain on the order of 10^8

neurons. If we make what Churchland takes to be the conservative assumption that each neuron can take on ten distinct levels of excitation, then each of these thousand or so typical brain regions will have 10 raised to the power of 10^8, that is, $10^{100,000,000}$ distinct states. So, if we assume that each distinct state of a typical brain region, rather than a single neuron, corresponds to a representation, then it would appear that we have more than enough potential representational states to meet Jackendoff's challenge.

It is perhaps worth interjecting on Churchland's behalf that the fact that one of these neuronal representational states is made up of parts does not thereby show that the state is a combinatorial state of the sort proposed by Classicism. Each neuron is certainly a part of the set of neurons that contributes to the total representational state of a given subregion, but in order to constitute a part in the sense of Classicism, it must have a semantic content unto itself that is context independent. If a neuron does not, then it is perhaps to be viewed in the way in which letters in words or pixels in dot matrix depictions of letters are generally viewed. Letters are parts of words, but they typically carry no meaning on their own. They are not morphemes. The individual pixels in a letter are parts of the letter, but they have no meaning on their own. They are parts, but not syntactically and semantically atomic parts.

While there are other dimensions of Horgan and Tienson's tracking argument that merit exploration and while there is certainly further room for argumentation here, the present conclusion is that, while it may be true that only Classicism can serve the vast representational needs of human cognition, we have no clear understanding of why this is so.

6.2 The Argument from Psychological Processes I

Fodor, (1985), notes that there is a parallelism between the logical order and the causal/cognitive order.[16] On the one hand, P&Q entails P, and, on the other, people who believe that P&Q also tend to come to believe that P. Similarly, on the one hand, P and P → Q entail Q, while on the other, normal people who believe that P and that P → Q also tend to believe that Q. How, one might ask, is this parallelism possible? Fodor contends that Turing provided us with an answer, an answer which he thinks is perhaps the only major advance cognitive science has yet seen. In a wide range of cases in the logical realm, inferential relations admit of formal characterization. Within certain limits, entailment relations can be mirrored with formal deductive relations. The fact that propositions of the form P&Q entail propositions of the form P has a syntactically specifiable, proof-theoretic analogue: anytime one has a symbol with the pattern "P&Q", one can write a symbol with the pattern "P". The fact that pairs of symbols of the form P and P →Q entail a symbol of the form Q likewise has a proof-theoretic analogue. In the causal realm, symbols have formal structure that can be recognized by mechanical means. Symbols can be given machine-readable forms, such as sequences of magnetic orientations (north and south) in a magnetic disk or a series of holes in 3x8 cards. Symbolic structure, thus, serves as a common ground by which logic and causation can be brought into alignment.

In running this argument from psychological processes, Fodor does not tell us whether or not we are to idealize from finite human performance to a bounded or an unbounded cognitive competence in the sense discussed in Chapter 3. Suppose, however, that the competence is strictly finite. In this case, the Pure Atomist has an explanation of the parallelism to which Fodor draws attention. The Pure Atomist will hypothesize that there exist n syntactic atoms to represent each set of premises from which a person can draw an inference and m syntactic atoms to represent each of the conclusions that a person can draw. There will then be at most n x m possible transitions from premises to conclusions. There is, therefore, no reason why these transitions cannot be computed by a look-up table in some Turing-equivalent formalism consistent with the Computational Theory of the Attitudes. So, on the assumption of a finite cognitive competence in psychological processes, there is no evident reason why a Pure Atomist must fail to provide an account of the parallelism between the logical and causal orders. If the finite competence version of the Argument from Psychological Processes I is to succeed, then it must have recourse to some principle of best explanation, some principle of the sort invoked in the systematicity arguments.

Suppose, then, that the argument from psychological processes presupposes an unbounded representational capacity. This would place the explanandum beyond the scope of any Pure Atomist account committed to the sort of Computational Theory of the Attitudes that was sketched in Chapter 1. No Turing-equivalent computational formalism may contain an infinite representational capacity. The appeal to an unbounded representational capacity does not render this argument from psychological processes invalid, insofar as some reason might be provided to support this appeal. Nevertheless, insofar as Fodor wishes to avoid recourse to an idealization to unbounded capacities, this limitation makes the Argument from Psychological Processes I something of a disappointment.

As a digression on a digression, it is worth separating the foregoing argument from psychological processes, which is directed against Pure Atomism, from a related argument directed against Associationism. These arguments appear in close proximity to each other in Fodor, (1985), hence are potentially conflated. This digression is motivated by a desire to clarify potential misunderstandings.

After broaching the idea of the parallelism between the logical and the cognitive/causal orders, and lamenting the embarrassment that was behaviorism, Fodor recounts how introspective psychology has it that thinking and reasoning are like giving arguments. Sequences of mental states are not mere sequences of contentful states, not mere free associations of contents; they are like inductive and deductive arguments. A sequence of states whose contents are "Reagan was the President of the United States," "Texas Hold 'Em is a kind of poker game," "French fries are not really French," and "Some people like to eat broccoli with steak," might constitute a sequence of mental contents, but would not constitute thinking. No doubt mere associations have some role in cognitive life, but it is the many cases of thinking as reasoning and inferring that prove to be the downfall of Associationism. If, as Associationists maintain, sequences of mental states are determined by such things as the relative frequency of their juxtapositioning of those same contents in experience, then we would find thought processes radically different than they are. If Associationists were correct, then we would have only sequences of mental states such as, "Salt and pepper are always on the table," "My wife cooks with a lot of salt and pepper," "And her Mother uses *a lot* of salt and pepper," "I remember one time when she had so much salt in her chicken soup that I could hardly eat any," "Then there was the time she had to tell me about her flowers," "I never thought I would get away," and "Talk about people who keep you trapped." The point is not that such sequences of mental contents do not occur; rather, if the Associationists were right, this would be all we have. There would be no account of the inferential transitions in thinking. Fodor is quite on the mark to note this, but all the foregoing shows is that thinking cannot be entirely a matter of associating. This is perfectly consistent with Pure Atomism. So, while Fodor has an apt critique of Associationism, his point misses the Pure Atomist mark.

6.3 The Argument from Psychological Processes II

In the Appendix to *Psychosemantics*, Fodor faces an interlocutor who believes in what we have called Pure Atomism, rather than Classicism. Thus, the interlocutor wants to know why a mental representation underlying the thought that John loves Mary, should be supposed to have the syntactic structure, say, $\alpha\beta\gamma$, with a concomitant combinatorial semantics, rather than the structure, say, ♣, with a concomitant atomistic semantics. This argument from psychological processes is meant to show that cognitive psychologists, such as psycholinguists, postulate processes that operate over mental representations and that such processes are ineliminably committed to syntactically and semantically complex representations, rather than only syntactically and semantically atomic

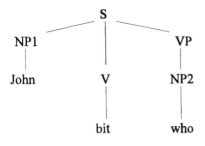

Figure 6.1. A tree structure before wh-movement.

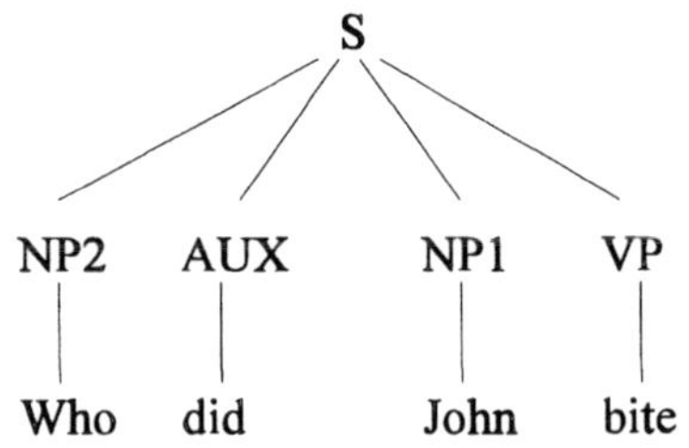

Figure 6.2. A tree structure after wh-movement.

representations.[17]

Fodor imagines that the production of English wh-questions involves, among other things, first being in a state representing the information in the phrase structure tree shown in Figure 6.1, followed by being in a state representing the information in the phrase structure tree shown in Figure 6.2. In other words, production of English wh-questions involves representations with the contents shown in Figures 6.1 and 6.2. Fodor suggests that the standard sort of psychological account of the transition from the state representing the information in Figure 6.1 to the state representing the information in Figure 6.2 is that a) the states representing the information in the figures involve the syntactic atoms "John," "bit," "who," "S," "NP1," "VP," "V," etc., with the obvious semantics, and that b) one gets from the first state to the second state *"by moving a piece of the parsing tree* (e.g., by moving the piece that represents 'who' as a constituent of type NP2)" (Fodor, 1987, p. 146). Fodor is willing to admit that syntactic atoms, such as ♣ and ♦, can represent the information illustrated in Figures 6.1 and 6.2, but he contends that Pure Atomism doesn't provide a way of understanding what psycholinguists talk about when they talk about moving a piece of the parsing tree. Thus, there is some defeasible reason to believe in Classicism as against Pure Atomism.

This is not the end of the matter, however. Fodor allows for the possibility that, in talking about wh-movement, psycholinguists may be indulging in mere loose talk. Nevertheless, he maintains that "Given a well-evidenced empirical theory [such as the foregoing bit of psycholinguistic theory], either you endorse the entities [and processes] that it's committed to or you find a paraphrase that preserves the theory while dispensing with the commitments" (Fodor, 1987, p. 146). This last part–the clause about finding a paraphrase–provides the route to a Pure Atomist account of wh-movement. Suppose that ♣ is a syntactic item that represents the information in Figure 6.1 (e.g., ♣ is a Turing machine tape symbol with the content depicted in Figure 6.1) and that ♦ is a syntactic item that represents the information in Figure 6.2 (e.g., ♦ is a Turing machine tape symbol with the content depicted in Figure 6.2). Then let the psycholinguistic process underlying wh-movement be realized in a Turing machine that starts in state s_0 with the symbol ♣ under the read-write head and the program "s_0 ♣ ♦ s_0" (if in state s_0 and scanning a ♣, write a ♦ and go into state s_0). Thus, we have a computational process that takes us from the state with the content shown in Figure 6.1 to a state with the content shown in Figure 6.2. The Pure Atomist can maintain that talk of moving parts of a parse tree is loose talk that need not be taken literally, as Fodor assumes it to be. Instead, talk of movement is be understood as a description of a range of functionally equivalent processes. Thus, one way of implementing "movement" would be through real spatial movement of physical items, but it might also be a matter of having particular circuits in the brain (those corresponding to "who" on the right) stop firing while others (those corresponding to "who" on the left) start firing. This latter is not literally spatial movement, but is functionally equivalent to movement. Similarly, we might include in the equivalence class of wh-movement operations, the replacement of ♣ with ♦. All that would seem to be in need of preservation in the talk of wh-movement is the structural information in the two representations. So, Pure Atomism has a paraphrase that preserves the theory while dispensing with the commitment to literal spatial movement.

In a separate discussion of this argument, Fodor notes that he is "appalled" that so much of contemporary philosophy of mind has been willing to do without a theory of mental processes. He reports that "It was a scandal of mid-century Anglo-American philosophy of mind that though it worried about the nature of mental states (like the attitudes) it quite generally didn't worry much about the nature of mental *processes* (like thinking)" (Fodor, 1985, p. 19). Yet, if what is needed to set aright this scandalous situation is simply a theory of mental processes, then *prima facie* Pure Atomism has one. Cognitive processes are simply a matter of moving through a sequence of atomic representational states. So, one can imagine a set of syntactically and semantically atomic representations, { ♣, ♦, ♥, . . . , ♠} with contents matching the contents of all possible occurrent cognitive states satisfying both Representationalism and the Computational Theory of the Attitudes. Further, the program of the mind might have essentially the form

s_0 ♣ ♦ s_{126}

s_{13} ♣ ♦ s_{763}

.   .   .

s_{461} ♣ ♠ s_{832}

s_{98} ♥ ♠ s_0

s_{831} ♥ ♣ s_0

s_{53} ♣ ♦ s_0

s_{71} ♠ ♦ s_0.

The Pure Atomist would, thus, have some story to tell about cognitive processes. Granted a Pure Atomist might never have before advanced such a theory, but one is obviously ready to hand, provided only that the processes occur over strictly finite domains.

As with the previous argument from psychological processes, Fodor does not specify whether he supposes that finite human performance in these cases is supposed to idealize to unbounded representational competence. If human psycholinguistic competence is assumed to be simply finite, then this second argument from psychological processes can be answered by the Pure Atomist. If, however, psycholinguistic competence is assumed to be unbounded, then the argument is but a special case of the productivity argument. It succeeds given tendentious assumption that Fodor has foresworn in the systematicity arguments. Again we can see how our detailed review of the systematicity and productivity arguments sheds light on other significant Classicist arguments.

7 TAKING STOCK

At this point, we have finished our first pass through the systematicity and productivity arguments, setting forth as clearly as possible the form of the argument, the proposed explananda and clearing away misguided objections. In this first pass, we have focused on Classicism and Pure Atomism. This has allowed us to focus on the principal logical and empirical objections to the arguments that have been found in the literature, establishing the nature and logical legitimacy of the arguments and the explananda. Our principal conclusions have been that, while neither Classicism nor Pure Atomism can explain the systematicity of inference, the counterfactual dependence among thoughts, or the content-relatedness of occurrent thoughts, Classicism does have the strength that it can explain a pair of co-occurrence regularities. Classicism can explain why it is that counterfactually dependent thoughts are at the same time contentfully related and why diachronically systematic minds are also synchronically systematic. The discussion of the co-occurrence arguments, in fact, invites a more thorough investigation, as there seem to be numerous possible combinations of regularities that might fruitfully be explored.

Chapters 2 through 6, thus, form an expository basis from which to extend the systematicity arguments, in Chapter 7, to the first of the more serious theoretical rivals to Classicism, namely, Connectionism. Chapter 8 extends the arguments to two species of Functionally Combinatorial theories of representation, namely, Gödel numerals and Smolensky's Tensor Product Theory. The extension will continue in Chapter 9 as we examine the bearing of the systematicity arguments on a theory of cognition that rejects Representationalism and the Computational Theory of the Attitudes, namely, Robert Cummins's Representational Theory of the Attitudes.

NOTES

1. Cf. Fodor & Pylyshyn, (1988), pp. 41-42, as it relates to language.

2. Van Gelder notes this as follows,

> For example, everyone who can have the thought that John loves the girl can also have the thought that the girl loves John. Although their discussion is not altogether clear on this point, Fodor and Pylyshyn (1988) suggest that these kinds of thoughts are systematically related in two ways: on a structural level, and also "from a semantic point of view" (pp. 31-42).

This is the difference between the "systematicity of cognitive representation" and the "compositionality of representations" (van Gelder, 1990, p. 376, fn 12).

3. The notion of content relatedness that is at work in the compositional of cognitive representations argument might benefit from more clarification than can be given here. The thought that John loves Mary and the thought that Mary loves John have related, but not identical contents. So, the relevant notion of content relatedness is weaker than content identity. Yet, we might also want to say that the thought that John loves Mary is more closely semantically related to the thought that Mary loves John than to the thought that John loves potatoes and the thought that John hates broccoli.

4. Here "compositionality of representations," the appropriate terminology from Fodor & Pylyshyn, (1988), replaces "systematicity" in Cummins's text.

5. Here I again insert the terminology of Fodor and Pylyshyn, (1988), into Cummins's text.

6. Cummins, (1996a) does, however, cover all bets when he indicates how his theory of cognitive architecture explains this dubious productivity and systematicity of thought.

7. Incidently, it is not clear why the combinatorial syntax and semantics of *natural language* should lead us to believe in the systematicity of thought either.

8. Of course, every competent speaker of English will know that the content of "Mary's favorite proposition" is Mary's favorite proposition. What we don't know, again, is the content of Mary's favorite proposition.

9. Cf. Fodor & Pylyshyn, (1988), p. 39.

10. The qualification "minimally sufficient" is vitally important. Its meaning and why it is important will be explained below.

11. Fodor and Pylyshyn incline to asking why systematically related thought capacities are also semantically related. Granted, they do also ask why systematic and compositionality are correlated, but the more common locution asks why systematically related thought capacities are also semantically related. That, to a considerable degree has shaped the way in which the co-occurrence argument has been developed here. One might, however, get much the same argument by asking why semantically related thought capacities are at the same time to some degree counterfactually related. The short answer is that they are semantically related and to some degree counterfactually related because they share common concepts. In this argument, one would have to use a notion of counterfactual dependence that differs from the one we have latched onto, namely, one in which counterfactual dependence is understood in terms of the nomologically necessary and sufficient. The reason is that, while the thought that John loves Mary is contentfully related to the thought that John sleeps, the thought that John loves Mary is not nomologically necessary and sufficient for the thought that John sleeps. Through personal communication I have gotten the sense that Brian McLaughlin inclines to ask why semantically related thought capacities are at the same time counterfactually dependent to some degree.

12. Exactly how this might work is not transparent. Perhaps one and the same program will both effect the counterfactual dependence among thoughts and provide the semantic interpretation of the program through a species of pure functional role semantics, where the meanings of symbols are determined by their mode of processing in the system's computational economy.

13. One might wonder whether this part about fitting new representations into an existing scheme of representation constitutes another auxiliary hypothesis that will lead to trouble. Even if it does count as a separate hypothesis, it turns out that it will be part of the minimally sufficient explanation of diachronic systematicity and with it one still gets for free the synchronic systematicity of thought. So, there's no problem. Of course, if diachronic systematicity needs this additional hypothesis, where synchronic systematicity does not, then the minimally sufficient explanation of the synchronic systematicity of thought will not automatically bring with it the diachronic systematicity of thought. We will then want some explanation of why it is that synchronically systematic minds are also diachronically systematic. Under such conditions, I don't know what the explanation of this is.

14. The foregoing description of development is meant to be neutral between empiricist and nativist theories of cognitive development. Perhaps new mental representations and cognitive grammatical constructions are learned or perhaps they simply unfold or emerge after some sort of triggering. In either case, there is a sense in which the number of capacities for distinct thoughts increases.

15. Here's what might be construed as another argument Jackendoff gives for thinking that language has a combinatorial basis. Normal adult speakers of English can understand an infinitude of sentences. Consider a trivial sampling:
   (1) Amy ate two peanuts
      Amy ate three peanuts
      Amy ate four peanuts

      . . .

      Amy ate forty-three million, five hundred nine peanuts.

      . . .

The only way a finite brain could be said to represent this infinitude of sentences is in virtue of having a system with the capacity or the competence to generate them. A finite brain can have such a competence, even if there some form of performance limitation keeping the system from actually generating this infinite. If we shift this argument from language to thought, however, it turns out to be essentially the productivity argument. Thus, it cannot serve to flesh out what Horgan and Tienson are after, namely, another reason for believing in a combinatorial system of representation.

16. This same observation might be found at Fodor & Pylyshyn, (1988), p. 46, but is not pressed into service of an argument from psychological processes. Instead, it is merely an introductory comment preparing for the systematicity of inference argument. Incidently, Fodor, (1998), pp. 9-12, appears to withdraw it.

17. Carruthers, (1996), p. 34, reviews this argument.

CHAPTER 7

THE SYSTEMATICITY ARGUMENTS APPLIED TO CONNECTIONISM

In Chapters 3 through 6, we saw how a range of systematicity and productivity arguments might be deployed against a Pure Atomist theory of cognitive representations that assumes the Computational Theory of the Attitudes. This gave us some familiarity with the explananda, the explanatory standard that appears to be at work in the arguments, and how one might meet some of the possible objections to these. The aim of the present chapter, however, is to show how the systematicity and productivity arguments can be applied to Connectionism. We will consider, first, a very simple Connectionist network described by David Chalmers, (1990), then a more complex network described by Robert Hadley and Michael Hayward, (1997). Of central importance will be showing how the explanatory principle that is involved in the systematicity arguments bears on Connectionism. What makes it so important to note this explanatory principle is the sheer difficulty of coming up with a Connectionist model that can even display any form of systematicity. This difficulty makes it hard to take notice of the still more difficult challenge of explaining the systematic relations in thought to a higher standard.

As was noted in Chapter 1, "Connectionism" is used to cover a wide range of ideas and theoretical approaches in a range of disciplines. Here, however, we are concerned with the strain of Connectionism that attempts to use the machinery of networks of nodes with modifiable weighted connections between them to explain cognitive processes. Thus, Connectionism must somehow come to grips with the putative systematic and productive nature of thought. In brief, the problem with Connectionist accounts of the systematic characteristics of thought is that, while one might be able to generate Connectionist models that display the sundry systematic regularities, they will do so by employing a range of arbitrary parameters comparable to the arbitrary parameters of Ptolemaic astronomy. A Connectionist model of any given phenomenon will have to postulate, at the least, a network topology, equations specifying the nature of the interactions among the inputs, activation values, outputs, and weights of the many interacting nodes in the network, and some specification of the way in which nodes represent objects, relations, or states of affairs. Further, if a network is to include a weight change theory of learning, there must be some specification of the training regimen. Such hypotheses must come into play and it will turn out that it is the need for such hypotheses and their lack of independent confirmation that will be the undoing of Connectionist attempts to explain the systematic relations in thought.

1 CHALMERS'S ACTIVE-PASSIVE TRANSFORMATION MODEL

Chalmers's (1990) simulations of Connectionist networks are of interest, first, because they are among the simplest networks one might think display systematic relations in processing and, second, because they continue to be endorsed as a (possible) refutation of Fodor and Pylyshyn's contention that Connectionism does not explain the content relations in thought.[1] Chalmers's idea is that a Connectionist network might explain what we have been calling the content relatedness of thought through non-Classical distributed representations.

Chalmers reports on a number of computer simulations of Connectionist networks, but for present purposes discussion of one simulation should suffice. In one task, a network is supposed to transform an "active" representation (roughly, one which would be expressed in English with a sentence having the syntactic form aRb, where a and b are individual terms and R is a two-place relation) into a "passive" representation (roughly, one which would be expressed in English with a sentence having the syntactic form b is R by a). So, for example, the network should map a representation with roughly the content expressed by the English sentence "John loves Mary" onto a representation with roughly the content expressed by the English sentence "Mary is loved by John". The domain for this task involves five relations (love, hit, betray, kill, hug) and five individual terms (John, Michael, Diane, Helen, Chris) each of which can occur as both the subject and the object of a sentence. This makes for a total of 125 possible "active" sentences as input and 125 possible "passive" sentences as output. In order to avoid merely implementing a Classical combinatorial architecture, Chalmers's network uses distributed representations. These are representations in which more than one node is dedicated to the representation of each concept.[2]

Chalmers creates two networks, a coding network and the actual transformation network. The coding network is a simple Recursive Auto-Associative Memory (RAAM) network that is used to create distributed representations for use in the transformation network. (See Figure 7.1). The actual transformation network, by contrast, is a simple three-layer feedforward network that maps the active distributed representations created by the first network onto the passive distributed representations created by the first network.

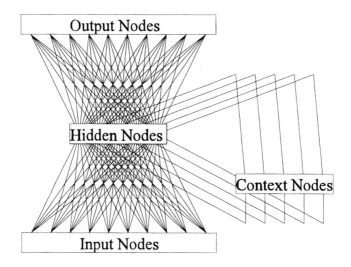

Figure 7.1. Chalmers's encoding network.

In the coding network, Chalmers supposes that the individual terms and relations are coded on 13 input nodes in a localist fashion that permits relatively easy semantic interpretation of each of the nodes:

```
JOHN        010000 10000 00
MICHAEL     010000 01000 00
HELEN       010000 00100 00
DIANE       010000 00010 00
CHRIS       010000 00001 00

LOVE        001000 10000 00
HIT         001000 01000 00
BETRAY      001000 00100 00
KILL        001000 00010 00
HUG         001000 00001 00

IS          000010 10000 00
BY          000001 10000 00
NIL         000000 00000 00.
```

In order to process sentences in the coding network, the sentences are assigned trees having a fixed branching of three. (See Figure 7.2.) The RAAM is then

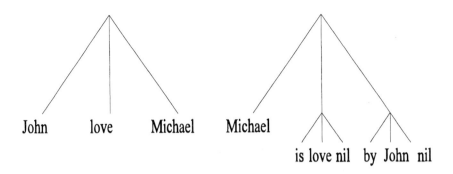

Figiure 7.2. Chalmers's scheme for representing propositions.

trained using a version of backpropagation to pair each of the 125 possible "active" representations and 125 possible "passive" sentences with itself. Since there is a bottleneck at the hidden layer, the localist representations given to the input layer produce distributed representations on the hidden layer. This produces 125 "active" distributed representations and 125 "passive" distributed representations which are available for use in the transformation network.

In the transformation network, each of the 125 "active" distributed representations is given to the network as input with its corresponding "passive" distributed representation used as target for supervised learning. As a result of training, the transformation network comes to pair each of the "active" distributed representations with its appropriate "passive" distributed representation. The three-layer network, thus, has the capacity to derive the "passive" form of aRb and the capacity to derive the "passive" form of bRa, while using non-classical distributed representations. In the three-layer network, the pattern of activation on the input nodes that corresponds to "John love Chris" does not literally contain a representation of John (i.e., 010000 10000 00), a representation of Chris (i.e., 010000 00001 00), or a representation of love (i.e., 001000 10000 00). Representations of individual terms and relations have been compressed into a single distributed representation. The representations in Chalmers's network, thus, do not have context independent meanings. They are, thus, non-Classical, hence an apparent solution to the Fodor and Pylyshyn challenge.

Perhaps the first feature of Chalmers's theory that bears some comment is the very distinction between the RAAM network that creates the distributed representations and the simple three-layer feedforward network that uses the distributed representations. This distinction presents in an exceptionally clear form one of the persistent ambiguities in a number of non-Classical accounts of the systematic and productive features of thought. These accounts postulate some sort of encoding process, on the one hand, and cognitive processes that must certainly use the products of this encoding, on the other. The non-Classicists clearly intend for the encoded representations to be real vehicles of semantic content that have causal roles in the cognitive economy. By contrast, they are less than clear what status is enjoyed by the encoding processes. Are these processes also to be supposed to be a part of the cognitive economy? This appears to be a dilemma. If the encoding processes are supposed to be a part of the cognitive economy, then insofar as they take Classical representations as input, then isn't the non-Classical account parasitic on the pre-existing Classical account? Yet, if the encoding processes are not supposed to be a part of a particular agent's cognitive economy, then what relation do they bear to that agent's cognitive economy? How is it, for example, that the distributed representations in the transformation network mean what they do and have the combinatorial semantic structure they do absent some historical or causal connection with the encoding network? How is it that, absent some historical or causal to the encoding processes, the distributed representations in the transformation network differ from simple Pure Atomistic representations? It is this latter case applied to Smolensky's Tensor Product Theory that apparently so greatly exercises Fodor, (1996). These are questions, perhaps, best left for Connectionists to answer.

In one Classicist critique of Chalmers's work, Brian McLaughlin, (1993b), points out that, when verb tense and noun-verb agreement are left out of any model of active and passive forms, one thereby abstracts from the very features of active and passive forms that lead Chomsky, (1957), to reject transformations on superficial structures and postulate deep structures from which active and passive forms are derived. All the empirical evidence that leads to the view that passive forms are not derived from active forms is, thus, supposed to constitute evidence that Chalmers's network is not a model of human psychological reality.[3] McLaughlin's claim, therefore, is that the network competence does not match human competence. Here we have an objection to the model based on data fit, a perfectly legitimate form of scientific criticism. In response, however, a Connectionist might claim that the point of the network simulation was not so much to account for all the available data concerning the formation of the active and passive forms of sentences in English as it was to show that a network using distributed representations is, in principle, capable of correctly processing a non-Classical representation with the content we would express with an English sentence having the form aRb just in case it can correctly process a non-Classical representation with the content we would express with an English sentence having the form bRa. This is something that one might have *prima facie* thought would constitute a genuine response to Fodor and Pylyshyn's challenge. The point of the network is to show that something one might have thought impossible for Connectionist networks is in fact possible for them.

While the Connectionist has a way of dodging McLaughlin's concerns about data fit, it is not clear that the Connectionist can finesse the challenge of providing the appropriate kind of explanation of the content relations among possible occurrent thoughts. It is not enough to show that a Connectionist network can fit the data. A Connectionist network, like any potential explanatory model, must provide an account of the systematic relations in thought that is not *ad hoc*. So, we may profitably turn to our familiar line of questioning in a guise suitable for Connectionism. Suppose that what a Connectionist needs to explain is why it is that a normal human being who can transform a representation with roughly the content expressed by "John loves Chris" into a representation with roughly the content expressed by "Chris is loved by John" can also transform a representation with roughly the content expressed by "Chris loves John" into a representation with roughly the content expressed by "John is loved by Chris." Chalmers's model exhibits this property, but does it explain it? No. To put the matter as would Fodor and Pylyshyn, the many properties and parameters in Chalmers's model could as easily have been set so as to enable the network to handle a contentfully related set of sentences as not. Given the same training set, but different network topology, different initial random weights, or different momentum or learning rate in the backprop procedure, the network would not have developed a set of weights that would allow it to handle a representation with (roughly) the content John loves Chris just in case it handles a representation with (roughly) the content Chris loves John. This is evidently what Fodor and McLaughlin had in mind when they wrote,

> the point of the problem that systematicity poses for connectionists . . .
> is not to show that systematic cognitive capacities are *possible* given the
> assumption of a Connectionist architecture, but to explain how
> systematicity could be *necessary*--how it could be a *law* that cognitive
> capacities are systematic--given those assumptions.
>
> No doubt it is possible for [a Connectionist] to wire a network so that
> it supports a vector that represents aRb if and only if it supports a vector
> that represents bRa. . . . The trouble is that, although the architecture
> permits this, it equally permits [a Connectionist] to wire a network so that
> it supports a vector that represents aRb if and only if it supports a vector
> that represents zSq; or, for that matter, if and only if it supports a vector
> that represents The Last of The Mohicans. The architecture would appear
> to be absolutely indifferent as among these options (Fodor &
> McLaughlin, 1990, p. 202, cf., Fodor & Pylyshyn, 1988, p. 50).

We have, of course, seen at least some of the inadequacies of Fodor and Pylyshyn's way of making their point, but we have also given reason to think that there was some point to be made. The historical examples constitute this reason. We also presented reasons for thinking that a better way to make the point Fodor and Pylyshyn were after was to say that the problem for Connectionism is that it must rely on auxiliary hypotheses that are arbitrary in the sense that these hypotheses cannot be confirmed independently of having antecedently confirmed the role of these hypotheses in a theory of the architecture of cognition. If one were to have confirmation of such things as network topology, training regimen, learning parameters, system of cognitive representation, and so forth, one would already have established some form of Connectionism as the architecture of cognition. For this reason, Chalmers's model is not able to provide the requisite type of explanation of the content relations in thought.

Consider, now, the potential Chalmers's network has for explaining the other features of thought that we have surveyed. Since the model has no provision for handling arbitrarily long sentences, it does not appear to be relevant to the explanation of the productivity of thought. Moreover, since there is no obvious way to connect the model to any patterns of inference, such as *modus ponens* or conjunction elimination, it does not appear to be able to explain the systematicity of inference. When it comes to the systematicity of cognitive representations, however, things look more promising. *Prima facie*, Chalmers's model can explain the counterfactual dependencies among thoughts. When Chalmers's three-layer network represents the content that John loves Chris with a pattern of activation distributed over the set of 13 input nodes, the loss of one of the nodes will have some impact on the representation of all inputs. The consequences may be such that we should say that the loss of the capacity to represent, say, John loves Chris brings with it the loss of the capacity to represent, say, Chris loves John. Thus, it appears that there is a kind of counterfactual dependency among thoughts. Under such conditions, one might think, the Connectionist has an explanation of the counterfactual dependency among thoughts.

One difficulty with this proposal is that lesioning of a node provides an implementational explanation of the counterfactual dependency among thoughts. Recall from Chapter 4 that the explanandum in the systematicity of cognitive representations argument is meant to be a psychological-level fact requiring a psychological-level explanation. It is some feature of a cognitive architecture, rather than of the implementation of a cognitive architecture, that is supposed to explain the counterfactual dependence. After all, were an implementational account of the systematicity of cognitive representations to count as an appropriate explanation, then essentially any cognitive architecture would have a ready account of the counterfactual dependencies among thoughts.

In response to the foregoing, however, one might suggest that we consider networks that have growth and pruning of connections. Perhaps a network with growth and pruning would have the counterfactual dependency among thought as a psychological level consequence. This is a clever idea, but nonetheless subject to our familiar line of criticism. Set aside the distinct possibility that growth and pruning of connections is an implementation theory. Not only must the envisioned class of networks rely on a range of unconfirmed auxiliary hypotheses regarding weight change procedure, network topology, activation functions, and the like, there is the very hypothesis of growth and pruning. Among the various types of Connectionist networks of nodes with weighted connections between them, there are those with growth and pruning and those without. So, in order to formulate an adequate non-implementational Connectionist account one must add some hypothesis essentially stipulating that the network uses growth and pruning. Such a hypothesis, however, is arbitrary in the sense that it has no confirmation independent of the truth of Connectionism. Such a hypothesis has the status of the Creationist's appeal to the plan of God in explaining biogeography. It is not necessarily false, but merely *ad hoc*, hence less credible.

Our more familiar sort of worry about the Chalmers model is that, while it shows how it is possible for one thought capacity to be dependent upon another thought capacity, it does not show how this is necessary. Such, of course, is the way that Fodor and McLaughlin might draw attention to the problem. Our alternative assessment would begin with the observation that there are connectionist networks that do not have this kind of dependency. One obvious possibility would be to build a super network that consists of 125 different independent three-layer feedforward networks, each one of which is responsible for one input-output mapping, such as the mapping from a representation of John loving Mary to a representation of Mary being loved by John. Clearly, in this case, there is no nomologically necessary and sufficient connection between the capacity to represent John loving Mary and the capacity to represent Mary loving John. These inputs are processed by distinct subnetworks that might be united only in virtue of there being pathways leading to or from the super network. In addition, one fails to find the appropriate kinds of counterfactual dependencies even within a single subnetwork of our supernetwork. While the capacity to represent John loving Mary may, in some sense, be necessary for the capacity to represent Mary loving John, the first capacity is clearly not sufficient for the second. Further, the capacity to represent Mary being loved by John is neither nomologically necessary nor sufficient for the capacity to represent John loving Mary. Take another connectionist network, only slightly more interesting, that might illustrate some of the same points. Consider a super network that has 125 separate input clusters and 125 separate output clusters each of which passes through a single hidden layer. (See Figure 7.3.) Let each of these 125 input clusters handle a distributed representation of one of the active form inputs and each of the 125 output clusters handle a distributed

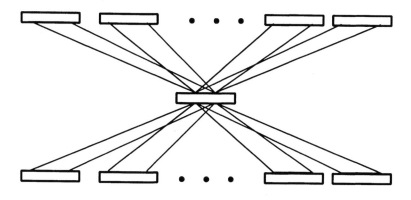

Figure 7.3. Schematic of a network lacking systematicity of cognitive representations.

representation of one of the passive form outputs. Clearly, in this network, the capacity to represent any of the active forms, such as John loves Mary and John loves Chris, is neither nomologically necessary nor sufficient for the other. Nor is the capacity to represent any of the passive forms, such as Mary being loved by John or Chris being loved by John, nomologically necessary or sufficient for the other. Perhaps there are some interesting connections between the representational capacities in this network, but evidently not enough to sustain an explanation of the systematicity of cognitive representations.

Having noted these networks that do not display systematicity of cognitive representations is just the beginning of our objection. At this point the Connectionist will surely note that she does not mean to hypothesize networks of the sort just described. Rather, networks such as those Chalmers devised are those that are on the table. Further, one might well find more than one way in which to ensure that only the desired networks are produced. This is surely correct. Yet, it is just the sort of thing we saw that the Classicist wanted to say about particular grammars or computer programs of the mind. Where in the Classicist case, there was a problem with providing the right sort of confirmation of an hypothesis concerning the grammar of the system of cognitive representation, in the present case, the problem takes the form of providing some confirmation of the hypothesis or hypotheses needed to ensure that the relevant Connectionist models are like the one Chalmers devised, rather than like the ones just sketched above. How is one to confirm some assumptions about the structure or properties of the relevant Connectionist networks, short of having confirmed that role of Connectionist mechanisms in cognition? No doubt this sort of challenge is irritating to Connectionists, in just the way that this sort of challenge was irritating to Classicists. Yet, that is the nature of the problem and it merits Connectionist attention.

What, then, about the co-occurrence of counterfactual dependencies in thought and content relations in thought and the co-occurrence of diachronic and synchronic counterfactual dependencies in thought? Since the model lacks the appropriate psychological-level counterfactual dependencies among thoughts, it cannot capture either of these explananda. Classicism is able to explain the co-occurrence of these features by invoking the context independence of content, an hypothesis that is both necessary on other grounds and that forges a link between the syntactic and the semantic. Insofar as Chalmers's model, or any Connectionist model, lacks such a hypothesis, it will fail to account for the syntactic/semantic co-occurrence.

2 HADLEY AND HAYWARD'S MODEL OF STRONG SEMANTIC SYSTEMATICITY

Throughout this book, it has been urged that the distinction between data fit and genuine explanation must be more consistently appreciated. Nowhere does this distinction appear to be more crucial in dealing with Connectionism than in Robert Hadley's (1994) discussion of alternative conceptions of systematicity. In this work, he draws distinctions between different types of systematic relations in thought and the extent to which particular Connectionist models display particular types of systematic relations, thereby focusing greater attention on fitting theory to data. While data fit is, of course, a crucially important element in theory choice, as a matter of addressing Fodor and Pylyshyn's critique of Connectionism, the issue is not joined until the explanatory considerations are addressed square on. As a case in point, Robert Hadley and Michael Hayward's (1997) model of strong semantic systematicity provides an excellent opportunity to join these issues.

Now, while our present interest in the Hadley-Hayward (HH) model stems from its relation to the numerous systematicity and productivity arguments, in all fairness, Hadley and Hayward's primary interest appears to be in developing a non-error-backpropagating connectionist network that can perform a particular sort of information processing task. Such a network is supposed to assign appropriate meanings to sentences after a weight change regimen in which the training corpus does not have all words occur in all syntactically well formed positions, that is, such a network is supposed to display what Hadley and

Hayward call "strong semantic systematicity." The HH model does this with a number of information processing virtues. Had Hadley and Hayward limited themselves to this information processing issue, then their model might not have warranted scrutiny in an examination of Fodor and Pylyshyn's systematicity arguments. Instead of limiting themselves in this way, however, Hadley and Hayward adopted an equivocal attitude about the bearing of their model on the systematicity arguments. Thus, Hadley and Hayward tell us that "we do *not* present our results as a counterexample to [Fodor and Pylyshyn]'s (1988) thesis" (Hadley & Hayward, 1997, p. 5), "we wish to emphasize that, in our view, the primary significance of our results lies *not* in whether our post-training network constitutes a counterexample to [Fodor & Pylyshyn]'s thesis" (ibid., p. 6), "we again stress that our goal here is not to refute [Fodor and Pylyshyn]" (ibid., p. 25), and "we have, for a number of reasons, not sought to answer [Fodor and Pylyshyn]'s challenge to connectionists" (ibid., p. 29). Despite these (sometimes emphatic) efforts to distance their work from Fodor and Pylyshyn's critique, there are other passages that suggest that their work should be understood as a response to, and indeed a refutation of, that critique. Note that, in claiming that the primary significance of their results does not lie in whether their network constitutes a counterexample to Fodor & Pylyshyn's thesis, there is the implication that part of the significance of their results *does* lie in its constituting such a counterexample. More directly, Hadley and Hayward claim that

> Turning now from considerations of representational systematicity to systematicity in external sentence comprehension, we believe our results may again cast doubt on [Fodor and Pylyshyn]'s claims" (ibid., p. 30).

Further,

> it appears that, using [Fodor and Pylyshyn]'s own criteria, we have produced a non-classical system which can systematically interpret sentences of the form *aRb* if and only if it can interpret sentences of the form *bRa*. The sentences in question may be novel to the network's experience. On the face of it, this would seem to refute certain views expressed in [Fodor and Pylyshyn] and in Fodor and McLaughlin, (1990).
>
> It will be objected though, that [Fodor and Pylyshyn]'s challenge required not only that a connectionist system exhibit systematicity, but that it provide the basis for an explanation of systematicity. The question arises, then, whether the network under consideration can provide such a basis? Our answer is that, within the realm of sentence comprehension, and subject to a limited range of syntax, our network does indeed provide a basis for such an explanation (ibid. pp. 30-31).

Perhaps there is some way to sort through these claims to remove the appearance of equivocation, but be this as it may authorial intent is not the only consideration here. A second consideration is that regardless of Hadley and Hayward's intent, others are apt to take the model as an adequate explanation of some of the content relations in thought. Yet a third reason to examine the HH model is that it provides us with an opportunity to explore the Classical theory in greater detail. In particular, it allows us to look a bit more closely at the Classical notion of structure sensitive processing. This issue could not arise for Pure Atomism, since by definition, there is no combinatorial structure to which computational mechanisms need be sensitive.

The task set for the HH model is to pair a "semantic representation" with a given sentence presented to the network as a sequence of words. Thus, the HH network has two layers of nodes: a lexical input layer and a "semantic" output layer. (Figure 7.4 illustrates a reduced version of the HH network that handles a lexicon of four words, along with one level of embedding.) Inputs to the network are sentences of a fragment of an English grammar wherein the words of the sentence are presented sequentially. The semantic nodes are of many types. Prominent among these are concept nodes corresponding to the words of the input lexicon. Thus, along with an input node for the English word "Bill" (the word standing alone at the bottom of Figure 7.4), there is a semantic node for the concept BILL (in gray, labeled with the letter B). Input nodes are completely connected to the concept nodes and to the "cores" of the pnodes (unlabeled white). The pnode cores are connected to additional nodes that indicate particular semantic roles that the concepts may fill. Thus, the pnode cores have one-way connections to and from the thematic site nodes: α = agent, β = action, γ = object, and π = modifier. Modifier pnodes have an additional modifier thematic site node π, indicating a modifier clause, where the master pnode, indicating the main clause of a sentence, does not. Finally, concept nodes and thematic site nodes are connected to binding nodes (diamonds).

In each pnode, the sites nodes (α, β, γ, and π) form a competitive winner-take-all cluster, that is, only one of the nodes in the cluster will be active while the others are inactive. In addition, the pnode cores together with the concept nodes form another winner-take-all cluster. Thus, in the HH model, there is a total of five winner-take-all clusters: one thematic site cluster in the master pnode, one thematic site cluster in each of three mod-pnodes, and one concept-and-pnode-core cluster. The modifiable connections in the network are those that run from the pnode cores to the thematic sites and those that run from the input nodes to the pnode cores and concept nodes. In Figure 7.4, the modifiable connections are represented by solid lines, where the fixed connections are represented by dotted

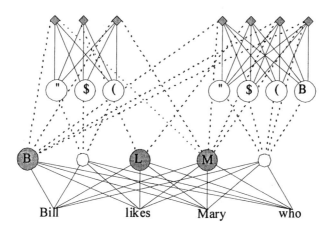

Figure 7.4. A reduced version of the Hadley-Hayward model.

lines. Weight training proceeds by a modified Hebbian rule.

Consider the processing of "Bill who likes Mary sees Jane," discussed by Hadley and Hayward, (ibid., p. 22). When "Bill" is presented as input, there is an *attentional spike* that activates the master pnode and its α thematic site node. Simultaneously, there is a winner-take-all competition among the concept nodes and pnode cores, which the BILL node wins. The BILL concept node becomes bound to the master pnode α thematic site, since the binding node between them becomes active. ("Bill" has thereby become the agent of the main clause.) This, in turn, leads to the activation of the master pnode β thematic site. When "who" is presented to the network, a mod-pnode core will win the competition and, in this mod-pnode, the α and π thematic site nodes will be equally activated. These α and π nodes then must bind and they do so with the most active concept node available, namely, BILL. ("Bill" is thereby interpreted as about to be modified by a relative clause.) When BILL is bound to the α and π sites, this sets up a competition in the mod-pnode between the β and γ nodes (from which the α and π sites are excluded). This competition is won by the mod-pnode's β thematic site node. This allows for subsequent binding of an action concept. When "likes" is entered, the LIKES conceptual node is activated. Since the activation of the BILL conceptual node has decayed and the β thematic site of the master pnode has decayed, the two most active nodes are the LIKES node and the β thematic site of the mod-pnode. The latter are, therefore, bound. ("likes" has thereby become the action concept modifying "Bill.") The binding of LIKES and the mod-pnode's β thematic site sets up a competition in the mod-pnode which the γ site wins (since the α, β, and π sites have been excluded from the competition). When "Mary" is given as input, the MARY concept node wins the ensuing competition among concept nodes and pnode cores. Since MARY is the most active concept node or pnode core (the other nodes having undergone further decay in activation), MARY is bound to the most active site node, namely, the γ node of the mod-pnode. ("Mary" thereby becomes the patient in the relative clause modifying "Bill.") This binding fills all the sites in the first mod-pnode, but leaves the β site of the master pnode unbound, but highly active. When "sees" is next input, the SEES concept node wins the winner take all competition and becomes the most active concept node. It is, therefore, bound to the β node of the master pnode. (Thus, "sees" becomes the main verb of the sentence.) This binding sets up a competition in the master pnode that the γ site (the only site in the competition) must win. Finally, when "Jane" is given as input, the JANE concept nodes wins the competition among the concept and pnode cores, hence is bound to the γ site of the master pnode. ("Jane" thereby becomes the patient in the main clause.)

In favor of the HH model, it must be said that it embodies a number of clever ideas for solving the problem of allowing a Connectionist network to learn to do the information processing task Hadley and Hayward set for it. As an explanation, or as a basis for an explanation, of Fodor and Pylyshyn's conception of the systematicity of cognitive representations, however, the model comes up short on two accounts: 1) it fails to meet the explanatory standard implicit in Fodor and Pylyshyn's critique and 2) it uses a Classical cognitive architecture. It is possible to fail in both regards since, as was one of the burdens of Chapters 3-6 to show, having a Classical cognitive architecture is not sufficient to explain the familiar systematic relations in thought. Each of these failings will be addressed in turn.

In Chapter 2, we drew attention to a notion of *ad hoc* explanations of empirical generalizations suggesting how these might be analyzed. The idea is that, in the explanation of empirical generalizations, one ought not rely on auxiliary hypotheses that are incapable of confirmation independent of the theory using them for the explanatory task at hand. The first failing of the HH model is that it runs afoul of this standard. Consider some of the *ad hoc* hypotheses at work in the HH model.

1. Minor changes to the network topology will alter the network's capacity. Without the one-way connections from pnode cores to thematic sites, with all other connections left in place, the network would not handle the task Hadley and Hayward desire.

2. Connectionism allows a range of weight change procedures. There is, for example, the family of backpropagation and Boltzmann machine weight change procedures differing among themselves in such things as learning rates, decay constants, and momentum terms. Within the family of Hebbian

weight change procedures, there is the simple rule to increase the weight between simultaneously active nodes, but also the modified Hebbian procedure that Hadley and Hayward use.[4] With the simple Hebbian procedure, the network would fail to learn properly, even though it can succeed with the modified Hebbian procedure.

3. In the processing of sentences, Hadley and Hayward postulate an initial attentional spike. With this hypothesis, against the backdrop of other assumptions, the network processes as Hadley and Hayward wish. Without this hypothesis, it would not.

4. Without the decay in activation values in the concept nodes and pnode cores, the concept and pnode cores would not be properly bound to thematic sites. Decay or no decay are perfectly free parameters for Connectionists

5. In the winner-take-all competition at thematic sites, bound nodes are excluded. One can make this assumption and, in the context of the other hypotheses about the network structure, thereby get the network to perform in the desired manner. On the other hand, by including bound nodes in the competition, the network would not perform as desired.

The list of hypotheses like the foregoing might well be extended. Assumptions about network topology, the precise character of the weight change procedure, and so forth, are like the Ptolemaic assumption about the colinearity of the deferents of the Sun, Mercury, and Venus. They are features of the model that can be adjusted to get the phenomena to occur, but can also be adjusted so that the phenomena to be explained do not occur, but for which there exists no independent confirmation. In their accounts of planetary motions, both Ptolemy and Copernicus can rely on the assumption that light propagates rectilinearly, since there is confirmation of this hypothesis independent of astronomical considerations. In accounting for the geographical distribution of Batrachians, Darwin can rely on the hypothesis that oceans constitute a migration barrier to these creatures since there is confirmation of this independent of questions about the biogeography of frogs, toads, and newts. What Hadley and Hayward need is some method of confirming these hypotheses outside of the fact that these hypotheses are needed to fit the data and without having previously established the truth of Connectionism.

Hadley & Hayward, (1997), at times, appear to overlook the explanatory standard invoked by Fodor, et al. Regarding the explanation of systematicity of cognitive representations, they have this to say:

It will be objected though, that [Fodor and Pylyshyn]'s challenge required not only that a Connectionist system exhibit systematicity, but that it provide the basis for an explanation of systematicity. The question arises, then, whether the network under consideration can provide such a basis? Our answer is that, within the realm of sentence comprehension, and subject to a limited range of syntax, our network does indeed provide a basis for such explanation. For, as previously noted, the processing behavior of our network is transparent. The preceding seven sections of the paper have explained in considerable detail how the network learns, and how role-node sequencing and spreading activation enable concept nodes to enter into *entirely novel* bindings with role sites. Presumably, then, the reader has already grasped how and why the network acquires systematicity. However, for convenience, we now summarize the explanation:

Crucially relevant is the interplay between the *combinatorial lattice* (involving role sites, binding nodes, concept nodes, and mod-pnodes) and the Hebbian learning. The basic structure of the combinatorial lattice may be regarded as 'innate,' although (presumably) some prior learning would be needed to assign 'identities' to the various concept nodes. Hebbian training ensures that lexical items will, regardless of their position within a sentence, excite the proper concept nodes. In addition, Hebbian training at pnode role sites ensures that thematic role nodes are activated in an appropriate sequence. The existence of binding nodes, together with spreading activation and activation decay ensure that the most recently activated concept node will bind with the appropriate role node. These factors also ensure that recently activated mod-pnodes bind with concept nodes that they should modify. The fact that the concept nodes always bind with appropriate role sites and mod-pnodes explains the network's systematicity of sentence 'comprehension.' (Hadley & Hayward, 1997, p. 30).

Although noting the distinction between a model's explaining the systematicity of cognitive representations and merely exhibiting systematicity of cognitive representations, Hadley and Hayward seem not to appreciate the standard at work in Fodor and Pylyshyn's critique. It appears that, for them, explanation involves simply reviewing the mechanisms in the model. Hadley, (1997a), however, adds that more is required than this. He adds, "At the very least, a formal description of the mechanism, together with certain laws of physics and logic, would need to figure in the explanation" (Hadley, 1997a, p. 572). Fair enough, but there is no concession to the sort of explanatory standard Fodor and Pylyshyn have in mind. In fact, Hadley suggests that the explanatory standard that has been at work in earlier chapters is not Fodor and Pylyshyn's.

The foregoing critique was first presented in Aizawa, (1997b), to which Hadley, (1997a), constitutes a response. In this response, Hadley refers to what he calls "Aizawa's standard of explanation." In so referring, he may mean only that this is a standard endorsed in Aizawa, (1997b). Fair enough. Yet, "Aizawa's standard of explanation" may suggest that the analysis is an idiosyncratic interpretation of the sundry systematicity arguments and that it is not what Fodor, et al., meant. If this is what Hadley has in mind, then one might want an alternative interpretation of the various passages in which Fodor, et al., appear to be endorsing some sort of explanatory standard of the sort described. Recall, for example, that Fodor and McLaughlin tell us that

> The point of the problem that systematicity poses for a non-LOT account is not to show that systematic cognitive processes are *possible* given the assumptions of a non-LOT architecture, but to explain how systematicity could be *necessary*--how it could be a *law* that cognitive capacities are systematic--given those assumptions (Fodor & McLaughlin, 1990, p. 202).

What could Fodor and McLaughlin be talking about, other than something roughly like the explanatory standard that was described in Chapter 2? Perhaps there is some answer to this, but there is textual evidence to be addressed.[5] Hadley, (1997a, p. 572), acknowledges these appeals to texts, but does not challenge the attributions.

The matter of exegesis aside, Hadley takes exception to the explanatory standard anyway.   Hadley, (1997a), argues that "Aizawa's standard of explanation undermines not only our own explanation, but a good deal of what has been accepted as explanation in cognitive science, biology, and perhaps even in physics" (ibid., p. 572). Setting aside possible reservations concerning the particular examples Hadley offers, the essential point is that not all scientific explanations conform to the standard we have here attributed to Fodor and Pylyshyn's critique. This is certainly correct. Recall that, in Chapter 2, we mentioned a few types of scientific explanations that do not conform to the pattern studied here. Hadley's observation, therefore, raises the following question. Given that not all explanations need be of this "preferred" form, what determines whether an explanandum should receive the "preferred" form? This is an excellent question for philosophy of science. Unfortunately, no easy answer is forthcoming. It is the sort of issue that one might think would require a robust theory of explanation. In lieu of having an answer to this question, how should we proceed? Presumably the answer is that (cognitive) science cannot wait for philosophers to provide a philosophically respectable answer to this question. Science must apparently limp along here using analogies. This has been the strategy adopted here. The argument has been that the Copernican and Darwinian accounts that we have studied have this virtue and that the systematicity arguments are in relevant respects analogous. If there is nothing superior about the Copernican and Darwinian cases or if there is some important point of disanalogy, let the critics spell out the problems. Here again, it seems that the existence of historical cases provides a constraint on how one should handle the systematicity arguments. Coming to grips with the systematicity arguments involves coming to grips with other explanatory arguments from the history of science.

Turn now to the second respect in which the HH model fails to meet Fodor and Pylyshyn's challenge, namely, the fact that it makes use of Classical cognitive architecture in its attempt to explain systematic relations in thought. Clearly, the HH model uses syntactically and semantically concatenative combinatorial representations that respect the Principle of Context Independence. The words of the input sentences are not, of course, presented to the input nodes all at the same time; rather, they appear sequentially. The words, thus, are not spatially concatenated, as is usually the case in printed text. Instead, they are temporally concatenated, as when single words of a sentence are presented one at time in spoken language. Consider the way in which Fodor and McLaughlin state this condition,

> for a pair of expression types E1, E2, the first is a *Classical* constituent of the second *only if* the first is tokened whenever the second is token. For example, the English word "John" is a Classical constituent of the English sentence "John loves the girl" and every tokening of the latter implies a tokening of the former (specifically, every token of the latter *contains* a token of the former; you can't say "John loves the girl" without saying "John") (Fodor & McLaughlin, 1990, p. 186).

So, in the HH model, you cannot give the model "John loves Mary" as input, unless you give it "John" as input. Further, the model can't token the semantic interpretation (JOHN-agent, LOVES-action, MARY-patient), unless it tokens the concepts, JOHN, LOVES, and MARY, and the thematic roles, agent, action, and patient. So, there is good *prima facie* reason to think that the HH model is thoroughly Classical.

Hadley & Hayward, (1997, p. 25) agree that their network uses Classical representations, but they further maintain that the model does not display structure sensitive processing, hence is not a *bona fide* Classical model. Aizawa, (1997b), presses a number of objections to Hadley and Hayward's case for saying that their model does not use structure sensitive processing, while Hadley, (1997a), attempts to rebut these objections. Since much of the argumentation in this exchange may be of limited general interest, the reader is simply referred to the original papers for the bulk of the discussion. Here, we will consider only what appears to be the principal issue in the foregoing exchange, namely, the proper interpretation of what Classicists mean by "structure sensitive processing." Aizawa, (1997b), attributes to Fodor & Pylyshyn, (1988), the minimal account of the structure sensitivity of processing which requires only that a system be causally sensitive, rather than causally oblivious, to the structure of representations it contains.[6] [7] Hadley, (1997a), however, explicitly rejects this minimal account, arguing that there is more to structure sensitive processing than simply having processing that is causally sensitive to structure.   Unfortunately, he is less than maximally clear in specifying what this additional component is. At one point (Hadley & Hayward, 1997, p. 26), there is a suggestion that structure sensitivity involves some sort of coherence and meaningfulness to processing. At other points, (e.g., Hadley & Hayward, 1997, p. 26, Hadley, 1997a, p. 575), there is the suggestion that structure sensitive processing is a matter of processing "by reference to form." Be these expository points as they may, it is common ground between Aizawa, (1997b), and Hadley, (1997a), that the issue comes down to the proper interpretation of what is meant by structure sensitive processing. So, what texts are there to adjudicate the matter?

Consider, first, the passage Fodor and Pylyshyn use to introduce the concept of structure sensitive processing:

> *Structure sensitivity of processes.* In Classical models, the principles by which mental states are transformed, or by which an input selects the corresponding output, are defined over structural properties of mental representations. Because Classical *representations* have combinatorial structure, it is possible for Classical mental *operations* to apply to them by reference to their *form.* The result is that a paradigmatic Classical mental process operates upon any mental representation that satisfies a given structural description, and transforms it into a mental representation that satisfies another structural description. (So, for example, in a model of inference one might recognize an operation that applies to any representation of the form P&Q and transforms it into a representation of the form P.) (Fodor & Pylyshyn, 1988, p. 13).

Hadley & Hayward, (1997), and Hadley, (1997a), appear to think that this passage supports some non-minimalist understanding of "structure sensitive processing." Yet, a close reading of this and related texts indicates that there is nothing here to support a non-minimalist understanding. In the first place, Hadley and Hayward's contentions notwithstanding, nothing in the foregoing indicates that structure sensitive processing must meet any sort of epistemic criterion, be it coherence, rationality, or ability to discriminate, over and above that necessary for mere causal sensitivity. So, this passage does nothing for that idea.

Second, there is Hadley and Hayward's idea that structure sensitivity requires "processing by reference to form" which is something over and above mere causal sensitivity. The passage does contain a reference to the notion of processing by reference to form, but does *not* say that structure sensitive processing *is* processing by reference to form. Rather, Fodor and Pylyshyn appear to mean that a computational mechanism that is causally sensitive to the structural features of representations is able to process representations by reference to semantically specified form. That is, because of the combinatorial syntactic structure of the representations and a computational mechanism's causal sensitivity to this structure, it is possible for a computational mechanism to perform processes such as those we semantically characterize as conjunction elimination. By being causally sensitive to the structural features of formulas, a mechanism can identify the main connective of a well-formed formula and perform conjunction elimination, should that main connective be a conjunction symbol. This interpretation of the Fodor and Pylyshyn passage on causal sensitivity is further supported if we consider it alongside a passage from Fodor's *Psychosemantics*,

> In fact, there's a deeper point to make. It's not just that, in a psychology of propositional attitudes, content and causal powers are attributed to the same things. It's also that causal relations among propositional attitudes somehow typically contrive to respect their relations of content, and belief/desire explanations often turn on this. Hamlet believed that somebody killed his father because he believed that Claudius killed his father. His having the second belief explains his having the first. How? Well, presumably vis some such causal generalization as 'if someone believes Fa, then ceteris paribus he believes $\exists x(Fx)$.' This generalization specifies a causal relation between two kinds of mental state picked out by reference to (the logical form of) the proposition they express; so we have the usual pattern of a simultaneous attribution of content and causal powers (Fodor, 1987, pp. 12-13).

So, the minimalist construal of structure sensitive processing stands. Structure sensitive processing, i.e., processing that is causally sensitive to the structure of representations, is not processing by reference to form, it enables processing by reference to form.

In a third attempt to extract some support from the Fodor and Pylyshyn passage, Hadley, (1997a) makes much of Fodor and Pylyshyn's reference to "paradigmatic" Classical mental processes transforming representations that satisfy one structural description into representations satisfying another structural description. This, however, is far from being all that Hadley needs. In the first place, just because it is *paradigmatic* for Classical mental processes to take representations that satisfy one structural description to representations that satisfy another structural description does not make it definitional that Classical mental processes do this. It is not surprising that Fodor, a sometimes psycholinguist, intimately familiar with the Chomskyan notion of movement during linguistic derivation, would find such a mental process paradigmatic. In fact, as the reader will recall from our discussion of the Argument from Psychological Processes II, Fodor discusses just such an idea in some detail.[8]

It should be emphasized that the difference between the paradigmatic and the definitional is not a mere quibble without some serious consequences. Take the notion of an acceptor from formal language theory. An acceptor is a device that decides whether or not given strings of symbols are well-formed members in a target language or not. It says, "yes" (writes a "1" on its output tape) if the string is in the language, and says "no," (writes a "0" on its output tape) otherwise. Just because the output appears to satisfy no structural description we should not, for that reason, say that an acceptor does not use structure sensitive processing. Presumably it is the acceptor's causal sensitivity to the structure of the sentence that enables it to make accurate assessments of candidate sentences. Such acceptors may, thus, not be paradigmatic examples of structure sensitive processors, but they are none the less structure sensitive processors.

So, the text that Hadley & Hayward, (1997), and Hadley, (1997a) cite in support of their interpretation does nothing for them. By contrast, if we review Fodor and Pylyshyn's discussion of structure sensitivity following the passage cited above, we see that it strongly supports that minimal conception of structure sensitivity of processing. The second paragraph following the cited passage is fairly clear about this:

> This bears emphasis because the Classical theory is committed not only to there being a system of physically instantiated symbols, but also to the claim that the physical properties onto which the structure of the symbols is mapped *are the very properties that cause the system to behave as it does*. In other words the physical counterparts of the symbols, and their structure properties, *cause* the system's behavior. A system which has symbolic expressions, but whose operation does not depend upon the structure of these expressions, does not qualify as a Classical machine since it fails to satisfy condition (2). In this respect, a Classical model is very different from one in which behavior is caused by mechanisms, such as energy minimization, that are not responsive to the physical encoding of the structure of representations. (Fodor & Pylyshyn, 1988, p. 14, italics in original).

This passage quite clearly indicates the physical mechanisms realizing or implementing a combinatorial system of representations must be causally sensitive to the combinatorial structure of the representations. Then there is also the opening passage from Fodor and McLaughlin's discussion:

In two recent papers, Paul Smolensky (1987, 1988b) responds to a challenge Jerry Fodor and Zenon Pylyshyn (Fodor and Pylyshyn, 1988) have posed for connectionist theories of cognition: to explain the existence of systematic relations between cognitive capacities without assuming that cognitive processes are causally sensitive to the constituent structure of mental representations. This challenge implies a dilemma: if connectionism can't account for systematicity, it thereby fails to provide an adequate basis for a theory of cognition; but if its account of systematicity requires mental processes that are sensitive to the constituent structure of mental representations, then the theory of cognition it offers will be, at best, an implementation architecture for a "classical" (language of thought) model (Fodor & McLaughlin, 1990, p.183).

In these texts, the minimal interpretation of structure sensitivity of processes is clearly vindicated.

Having established the correctness of the minimal interpretation of the structure sensitivity of processing, we have left to emphasize that the HH model is causally sensitive to the temporal structure of its input representations. The order in which a sequence of representations is presented to the network makes a causally efficacious difference in the temporal sequence of the changes in activation values of the various nodes in the network. The HH model is, therefore, thoroughly Classical *and*, like other Classical models, fails to explain the systematic features of thought.

As a final note, it might be worth emphasizing that the HH network is causally sensitive to the structure of its inputs both before and after training. This is worth emphasizing, since Hadley and Hayward hedge their bets about their model being Classical by suggesting that their model evolves from one that lacks structure sensitive processing to one that has structure sensitive processing (Hadley & Hayward, 1997, p. 25) The hedge, however, is of no help to Hadley and Hayward. If one moves from a system that *does not* have systematic cognitive representations, *does not* have contentfully related states, and *does not* use structure sensitive processing to one that *does* have systematic cognitive representations, *does* have contentfully related states, and *does* use structure sensitive processing, this does not show that Fodor and Pylyshyn are wrong to suppose that a Classical system of cognitive representation is required in order to explain the various systematic characteristics of thought. In fact, one might think Hadley and Hayward's result serves to reinforce the significance of Classical cognitive architecture. It shows that going Classical enables one to generate a model that at least displays the relevant properties. Granted, producing such a network that goes from not having systematic cognitive representations, not having semantically related representations, and not having sensitivity to causal structure to one that does have systematic, semantically related cognitive rpresentations to which mechanisms are causally sensitive could be an important information processing accomplishment for Connectionism. Nevertheless, producing such a network is simply not an adequate response to Fodor and Pylyshyn's challenge.

3 TAKING STOCK

Chapters 3-6 made the case that Classicism could explain the various productive and systematic features of thought better than could Pure Atomism. To some extent, this discussion was an expository aid to the work in the present chapter, where the case against Pure Atomism was turned into a case against Connectionism. Although the logic of the argument carries through quite nicely, there is a point of significant concern. Pure Atomism is a relatively simple theory of cognitive architecture, designed primarily for expository convenience. By contrast, Connectionism is a much looser configuration of hypotheses. In addition, the information processing features of Connectionist networks are in many respects not fully understood. This ambiguity and uncertainty in the Connectionist state of the art makes it difficult to say definitively that nothing going by the name of "Connectionism" could possibly provide an explanation of the productive and systematic features of thought. All that it appears one can say at this point is that existing Connectionist proposals have yet to explain the various systematic and productive dimensions of thought.

NOTES

1. Cf., Hadley and Hayward, (1997).

2. Although this is the most common analysis of what distributed representations are, it is not entirely clear that this could be all Connectionists are after. Surely, the difference between using one node to represent a concept and using many nodes to represent a concept is not in itself that momentous.

3. Incidently, recent work in Chomsky's (1995) Minimalist Program has proposed to abandon deep structures and D-structures as explanatory devices.

4. One of Hadley and Hayward's modifications of the simple Hebbian rule is the addition of a competitive element to the weight change by making the increment on a weight into node S proportional to the ratio of the current weight on the link into S to the average weight on links into S (ibid., p. 14). Another modification involves the random selection of which mod-pnode to include in the representation of a proposition in the training phase (ibid., p. 13).

5. Relevant passages include Fodor, (1987), p. 151, Fodor & Pylyshyn, (1988), pp. 48, 50, and Fodor, (1996), p. 109.

6. A problem case: Suppose that some Turing machine is such that, for any structured strings given as input, it erases the entire string, then goes into one particular state, say, s_{398432}, and then writes a string of three 1's. Surely the TM was causally sensitive to the input string, but its causal sensitivity to this input string had, in some sense, nothing to do with the output it eventually produced. What to say about this case? Who knows? This was the issue obliquely alluded to at Aizawa (1997b), p. 52. Since this possibility seems to be tangential to the question about the possible Classical status of the HH model, we will pass over it.

7. For what it is worth, van Gelder, (1990), also appears to attribute this view to Fodor & Pylyshyn, (1988):

> (The term "sensitive to," although widely used, is conveniently vague; in this context it can only mean something like "causally influenced by.") Thus, the fact that everybody who can infer P from (P&Q) can also infer P from ((P&Q)&R), is explained by reference to the structural similarity of the representations involved and the fact that there are cognitive processes which can pick up on (i.e., are casually influenced by) that structural similarity (van Gelder, 1990, p. 376).

8. Cf. Fodor, (1987), pp. 143-147.

CHAPTER 8

FUNCTIONAL COMBINATORIALISM

One of the leading Connectionist responses to the systematicity arguments is to postulate that cognition involves functionally combinatorial representations rather than Classical concatenative representations. In a functionally combinatorial representation, no token of a syntactic and semantic atom need be a literal part of a token of a syntactic and semantic molecule to which it gives rise. Rather, a syntactic and semnatic atom is merely an argument to a function whose value is a syntactic and semantic molecule.[1] Gödel numberings and Smolensky's Tensor Product Theory are often offered as examples illustrating this idea.[2] In this chapter, we shall consider what potential Gödel numberings and Tensor Product Theory have for explaining the numerous productive and systematic characteristics of thought. What we shall find is that, where Gödel numbers can explain the productivity of thought to the standard implicit there, neither theory of cognitive representation can explain the familiar systematic relations in thought. Further, neither of these forms of functionally combinatorial representations can explain the co-occurrence of the counterfactual dependence and content relatedness of possible occurrent thoughts. There is, therefore, some defeasible reason to prefer a Classical theory of cognition over a Functionally Combinatorial theory.

Before we begin, however, it is worth reviewing three features of the application of these arguments to Functional Combinatorialism (FC) and Connectionism. First, even if Functional Combinatorialism were to succeed in explaining the systematic relations in thought, this should not automatically be counted as an explanatory success for Connectionism. In FC accounts, what is supposed to be doing the explanatory work is the functionally combinatorial representations. If, however, such representations are doing the explanatory work and the Connectionist apparatus of nodes and weighted connections serves as a mere implementation of FC, then Connectionism *per se* does not explain the systematic relations in thought. Connectionism, therefore, would receive no explanatory confirmation. This is exactly the point Fodor and Pylyshyn were making when they said that it would not do for Connectionism to try to explain the many kinds of systematic relations in thought by implementing a Classical architecture.[3] The challenge is for a Connectionist network *qua Connectionist network,* rather than, say, Connectionist network *qua Turing Machine,* to explain the various systematic relations in thought. What goes for implementing a Classical architecture goes for implementing a non-Classical functional combinatorial architecture. The challenge to Connectionists is to show how a Connectionist network *qua Connectionist network,* rather than Connectionist network *qua realizer of a functionally combinatorial theory of cognitive representations,* is to explain the systematic and productive relations in thought.

The second point concerns the observation that, if FC were to explain the various kinds of systematic relations in thought, then it would be true that Connection*ists,* i.e., cognitive scientists who believe that cognition is worth studying in terms of processes involving nodes and weighted connections, will have succeeded in explaining the systematic and productive features of thought. In such a situation, there is a sense in which Connectionists have explained the sundry systematic and productive characteristics of thought. Yet, this is not the sense in which Connectionists are challenged to explain systematicity. When it is urged that Connectionists are to explain the systematic characteristics of thought, this is elliptical for the idea that Connectionists must explain the various systematic relations in thought *using the theory of nodes with weighted connections between them.* The numerous systematicity and productivity arguments are concerned with confirming, or disconfirming, theories of cognitive architecture, not with saying something about those who study those cognitive architectures. To put matters in another way, the Classicist's arguments are meant to confirm certain sets of hypotheses concerning the architecture of cognition. If none of the principles of nodes and weighted connections figure into the explanation of the systematic features of thought, then principles of nodes and weighted connections receive no empirical confirmation through the systematicity arguments. The principles do not explain what has been argued that they should explain.

The third feature of the arguments concerns the observation that the theory of nodes with weighted connections may be said to have inspired theorists, such as Paul Smolensky, to develop functionally combinatorial theories of representation. This, it may be thought, lends some credibility to Connectionism. Yet it is far from clear that if A inspires B and B is confirmed, then A is confirmed. That is certainly not any principle that is at work in the argumentation we have seen. In other words, even if Connectionism does inspire a theory that explains the systematic and productive features of thought, that is not enough to confirm Connectionism. So, the upshot of the foregoing three observations is that, even in the event that either of the species of Functional Combinatorialism that we examine turns out to explain the systematic and productive relations in thought, this does nothing in and of itself to confirm a Connectionist theory of cognition.

1 GÖDEL NUMERALS

To begin with, we should recall the distinction between numbers and numerals. Numbers are abstract objects, where numerals are syntactic objects used for representing numbers. The vast majority of us use the Arabic system of numerals, although many of us are familiar with at least a significant portion of the Roman numeral system. Computing devices, being physical objects, do not manipulate abstract objects such as numbers. Instead, they manipulate symbols or tokens of syntactic objects. It is, in part, in virtue of manipulating symbols for numbers, i.e., numerals, that computing devices are said to compute, for example, arithmetic functions. So, Turing machines do not, strictly speaking, print numbers on the squares of their tapes. Instead, they print numerals, i.e., strings of symbols that represent numbers. For most purposes, no harm is done by the familiar practice of speaking of Gödel numbers. In the present context of a theory of the structure of cognitive representations, however, it is best that we abandon the informal and instead develop a theory of the way in which Gödel *numerals* might constitute a system of cognitive representation.

As another preliminary point, we must observe that, despite the frequent reference to Gödel numerals as perfectly legitimate forms of functionally combinatorial representations, no Non-Classicist has ever seriously developed the proposal as a means of trying to explain the range of productive and systematic features of thought. Indeed, it is unlikely that any Non-Classicist wants to maintain that cognitive representations really are Gödel numerals or even that Gödel numerals are serious contenders as cognitive representations. Instead, Gödel numerals appear to be intended only to serve as an illustration of one way one might try to explain the many productive and systematic relations in thought. Two observations are, therefore, relevant here. First, we can only examine the Gödel numeral proposal in a preliminary sort of way. Just as Gödel numerals have so far only been intended to serve as a concrete illustration of how functional combinatorialism might work, so they are only intended here to serve as a concrete illustration of one way in which functional combinatorialism does not work. Second, since there has been no serious attempt to explain how Gödel numerals might be used to explain the systematic and productive relations in thought, we will have to develop such a proposal here. This brings with it the risk that the present proposal will not be as sympathetic to the Connectionist cause as is possible, but there seems to be no other way to proceed at this point. Let the Connectionists show us a more impressive use of Gödel numerals. This seems to be the way to advance the discussion.

So, consider a very simple-minded way in which to use Gödel numerals in a cognitive architecture: keep as much of the Classical framework as is possible, substituting Gödel numerals for Classically structured representations. Let us call this theory GN. According to GN, the familiar computational architecture of Turing-equivalent digital computers uses Gödel numerals, rather than Classically structured representations. Thus, GN is a species of Representationalism. Further, GN adopts the Computational Theory of the Attitudes, according to which having an attitude, such as thinking, believing, hoping, or fearing, is a matter of standing in a particular kind of computational relation to a representation. GN will, thus, differ from Pure Atomism and Classicism in the structure of the hypothetical cognitive representations. Rather than supposing that the contents of propositional attitudes are represented by syntactically and semantically atomic representations, a la Pure Atomism, or that these contents are represented by a system of syntactically and semantically concatenatively combinatorial representations respecting context independence, a la Classicism, the Gödel proposal is that these contents are represented by a particular kind of numeral system.

In a GN theory of cognition, the Gödel numerals that constitute the cognitive representations that underlie particular occurrent thoughts are permitted to have a concatenative combinatorial syntax. For simplicity, we shall use the familiar syntactic atoms and concatenative combinatorial syntax of Arabic numerals. These complex syntactic molecules are related to their syntactic and semantic atoms via encoding processes. The encoding processes use intermediate numerical representations that do double duty as representations of numbers, on the one hand, and as representations of such other things as terms, relations, punctuation marks, and propositions, on the other. For convenience, we shall suppose that these intermediate numerical representations, like the final Gödel numerals, use the familiar syntax of Arabic numerals. We will, however, use italic Arabic numerals for these intermediaries in order to contrast them with the final Gödel numerals. So, take the following set of propositions

{John loves John,
John loves Mary,
Mary loves John,
Mary loves Mary,
John loves John and John loves John,
John loves John and John loves Mary,
John loves John and Mary loves John,
John loves John and Mary loves Mary,
John loves Mary and John loves John,
John loves Mary and John loves Mary,
John loves Mary and Mary loves John,
John loves Mary and Mary loves Mary,
Mary loves John and John loves John,
Mary loves John and John loves Mary,

Mary loves John and Mary loves John,
Mary loves John and Mary loves Mary,
Mary loves Mary and John loves John,
Mary loves Mary and John loves Mary,
Mary loves Mary and Mary loves John,
Mary loves Mary and Mary loves Mary,
John loves John and John loves John and John loves John,
John loves John and John loves John and John loves Mary,
...}

One way to provide Gödel numerals for these propositions would begin by taking representations for John, loves, Mary, and conjunction as our "atomic" representations. Another would begin by taking representations of conjunction and the propositions that John loves John, that John loves Mary, that Mary loves John, and that Mary loves Mary as our atomics. We shall take this latter course. Thus, we suppose that conjunction and each of the propositions in our set can be associated with a sequence of numerals as follows:

$<1>$ with John loves John,
$<2>$ with John loves Mary,
$<3>$ with Mary loves John,
$<4>$ with Mary loves Mary,
$<5>$ with conjunction.
$<1, 5, 1>$ with John loves John and John loves John,
$<1, 5, 2>$ with John loves John and John loves Mary,
$<1, 5, 3>$ with John loves John and Mary loves John,
$<1, 5, 4>$ with John loves John and Mary loves Mary,
$<2, 5, 1>$ with John loves Mary and John loves John,
$<2, 5, 2>$ with John loves Mary and John loves Mary,
$<2, 5, 3>$ with John loves Mary and Mary loves John,
$<2, 5, 4>$ with John loves Mary and Mary loves Mary,
$<3, 5, 1>$ with Mary loves John and John loves John,
$<3, 5, 2>$ with Mary loves John and John loves Mary,
$<3, 5, 3>$ with Mary loves John and Mary loves John,
$<3, 5, 4>$ with Mary loves John and Mary loves Mary,
$<4, 5, 1>$ with Mary loves Mary and John loves John,
$<4, 5, 2>$ with Mary loves Mary and John loves Mary,
$<4, 5, 3>$ with Mary loves Mary and Mary loves John,
$<4, 5, 4>$ with Mary loves Mary and Mary loves Mary,
$<1, 5, 1, 5, 1>$ with John loves John and John loves John and John loves
    John,
$<1, 5, 1, 5, 2>$ with John loves John and John loves John and John loves
    Mary,

In the foregoing list, the angle brackets, <, >, indicate that the order of the terms enclosed makes a difference; in other words, the numerals form an order n-tuple. Next, we take the n numbers represented by the n numerals in the sequence and use them as the powers of the first n prime numbers. The product of these n exponentiated prime numbers yields another number whose Arabic representation we can then take to be the representation of our proposition. Thus, we take the three-member sequence <2, 5, 3> (which is associated with the proposition that John loves Mary and Mary loves John) and apply it to the first three prime numbers to give us the number one hundred twenty-one thousand, five hundred ($= 2^2 \times 3^5 \times 5^3$) which is written in our Arabic notation "121500." Thus, in our GN system, "121500" represents the proposition that John loves Mary and Mary loves John. Similarly, we take the three-member sequence <3, 5, 2> (which is associated with the proposition that Mary loves John and John loves Mary) and apply it to the first three prime numbers to give us the number forty-eight thousand, six hundred ($= 2^3 \times 3^5 \times 5^2$). Thus, in our GN system, "48600" represents the proposition that Mary loves John and John loves Mary. Following this arrangement, we represent our set of propositions with the following Gödel numerals:

"2" (2) means John loves John,
"4" (2^2) means John loves Mary,
"8"(2^3) means Mary loves John,
"16" (2^4) means Mary loves Mary,
"2430" ($2 \times 3^5 \times 5$) means John loves John and John loves John,
"12150" ($2 \times 3^5 \times 5^2$) means John loves John and John loves Mary,
"60750" ($2 \times 3^5 \times 5^3$) means John loves John and Mary loves John,
"303750" ($2 \times 3^5 \times 5^4$) means John loves John and Mary loves Mary,
"4860" ($2^2 \times 3^5 \times 5$) means John loves Mary and John loves John,
"24300" ($2^2 \times 3^5 \times 5^2$) means John loves Mary and John loves Mary,
"121500" ($2^2 \times 3^5 \times 5^3$) means John loves Mary and Mary loves John,
"607500" ($2^2 \times 3^5 \times 5^4$) means John loves Mary and Mary loves Mary,
"9720" ($2^3 \times 3^5 \times 5$) means Mary loves John and John loves John,
"48600" ($2^3 \times 3^5 \times 5^2$) means Mary loves John and John loves Mary,
"243000" ($2^3 \times 3^5 \times 5^3$) means Mary loves John and Mary loves John,
"1215000" ($2^3 \times 3^5 \times 5^4$) means Mary loves John and Mary loves Mary,
"19440" ($2^4 \times 3^5 \times 5$) means Mary loves Mary and John loves John,
"97200" ($2^4 \times 3^5 \times 5^2$) means Mary loves Mary and John loves Mary,
"486000" ($2^4 \times 3^5 \times 5^3$) means Mary loves Mary and Mary loves John,
"2430000" ($2^4 \times 3^5 \times 5^4$) means Mary loves Mary and Mary loves Mary,
"449251111" ($2 \times 3^5 \times 5 \times 7^5 \times 11$) means John loves John and John loves John and John loves John,

"4941762221" ($2 \times 3^5 \times 5 \times 7^5 \times 11^2$) John loves John and John loves John and John loves Mary,

...

These are the numerals must without a doubt occur in a GN theory of cognition. Since the coding process we have just described can be carried out by digital computation and provides a unique mapping from propositions onto Gödel numerals. In addition, the process of going from a given Gödel numeral to its atomic representations can also be carried out by digital computation and provides a unique mapping from Gödel numerals to propositions.

The GN system of cognitive representations involves syntactic concatenative combinatorialism insofar as the syntactic objects that are supposed to be part of the cognitive economy are simply the Arabic numerals. GN representations are, to this extent, Classical. They are not, however, thoroughly Classical insofar as they do not invoke the Classicist's Principle of Context Independence. It is not the case that a given syntactic object in a Gödel numeral that is produced by the encoding process makes the same semantic contribution to each context in which it occurs. In fact, the meaning of, say, "48600" is not a function of the meaning of the rightmost "0". Imposing the condition that a single numeral make the same semantic contribution to every context in which it occurs would thwart the whole system. It would render the system thoroughly Classical. With Gödel numerals, we might speak metaphorically and say that there is no "alignment" between the combinatorial syntax of the Arabic numerals and the combinatorial semantics that is somehow supposed to derive from the encoding process. So, we can see how it is that Gödel numerals form a non-Classical system of representation.

With a version of the GN theory on the table, we run can through the various explananda. Consider, first, the productivity of thought. Recall that, in Chapter 3, we argued that the productivity of thought argument does not invoke our principle regarding better explanations, according to which such explanations should not rely on arbitrary hypotheses in the sense articulated in Chapter 2. Instead, what is needed in the productivity argument is some sort of plausible, non-Classical account of how finite means might be used to generate an unbounded number of semantically distinct representations. Yet, the foregoing sketch clearly provides this. There is no bound on the number of prime numbers that can correspond to our syntactic atoms. There is an unbounded supply of prime numbers for which these might be exponents. There is no bound on the domains or ranges of the arithmetic functions involved in the construction of our Gödel numerals. In addition, the processes that mediate state transitions in our GN cognitive architecture are as philosophically kosher as the processes that mediate state transitions in Classical cognitive architectures, since both the GN processes and the Classical processes are Turing-computable. So, the GN version of functional combinatorialism can explain the productivity of thought.

How does our GN architecture handle the systematicity of inference? For simplicity, we can consider merely a limited degree of systematicity of conjunction elimination. Taking advantage of our coding above, we want the GN architecture to explain how it is that a person who can infer that John loves Mary from Mary loves John and John loves Mary can also infer that John loves Mary from John loves John and John loves John and John loves Mary. Since our GN architecture represents the proposition that John loves Mary using "4," the proposition that Mary loves John and John loves Mary using "48600," and the proposition that John loves John and John loves John and John loves Mary using "4941762221," the inferential task becomes one of having a computer program of the mind that will take both "48600" and "4941762221" as input and produce "4" as output. There are many ways of doing this.[4] One is simply to have the GN computer program of the mind erase either a "48600" or a "4941762221" and replace it with a "4." Since the systematicity of conjunction elimination, like the systematicity of inference, is a task over a finite domain, a "look-up table" approach will suffice.

The problem with the foregoing GN account of the systematicity of inference is the one we should have come to expect. Speaking loosely in a Fodorian sort of way, it is just as easy to produce a computer program that writes "4" as output to both "48600" and "4941762221," as it is to produce a computer program that writes "4" as output to "48600" but not on "4941762221." To put the matter as we proposed in Chapter 2, we should say that the account that is invoked to explain the systematicity of inference relies on an arbitrary hypothesis about the structure of the computer program of the mind. The arbitrary hypothesis will have to do with the particular instructions in the program, namely, that those instructions enable the GN computer program of the mind to handle inputs in one way as well as another. The hypothesis that the GN program of the mind has such instructions cannot be confirmed short of confirming the hypothesis that the system uses Gödel numerals as cognitive representations. Given this reliance on an arbitrary hypothesis, we do not have an appropriate GN account of the systematicity of inference.

What about the counterfactual dependence among thought capacities? What about the idea that some thought capacities are nomologically necessary and sufficient for others? It is difficult to see how the capacity to token one numeral, such as "48600" might be nomologically necessary and sufficient for tokening another numeral, such as "4941762221". There are clearly computer programs that will write only one of these numbers, but not the other. The best that a GN theory seems to be able to do is provide some account of a more limited kind of counterfactual dependency or "intrinsic connection", a notion somewhat weaker than a nomologically necessary and sufficient connection. *Prima facie*, the Gödel numeral theory of cognitive representation can explain the existence of weak dependencies among thoughts in virtue of the fact that the various Arabic base ten representations of propositions have common syntactic elements. In our scheme above, the representation of John loves Mary and Mary loves John is the Arabic numeral "121500," where the representation of Mary loves John and John loves Mary is the Arabic numeral "48600." Thus, in virtue of the fact that both of these representations involve a "0" in the tens place and a "0" in the ones place, there will be an intrinsic connection between the capacity for the John loves Mary and Mary loves John thought and the capacity for the Mary loves John and John loves Mary thought. Inspection of our list of examples will reveal further dependencies, hence we have a *prima facie* acceptable GN account of a weaker notion of the systematicity of cognitive representations. In contrast to the stronger notion of nomologically necessary and sufficient conditions, where there was no apparent story to tell, there is in the present weaker case, some account that might be ventured.

We now have to consider whether or not there is some arbitrary auxiliary hypothesis in the account. Morever, as we may have come to expect, there is. So far we have seen one Gödel numeral scheme that leads to counterfactual dependencies among thoughts. One assumption underlying this system is the assumption that the Gödel numerals (i.e., the products of the exponeniated primes) are expressed in the familiar base ten notation of Arabic numerals. This is an assumption about the nature of the concatenatively combinatorial syntax of cognitive representations. In virtue of this assumption and the choice of numerals for the atomic representations, it turns out that some of the Gödel numerals for the propositions have common elements, hence that there is a kind of intrinsic connection between them. An alternative assumption, however, is that the Gödel numerals occur in a base 100,000 system in which none of the 100,000 syntactically atomic symbols have anything syntactic in common. So, the set of atomic numerals in the system might be something like $\{0, 1, 2, 3, 4, 5, 6, 7, 8, 9, a, A, b, B, \ldots, z, Z, \ldots, \heartsuit, \diamondsuit, \clubsuit, \spadesuit\}$. In such a system, none of the numerals for our propositions would have common elements, hence there would be no intrinsic connections or counterfactual dependencies among any of the numerals representing the propositions in our set, hence no intrinsic connections or counterfactual dependence among the corresponding thoughts.[5] So, it cannot be that, in virtue of having Gödel numerals as the cognitive representations in a Computational Theory of the Attitudes, one has systematic thoughts. One must add some additional hypothesis that does the work of the hypothesis that the system of cognitive representation uses the syntax of the Arabic numeral system. The hypothesis need not be this hypothesis in particular. It might work, for example, to stipulate that the cardinality of the set of atomic representations is smaller than the cardinality of the set of representations that are to be counterfactually dependent. Yet, what Fodor and Pylyshyn would say is that such an assumption is one that we can as easily keep as drop, all the while remaining within the framework of a Gödel numeral system. To put matters in the manner developed in Chapter 2, the hypothesis that a Gödel numeral system of representation is a base ten system is not confirmed independently of the present explanatory challenge. The idea is that it is impossible to confirm that a system has a set of syntactic atoms of a given cardinality in a hypothetical GN cognitive architecture short of knowing that the system is a GN system. So, GN cannot explain the systematicity of cognitive representations to the standard Fodor and Pylyshyn have in mind.

Next there is the content relatedness of possible occurrent thoughts. In our scheme above, the Gödel numerals are indeed contentfully related. This shows that Gödel numerals can exhibit compositionality. But, again, we must ask whether or not there are arbitrary auxiliary hypotheses that prevent Gödel numerals from explaining semantic relatedness. Consider, to begin with, the assumption that the content of a Gödel numeral is a function of the content of the arguments and the ordering of the arguments which generated the Gödel numeral. This is the Gödel numeral version of the Principle of Semantic Compositionality. Yet, as we discussed before, this is a rather weak semantic assumption. It is consistent with a scheme in which one uses the same arguments and combinatorial processes as was used above, but in which the contents of the resulting Gödel numerals are totally unrelated as in

"2430" means John loves Mary,

"12150" means Paris is the capital of France,

"60750" means time heals all wounds,

"303750" means the sum of the internal angles of a triangle equal 180°,

"4860" means π is less than 4

"24300" means Dover is the capital of Delaware

...

This suggests that the GN theory needs some version of the Principle of Context Independence. Recall that this principle says that a given syntactic item makes the same semantic contribution to all contexts in which it occurs. Thus, according to this principle, "John" means the same thing, namely, John, in the context of "___ loves Mary" and in the context of "Mary loves ___." We say that GN needs some version of this principle, since as it stands the principle will not work for GN. GN does not want, say, "5" to mean the same thing in the context of "121__00" and in the context of "607__0." GN does not want this principle to hold for the numerals that are the product of its encoding process. The GN version must hold for the encoding process itself. What GN needs, roughly, is to have a given syntactic atom make the same semantic contribution to every value of the encoding function of which it is an argument. This is not the Classical hypothesis, but it serves a similar function. Yet, such a principle has the weakness we have seen in other auxiliary hypotheses. It appears to be impossible to confirm this auxiliary short of confirming that the mind uses a Gödel numeral system of cognitive representation. How could one know that the GN encoding process satisfies the GN version of the principle of context independence, or even a version of the principle of semantic compositionality, without having antecedently established the existence of such an encoding and the truth of the GN theory of cognitive architecture?

This brings us to the co-occurrence of counterfactual dependency and semantic relatedness. How do Gödel numerals fare here? Clearly, if there is no GN account of the systematicity of cognitive representations that explains why it is that one thought capacity is nomologically necessary and sufficient for another, then *a fortiori* there will be no account of how it is that the thought capacities that are mutually nomologically necessary and sufficient are at the same time contentfully related. Nevertheless, we might examine the cases in which there is some degree of "intrinsic connection" among thoughts capacities that are contentfully related. So, for example, in our discussion above, the representations "121500" and "48600" show some degree of "intrinsic connection" or mutual dependence in virtue of having "0"s in the ones and tens places. Moreover, their contents are related. "121500" means that John loves Mary and Mary loves John while "48600" means that Mary loves John and John loves Mary. So, there is at least some *prima facie* acceptable GN account. Yet, given a computing device that realizes the GN theory of cognitive architecture and produces some degree of "intrinsic connection" or dependence among thought capacities, there is no guarantee that the thought capacities will be semantically related. An illustration of this is given in Appendix A. So, GN *per se* does not provide the desired form of explanation of the co-occurrence of systematicity and content relatedness. An auxiliary hypothesis might be brought in to insure that the thought capacities that are to some degree dependent upon one another are also semantically related, but this auxiliary has all the markings of what we have taken to be an arbitrary auxiliary hypothesis. It appears to be one which we would not be able to confirm short of confirming the GN theory of cognitive architecture.

Finally, there is the co-occurrence of diachronic and synchronic systematicity. Why is it, according to a GN theory, that the number of possible occurrent thoughts increases by leaps and bounds during development and that these same thoughts are, at any given time, counterfactually dependent upon one another? Recall that the developmental idea is that, during some initial cognitive stage, a human being might have the capacity to have the thoughts

| John loves John | John loves Mary |
| Mary loves John | Mary loves Mary, |

then at a later stage have the capacity to have the thoughts,

| John loves John | John loves Mary | John loves Jane |

Mary loves John	Mary loves Mary	Mary loves Jane
Jane loves John	Jane loves Mary	Jane loves Jane
John hates John	John hates Mary	John hates Jane
Mary hates John	Mary hates Mary	Mary hates Jane
Jane hates John	Jane hates Mary	Jane hates Jane.

One proposal GN might offer is that cognitive development involves plugging new atomic representations into the function that computes Gödel numerals. Since each new atomic representation will serve as an argument on many different values of the function, the number of possible occurrent thoughts will increase by leaps and bounds as is required by the explanandum. Moreover, one might expect there to be counterfactual dependencies among the values of these functions, hence the system will be at once both diachronically and synchronically systematic. So, we have at least one scheme on which GN appears to be in the running.

The problem for this scheme is that it is possible to get diachronic systematicity without synchronic systematicity, hence that there is a need for some auxiliary hypothesis that will block this. Yet, such an auxiliary is a prime candidate for a hypothesis that does not admit of confirmation independent of GN architecture. To see how to separate diachronic from synchronic systematicity, one can keep the story about diachronic systematicity. Synchronic systematicity will elude a GN architecture if, rather than using the familiar syntactic combinatorial apparatus of Arabic numerals, one uses a numeral system with a very large stock of atomic representations. This is the observation we made in pressing the synchronic systematicity argument against Classicism and in our first pass through the synchronic systematicity argument against GN. So, we have reason to think that the GN approach will not adequately explain the various systematic relations in thought.

2 SMOLENSKY'S TENSOR PRODUCT THEORY

Although the Gödel Numerals theory of cognition surfaces from time to time as a possible non-Classical explanation of the systematic and productive features of thought, by far the more seriously developed account is Paul Smolensky's

(1987, 1991, 1995) Tensor Product Theory (TPT). Although it is, in principle, possible to see how much of the argumentation from previous sections undermine TPT accounts, there are sufficiently many points of detail to be introduced that it is worth explicitly setting out how the extensions of the arguments are to be made.

Smolensky develops TPT as a system for representing propositions. For convenience he supposes that propositions can be represented by binary branching structures. Thus, the proposition that John loves Mary could have the binary branching representation,

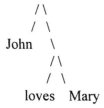

where the proposition that John really loves Mary would have the binary branching representation,

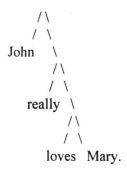

According to TPT, these binary branching structures do not constitute mental representations. Instead, TPT postulates tensor codes for these binary branching trees and the cognitive economy traffics in tensors.

As with Chalmers's active-passive transformation network in Chapter 7 and the Gödel Numeral theory introduced in the previous section, Tensor Product Theory postulates both encoding procedures and products of these encoding procedures. In Chalmers's model, the encoding process was a simple auto-associative feed-forward network. In the GN theory, the encoding process was the computational procedures used to compute the Gödel numerals. In TPT, the processes are operations on tensors.

The TPT encoding process involves two fundamental vectors, which we may designate L and R. For technical reasons, L and R must have the property of

being linearly independent, that is, there cannot exist some constant c such that
L = cR. There are many pairs of vectors that have this feature, but for the sake
of easy exposition we can let L = |1 2 3 | and R = | 3 2 1 |. L and R are in some
respects like the functional categories in transformational grammars. They do
not have content in the way that lexical items, such as vectors representing John,
loves, and Mary, do. Instead, L and R indicate roles or positions items may have
in binary branching structures.[6] L is a vector that combines with another vector
X to indicate that X is the left branch at a binary branching, where R is a vector
that combines with X to indicate that X is the right branch at a binary branching.
To articulate the theory, let us suppose that we have "lexical" vectors such that

| 4 3 | means John,
| 5 8 | means loves,
| 7 9 | means Mary, and
| 3 6 | means really.

Tensor codes for propositions are built up from these "lexical" vectors and the
"functional" vectors, L and R, using two mathematical operations on vectors:
vector addition and vector multiplication.

Both L and R combine with any other vector X via vector multiplication, that
is, each component of the L and R vectors is multiplied by each component of
the X vector in order to produce a higher rank tensor. Thus, if we combine L
and R with each of our lexical vectors via vector multiplication we get

| 4 8 12 | means "(John) on the left" | 12 8 4 | means "(John) on the right"
| 3 6 9 | | 9 6 3 |

| 5 10 15 | means "(loves) on the left" | 15 10 5 | means "(loves) on the right"
| 8 16 24 | | 24 16 8 |

| 7 14 21 | means "(Mary) on the left" | 21 14 7 | means "(Mary) on the right"
| 9 18 27 | | 27 18 9 |

| 3 6 9 | means "(really) on the left" | 9 6 3 | means "(really) on the right."
| 6 12 18 | | 18 12 6 |

These tensors constitute intermediates in the construction of propositional
tensors, i.e., tensors that represent propositions.   Yet, there are further
intermediates between the foregoing tensors and the tensors that represent
propositions. Suppose we wish to construct a tensor that means that John loves
Mary. If so, then we next construct another intermediate tensor that means

"(loves) on the left - (Mary) on the right". This is done by vector addition, the simple addition of components of the "(loves) on the left" vector and the "(Mary) on the right" vector. Thus, our next intermediate tensor is

| 26 24 22 | means "(loves) on the left - (Mary) on the right."
| 35 34 33 |

Since we want this to be the right branch of our root node, we perform another tensor multiplication of this tensor with R:

| 26 24 22 | ⊗ | 3 2 1 | = | 78 72 66 |
| 35 34 33 | |105 102 99 |
| 52 48 44 |
| 70 68 66 |
| 26 24 22 |
| 35 34 33 |.

This gives us a 3 x 2 x 3 matrix for the tensor representation of "((loves) on the left - (Mary) on the right) on the right." At this point, the theory suggests that we perform tensor addition of the "(John) on the left" representation with the representation we have just generated. But, because these tensors have different rank, i.e., there are a different number of components in each of the matrices, an *ad hoc* move is needed to overcome this technicality. One option is simply to increase the rank of the "(John) on the left" tensor by adding null components to make it agree with the rank of the "((loves) on the left - (Mary) on the right) on the right." tensor. This is what we do. Thus,

4 8 12		78 72 66		**82 80 78**
3 6 9		105 102 99		**108 108 108**
0 0 0	+	52 48 44	=	**52 48 44**
0 0 0		70 68 66		**70 68 66**
0 0 0		26 24 22		**26 24 22**
0 0 0		35 34 33		**35 34 33** |,

gives us our final representation of the proposition that John loves Mary, here rendered in bold.[7]

How, then, is it that thought is productive according to TPT? The short answer is that there is no bound on the number of times that one can iterate the operations of vector multiplication and vector addition, hence there is no bound on the size of a tensor product representation. Hence, there is no bound on the number of possible thoughts that might occur to a person possessing tensor product representations.

This is certainly a clever idea. Yet, there are difficulties that keep this proposal from getting entirely clear of the woods. The concern centers on a problem to which Smolensky is sensitive, namely, the evident need for a tensor to have n dimensions to represent a proposition with n "lexical" elements. So, a representation of John's loving Mary requires three dimensions, a representation of John's really loving Mary requires four dimensions, a representation of John's really, really loving Mary requires five dimensions, and so on. What then of the neural substrate for these n dimensions? Although neural networks are not essential here, the nature of the problem can be made clearer by thinking of the implementation of TPT in neural networks. A representation of n dimensions will require at least n nodes.[8] However the mathematical apparatus of a node is realized in brain tissue, whether as a single neuron, a cluster of neurons, or a fragment of a neuron, there will evidently be some maximal number of nodes the brain can implement, hence some "largest" possible thought. If, however, there is largest possible thought, then thought will have a strictly finite cognitive capacity, hence not be productive. Thus, a finite brain using tensor product representations cannot literally embody an arbitrarily large representation, hence cannot be said to have a capacity for an unbounded number of distinct thoughts.

Smolensky, (1995), responds to this problem in the natural way by appeal to a competence/performance distinction. He observes that there is a simple finite specification of these unbounded networks (Smolensky, 1995, pp. 259-260). Although Smolensky does a fair amount of work to provide the technical details underlying how one is to provide this finite specification, he is less than maximally clear about how this finite specification bears on the competence/performance distinction. After all, there are several paragraphs on the technical issue, but only one sentence on how that technical apparatus will give rise to a version of the competence/performance distinction that will help TPT. Be that as it may, we can venture the following conjecture. Consider a Turing machine that computes the successor function $S(x) = x + 1$. One such Turing machine has the following program,

s0 1 R s0
s0 0 1 s1.

The program simply scans to the right end of a string of 1's, adds one more, then halts. There is a sense in which any finite physical object realizing this program will have a bounded capacity for computing successors. There is some number x such that the physical object realizing this program cannot compute $S(x)$, since the object will run out of tape squares. Thus, the actual performance of the object will be bounded. Be this as it may, the physical object may be said to embody a competence for unbounded computation of the successor function.

There exists some finite specification of what the physical object is supposed to do, namely, our two-line program. This is, apparently, what Smolensky has in mind when he appeals to the finite specifiability of his unbounded networks. The finite specification constitutes a network's competence for unbounded computation.

Will this work?   Can Smolensky appeal to this dimension of the competence/performance to vindicate the TPT account of productivity? Apparently not. It is not enough that there exist a finite specification of how the task is to be done or how representations are to be constructed. The physical object that is said to have the competence must actually embody that finite description. The physical object must actually contain some finite number of physical components that constitute the realization of that competence. The requirement here is quite weak. It is not, for example, a requirement that the finite competence be realized in some finite quantity of physical matter *constituting explicit rules*, it is only the requirement that the finite competence be realized in some finite quantity of material.[9] In the case of the physical object realizing the Turing machine described above, the finite physical basis is whatever happens to realize the two lines of the program. If the lines of the program were merely something that we as observers possessed, but were not part of the physical object realizing the Turing machine, then barring some other source of the object's competence, the machine would lack the competence for computing the successor function. So, does a connectionist network realizing TPT have this finite physical basis? If we sift through the technical details of Smolensky's proposal, we find that his simple characterization involves an *unbounded* recursion matrix $\mathbf{R}$ given by $\mathbf{R} = 1 + \mathbf{I} \otimes \mathbf{I} + \mathbf{I} \otimes \mathbf{I} \otimes \mathbf{I} + \ldots$, where $\mathbf{I}$ is an identity matrix containing 1's on the diagonal and 0's everywhere else.[10] Given the way that Smolensky proposes to have networks realize matrices, a finite network cannot physically realize $\mathbf{R}$. So, this particular take on the competence/performance distinction will not work, hence TPT has yet to provide a way of explaining the productivity of thought. That is, Smolensky has given us no way to account for the sense in which a normal human being can produce an unbounded number of distinct thoughts. Granted the details of the weakness in Smolensky's account differs from the details of the weakness in the Pure Atomistic case. Nevertheless Smolensky's TPT has yet to provide a satisfactory explanation of the productivity of thought.

What of the other systematic features of cognition? Smolensky says that TPT has not yet advanced to the point where it can be applied to the systematicity of inference, so that he has little to say, other than that it is possible to adopt a Classical account of the systematicity of inference (Cf., Smolensky, 1995, p. 263, pp. 269-271). Accordingly, there is not much to say here either, save perhaps for the fact that relying on the Classical explanation of the systematicity of inference does nothing to meet the challenge Fodor and Pylyshyn lay down. Again, the challenge to TPT is to have TPT *qua TPT*, rather that TPT *qua realizer of Classicism*, explain the systematicity of inference. Further, relying on the Classical explanation does nothing to confirm TPT. Consider, then, the content relations among possible occurrent thoughts. Clearly on the TPT account, it is possible to represent both John loves Mary and Mary loves John. The "lexical" vectors can occur in either of two places in the binary branching trees, hence can be either subject or object of the proposition.[11] So, it would appear that there is a TPT account of the compositional character of thought.

The problem facing this account of the content relations in thought is a dilemma. TPT allows well-formed representations of John loves Mary and Mary loves John, but it also allows well-formed representations of loves loves loves, John loves loves, Mary Mary John, and a host of other pseudo-propositions. Thus, it would appear to be a consequence of TPT that any normal human being who has the capacity to think that John loves Mary will also have the capacity to think that Mary loves John, loves loves loves, John loves loves, Mary Mary John, and a host of other preposterous "thoughts." So, unadorned the theory runs afoul of a kind of superabundance of representational power. Yet, we can surely imagine that Smolensky wants some principles that allows different subsets of the set of all possible strings to count as grammatical. In particular, he appears to want the principles of Harmony Theory to do this. Without going into any of the technical details, we can say that the central idea of Harmony Theory is that the weights on connections determine relative well-formedness. As we saw, in Chapter 6, though, what weights are placed on connections is not currently subject to independent confirmation. Were we to know that the weights on the connections in a connectionist network play this kind of role in cognition, then Connectionism would already be established as the architecture of cognition. This conclusion is exactly what we should expect given what we encountered with Classicism. Insofar as the principles of Harmony Theory are supposed to provide the mechanism whereby a connectionist network can be said to compute one grammar, rather than another, these principles will be just as much lacking in independent empirical support as are the rules constituting a Classical grammar.

What of the systematicity of cognitive representations? Is there some way in which TPT can make the capacity for one thought nomologically necessary and sufficient for another thought capacity? The tensor on the left is a TPT representation of John's loving Mary, while the tensor on the right is a TPT representation of Mary's loving John.

82 80 78		58 68 78
108 108 108		60 84 109
52 48 44		34 36 38
70 68 66		34 44 27
26 24 22		17 18 19
35 34 33		12 22 27 |.

It is not at all clear what TPT might say to have these capacities, or any others, be mutually nomologically necessary and sufficient for the other. The whole Classicist approach of explaining mutual necessary and sufficiency in terms of completely shared cognitive capacities is simply unavailable. No case is here offered that TPT can't meet the challenge, but there is really nothing on offer. Smolensky simply does not address this kind of systematicity.

There is, however, a possibility that merits some exploration. We might notice that both of the tensors above have a 78 component in the upper right portion of the matrix. This suggests that there is at least some basis for a TPT account of a limited degree of systematicity of cognitive representations. Two representations have a kind of weak intrinsic connection insofar as they share common elements. That is, the reason the capacity for the thought that John loves Mary is to some extent dependent on the capacity for the thought that Mary loves John is that they have a common underlying capacity. Here TPT takes a cue from Classicism in trying to explain a weak intrinsic connection in terms of shared capacities. Nevertheless, the TPT account is non-Classical. Even though the common capacity to which TPT appeals is in some sense a common syntactic item, or part of a syntactic item, this item does not have a semantic value unto itself. It is, therefore, to that extent, non-Classical. Thus, there appears to be a non-Classical explanation of the dependencies among thoughts.[12]

Still, this attempt to explain even a limited degree of systematicity does not succeed. The fact that the representation for John loves Mary and the representation for Mary loves John share but one common component may suggest that systematicity of cognitive representations displayed by TPT is merely a chance feature of particular parameters chosen in our scheme of tensor product representations. Given our initial choice of vectors for L and R, along with the vectors that constitute our "lexical" representations, we find tensors in which there are common elements, hence among which there are dependencies. Yet, it is also possible to select "lexical" and "functional" vectors that do not give rise to dependencies. In particular, if we have "lexical atoms" such that

| 4 3 | means John,

| 5 8 | means loves, and
| 7 9 | means Mary,

and let, L = |3 5 7| and R = | 2 3 11 |, then we get tensor product representations of John loves John, John loves Mary, Mary loves John, and Mary loves Mary, such that there are no common components in the tensors. (The details are provided in Appendix B below.) Thus, given a tensor product system of representation, we can as easily have the systematicity of cognitive representations as not. It is not entirely clear how much freedom the choice of L, R, and the "lexical" vectors gives us in making tensor product representations mutually independent. Nevertheless, hypothesizing that cognition uses tensor product representations does not imply that cognition involves even weak intrinsic connections among thought capacities. Of course, even if we were to add some hypothesis that leads a tensor product system to generate a weakly systematic set of representations, we would have to have some independent confirmation of this hypothesis in order to meet the challenge of Fodor and Pylyshyn's explanatory standard. This, however, would appear to be hard to come by. There is surely no independent confirmation for one particular choice of L and R over another, short of the verification of TPT. Moreover, there is no independent confirmation for the choice of one set of vectors to constitute the "atomic" representations over another set. These sorts of hypotheses, thus, have the arbitrary character that we have come to reject as an insufficient basis for explaining the counterfactual dependencies in thought.

What can TPT say about the co-occurrence regularities? Is there any TPT reason why content relations among representations should co-occur with mutual dependencies? Evidently not. On the one hand, it is possible to get contentfully related tensor product representations that do not have common elements. This was mentioned above and is illustrated in Appendix B. On the other hand, it is also possible to get dependencies among tensor product representations even when the tensor product representations are not contentfully related. An illustration of this point is worked out in Appendix C. As for the co-occurrence of synchronic and diachronic systematicity, we are at something of a loss, since there is no provision for concept acquisition, hence diachronic systematicity, in TPT.

At this point, anyone who has followed the debate between Smolensky and Fodor, et al., will have noticed that the Classicist critique of TPT that has been offered here diverges quite dramatically from that in Fodor, (1996). Fodor contends that the TPT explanation of the systematic family of cognitive properties is parasitic on the Classical explanation:

Smolensky proposes that the classical theory will do the hard work of explaining compositionality, systematicity, etc., and then [TPT] will give the *same* explanation except for replacing "constituent" with "derived constituent" and "explain" with "acausally explain" throughout. . . . This way of proceeding has, in Russell's famous phrase, all the virtues of theft over honest toil (Fodor, 1996, p. 116, cf. p. 109).

Despite our tendency to take a Classicist line in these debates, there appear to be some easy responses available to Smolensky. In fact, some of the points we have raised in the course of our discussion of the various systematicity arguments in this and earlier chapters will help make this clearer.

To begin with, there is Fodor's charge that the TPT account is parasitic on the Classical account. There is, of course, some basis for concern about this. Smolensky proposes to use tensors to code binary branching trees. Tree structures, however, are paradigmatic examples of Classical representations insofar as they have a concatenative combinatorial syntax and semantics and insofar as they satisfy the Principles of Semantic Compositionality and Context Independence. Yet, it is in principle possible for Smolensky to dodge this objection insofar as he is able to develop TPT in a way that does not depend on postulating Classical cognitive representations. Clearly, there is no need to say that the binary branching trees that are being coded are cognitive representations, rather than, say, sentences of a natural language. That is to say that the input to the coding process can be sentences of a natural language, rather than sentences of a putative mentalese. Smolensky can, therefore, say that the Tensor Product Theory of cognitive representations does not depend on the Classical Theory *of cognitive representations*.

What if Fodor notes that a Tensor Product Theory built on encodings of the combinatorialism in natural language sentences is still parasitic on a Classical version of some sorts of representations? Smolensky might then develop the Tensor Product Theory on the basis of the structure of propositions. Since Classicism is not a theory of the structure of propositions. It would appear to take some heavy metaphysics to keep Smolensky from finding something sufficiently non-Classical to have TPT encode. So, the first thing to observe in response to Fodor's critique is that TPT is not, in Fodor's phrase, "hopelessly parasitic" on the Classical account.

The second thing to observe is that Smolensky does not really propose to explain the systematicity of cognitive representations, etc. in the way sketched by Fodor. More cautiously, Smolensky does not really *have to* propose to explain the systematicity of cognitive representations, etc. in the way Fodor sketches. It is not, or need not, be the case that Classicism explains the semantic relatedness of possible thoughts, the systematicity of cognitive representations, etc., while TPT gives the same explanations except for replacing "constituent" with "derived constituent" and "explain" with "acausally explain." The TPT account of the productivity of thought does not work this way. Nor does the TPT account of the content relatedness of possible occurrent thoughts cited above work this way.[13] Nor does the account we offered of the dependencies of thought go this way. In fact, in each case, the dubious notion of an "acausal" explanation need not be invoked. Instead, the causal properties of actually tokened tensors might be supposed to be doing the explanatory work. Smolensky himself may choose to go a more metaphysically exotic route, but at the least one can envision a version of TPT were the Fodorian metaphysics of explanation is respected. The short of this seems to be that the more telling criticism of TPT is to be found in the earlier work of Fodor & Pylyshyn, (1988), and Fodor & McLaughlin, (1990), rather than in Fodor, (1996).

3 TAKING STOCK

In some respects this chapter constitutes the high point of our discussion. Each of the preceding chapters has developed ideas and analyses that have shaped the analysis we have just given of Smolensky's Tensor Product Theory, the view that is widely taken to be the most significant response to the Classical challenge based on the many kinds of productivity and systematicity. Chapter 2 presented some historical cases of explanatory confirmation in action, then attempted to develop a theoretical analysis of what is common to these cases and how this bears on the systematicity and productivity arguments. Chapters 3 through 6 clarified and refined the productivity and systematicity arguments using the simplest possible alternative to Classicism, namely, Pure Atomism. The simplicity of Pure Atomism allowed us to focus on what one might call the logic of the arguments and postpone exegetical issues surrounding Connectionism and the species of Functional Combinatorialism. Chapter 7 was the first chapter that showed how to extend the analysis of the systematicity and productivity arguments to Connectionist models that have to a greater or lesser degree been construed as responses to Fodor and Pylyshyn's challenge. Those with vaguely Connectionist sympathies have often inclined to theories of Functional Combinatorialism as the proper strategy for responding to Fodor and Pylyshyn's challenge. Within the Functional Combinatorial approach, the idea of Gödel numerals has been to used to demonstrate the philosophically unproblematic character of such functionally combinatorial representations, while Smolensky's Tensor Product Theory has often been heralded as delivering the goods on an adequate response to the Classical challenge. This last, despite various cautionary, if sometimes optimistic, comments from Smolensky.[14]

In this chapter we first explored the idea that Functional Combinatorialism can explain the productive and systematic features of cognition using one version of Functional Combinatorialism, namely, a kind of Gödel numerals theory of cognition. There we saw that the Gödel numerals theory provides a computationally adequate account of productivity. By contrast, it suffers from the same sorts of problems as does Classicism when it comes to the familiar conceptions of the systematicity of cognitive representations, the compositionality of representations, and systematicity of inference. Further, we saw that the Gödel numerals theory proves to be weaker than Classicism when it comes to the explanation of the co-occurrence regularities. Classicism provides a compelling explanation of these co-occurrences, where the Gödel numerals theory does not.

As for the much acclaimed Tensor Product Theory, we have reason to think it does not rise to any of the Classical challenges. Despite considerable efforts to explain the productivity of thought, Smolensky provides no adequate sense in which a finite being can be said to possess a capacity for an unbounded number of distinct thoughts. His account founders on the fact that he can provide no finite basis that would constitute a human being's capacity to generate arbitrarily many representations. To put the matter informally, the problem is that he shows no finite component that would constitute a finite being's "know how" in constructing an unbounded number of distinct representations. With regards to the systematicity of inference, Smolensky offers no account, only some optimistic comments about the prospects for TPT. The co-occurrence of diachronic and synchronic systematicity is in a similar state. We simply have no TPT account of diachronic systematicity.

With regards to the systematicity of cognitive representations, i.e., one thought capacity being nomologically necessary and sufficient for another, Smolensky gives us no account of how this could occur. The Classicist idea of fully common representational capacities is the only idea on the table. Smolensky does, however, provide resources with which one can use the Classicist idea of sharing of representational capacities to generate some "weak intrinsic connections" between TPT representations. These resources cannot, however, do this without relying on some arbitrary hypothesis. The use of, for example, Harmony Theory to specify the weights on connections between nodes may, in principle, allow TPT to generate one grammar rather than another, hence some weak intrinsic connections, rather than no intrinsic connections. The problem with this approach is that hypotheses about particular weights playing a particular role in specifying a grammar, or the connections among thought capacities, cannot be confirmed independent of the truth of TPT.

The compositionality of representations fares much as does the systematicity of cognitive representations. It is possible for tensor product representations to display semantically related contents. In fact, it might appear that tensor product theory suffers from a superabundance of compositionality insofar as it allows any content bearing vector to be combined with any other content bearing vector, leading to representations of loves John Mary, Mary Mary Mary, and so forth. If, however, principles regarding weights on connections are introduced, a la Harmony Theory, then we have a situation in which tensor product theory must rely on arbitrary hypotheses.

Finally, there is the challenge of explaining why content related occurrent thoughts are also mutually dependent. Although it is possible to select values of the "functional" and "lexical" vectors in a Tensor Product Theory to get semantically related thought capacities to have some degree of intrinsic connection, it is also possible to select values such that they do not occur. Although one can envision adding hypotheses that force systematicity and compositionality to co-occur, they will not suffice to meet the explanatory challenge that Fodor and Pylyshyn have in mind. There is no way that the set of hypotheses that is necessary for explaining the nomologically necessary and sufficient connections between thought capacities can entail that thought capacities are semantically related and no way that the set of hypotheses that is necessary for explaining why thought capacities are semantically related can entail that thought capacities are mutually nomologically necessary and sufficiently connected.

In our discussion of David Chalmers's active-passive transformation network in Chapter 7, we noted a distinction between an encoding network that produces distributed representations of active and passive sentences and the transformation network that maps distributed representations of active sentences onto distributed representations of passive sentences. In that discussion, we wondered about the role of the encoding network in a hypothetical cognitive economy. In the GN theory and TPT, we again have a distinction between encoding processes and the products of these encoding processes. Although we have explored one way in which GN might try to explain the systematicity and productive features of thought, the relationship between the encoding processes and the products of the encoding processes may leave some room for developing alternative attempts to explain the systematic and productive features of thought. Yet, it is an area from which no obvious accounts of systematicity and productivity emerge.

Having addressed the principal lines of response to the systematicity and productivity arguments, we will in the next chapter consider a less familiar alternative, Robert Cummins's theory of content, targets, and propositional attitudes.

APPENDIX A

There exist Gödel numeral representations in which weakly intrinsically connected thought capacities are not contentfully related, hence GN cannot explain the co-occurrence of even weak intrinsic connections and content relations in thought. Here is an example. Let our atomic representations be:

<1> with John loves Mary,
<2> with Ted hates Mark,
<3> with conjunction, and
<4> with disjunction.

For our intermediate ordered n-tuples we will use the following pairing:

<1> with John loves Mary,
<2> with Ted hates Mark,
<1, 3, 1> with John loves Mary and John loves Mary
<1, 3, 2> with John loves Mary and Ted hates Mark
<2, 3, 1> with Ted hates Mark and John loves Mary
<2, 3, 2> with Ted hates Mark and Ted hates Mark
<1, 4, 1> with John loves Mary or John loves Mary
<1, 4, 2> with John loves Mary or Ted hates Mark
<2, 4, 1> with Ted hates Mark or John loves Mary
<2, 4, 2> with Ted hates Mark or Ted hates Mark
. . .

Thus, our Gödel numerals will be:

"2" (2) means John loves Mary,
"4" (2^2) means Ted hates Mark,
"90" ($2 \times 3^3 \times 5$) means John loves Mary and John loves Mary,
"450" ($2 \times 3 \times 5^2$) means John loves Mary and Ted hates Mark
"60" ($2^2 \times 3 \times 5$) means Ted hates Mark and John loves Mary
"300" ($2^2 \times 3 \times 5^2$) means Ted hates Mark and Ted hates Mark
"810" ($2 \times 3^4 \times 5$) means with John loves Mary or John loves Mary
"4050" ($2 \times 3^4 \times 5^2$) means with John loves Mary or Ted hates Mark
"1620" ($2^2 \times 3^4 \times 5$) means with Ted hates Mark or John loves Mary
"8100" ($2^2 \times 3^4 \times 5^2$) means with Ted hates Mark or Ted hates Mark
. . .

On this scheme, there are weak intrinsic connections between "90" and "8100" yet these representations are completely semantically unrelated.

Incidently, even though "2" is semantically related to "90", "450", "300", "810", and "4050", there is no intrinsic connection between it and the other representations.

APPENDIX B

There exists a tensor product system of representation wherein representations with common contents lack common components. We show this for tensor product representations of John loves Mary and Mary loves Mary. In doing this, we assume that some principles, such as those of Harmony Theory, allow us to specify a grammar containing just the representations of these propositions.

$L = |3\ 5\ 7|$ and $R = |\ 2\ 3\ 11\ |$ are independent since there does not exist a value of c such that $|\ 3\ 5\ 7\ | = |c_2\ c_3\ c_{11}|$. If

|4 3 | means John,
|5 8 | means loves, and
|7 9 | means Mary,

and we combine them with L and R, we get,

| 12 20 28 | means "(John) on the left" | 8 12 44 | means "(John) on the right"
| 9 15 21 | | 6 9 33 |

| 15 25 35 | means "(loves) on the left" |10 15 55 | means "(loves) on the right"
| 24 40 56 | | 16 24 88 |

| 21 35 49 | means "(Mary) on the left" | 14 21 77 | means "(Mary) on the right"
| 27 45 81 | | 18 27 99 |

For our representation of John's loving Mary, we first combine the tensors for "(loves) on the left" and "(Mary) on the right". Thus, we have

| 29 46 112 | means "(loves) on the left - (Mary) on the right."
| 32 67 155 |

To make this the right branch of our root node, we perform tensor multiplication of this tensor with R:

| 29 46 112 | ⊗ | 2 3 11 | = | 58   92 224 |
| 32 67 155 | | 64 134 310 |
                                            | 87 138 336 |
                                            | 96 201 465 |
                                                   | 319 506 1232 |
                                                   | 352 737 1705 |.

Finally, we increase the rank of the "(John) on the left" tensor by adding null components and perform the relevant vector addition:

12 20 28		58 92 224		**70 112 252**
9 15 21		64 134 310		**73 149 331**
0 0 0	+	87 138 336	=	**87 138 336**
0 0 0		96 201 465		**96 201 465**
0 0 0		319 506 1232		**319 506 1232**
0 0 0		352 737 1705		**352 737 1705**

This gives us our final representation of John loves Mary.

For our representation of Mary loves John, we first use tensor addition to get

| 23 37 79 | means "(loves) on the left - (John) on the right."
| 30 49 89 |

Next we combine this tensor and R via tensor multiplication to get

| 23 37 79 | ⊗ | 2 3 11 | = | 46 74 158 |
| 30 49 89 | | 60 98 178 |
                                          | 69 111 237 |
                                          | 90 147 267 |
                                                 | 253 407 869 |
                                                 | 330 539 979 |.

Finally, vector addition of the expanded Mary-on-the-left representation gives us

$$
\begin{vmatrix} 21 & 35 & 49 \\ 27 & 45 & 81 \\ 0 & 0 & 0 \\ 0 & 0 & 0 \\ 0 & 0 & 0 \\ 0 & 0 & 0 \end{vmatrix} \quad + \quad \begin{vmatrix} 46 & 74 & 158 \\ 60 & 98 & 178 \\ 69 & 111 & 237 \\ 90 & 147 & 267 \\ 253 & 407 & 869 \\ 330 & 539 & 979 \end{vmatrix} \quad = \quad \begin{vmatrix} \mathbf{67} & \mathbf{109} & \mathbf{207} \\ \mathbf{87} & \mathbf{143} & \mathbf{259} \\ 69 & 111 & 237 \\ 90 & 147 & 267 \\ 253 & 407 & 869 \\ \mathbf{330} & \mathbf{539} & \mathbf{979} \end{vmatrix}.
$$

Clearly, the content-related representations of John's loving Mary and Mary's loving John, indicated in bold, have no common elements.

APPENDIX C

Here we show a system of tensor product representations in which two semantically unrelated representations are weakly intrinsically connected to one another. For this, we let L = |1 0 0| and R = |0 1 1|. As "lexical" vectors, let

| 4 3 | mean John,
| 5 8 | mean loves,
| 7 9 | mean Mary,
| 3 6 | mean Bill,
| 1 4 | mean calls, and
| 3 5 | mean Paul.

If we combine L and R with our lexical vectors we get

| 4 0 0 | means "(John) on the left" | 0 4 4 | means "(John) on the right"
| 3 0 0 | | 0 3 3 |

| 5 0 0 | means "(loves) on the left" | 0 5 5 | means "(loves) on the right"
| 8 0 0 | | 0 8 8 |

| 7 0 0 | means "(Mary) on the left" | 0 7 7 | means "(Mary) on the right"
| 9 0 0 | | 0 9 9 |

| 3 0 0 | means "(Bill) on the left" | 0 3 3 | means "(Bill) on the right."
| 6 0 0 | | 0 6 6 |

| 1 0 0 | means "(calls) on the left" | 0 1 1 | means "(calls) on the right"
| 4 0 0 | | 0 4 4 |

| 3 0 0 | means "(Paul) on the left" | 0 3 3 | means "(Paul) on the right."
| 5 0 0 | | 0 5 5 |

For our comparison, we want a representation of John loving Mary and Bill calling Paul. Take, first, the construction of the John-loves-Mary representation. We perform vector addition to get our tensor that means "(loves) on the left" and "(Mary) on the right":

| 5 7 7 | means "(loves) on the left - (Mary) on the right."
| 8 9 9 |

To make this the right branch of our root node, we perform a tensor multiplication of this tensor with R:

| 5 7 7 | ⊗ | 0 1 1 | = | 0 0 0 |
| 8 9 9 | | 0 0 0 |
                        | 5 7 7 |
                        | 8 9 9 |
                        | 5 7 7 |
                        | 8 9 9 |.

Finally, we increase the rank of the "(John) on the left" tensor by adding null components and perform a tensor addition to yield our representation of John loving Mary,

4 0 0		0 0 0		**4 0 0**
3 0 0		0 0 0		**3 0 0**
0 0 0	+	5 7 7	=	**5 7 7**
0 0 0		8 9 9		**8 9 9**
0 0 0		5 7 7		**5 7 7**
0 0 0		8 9 9		**8 9 9** |.

Now consider the construction of the Bill-calls-Paul tensor. Our initial vector addition gives us

| 1 3 3 | means "(calls) on the left - (Paul) on the right."
| 4 5 5 |

Performing tensor multiplication gives us the representation of "((calls) on the left - (Paul)on the right) on the right" with R gives us

$$
\begin{vmatrix} 1\ 3\ 3 \\ 4\ 5\ 5 \end{vmatrix} \otimes \begin{vmatrix} 0\ 1\ 1 \end{vmatrix} \;=\; \begin{matrix} |0\ 0\ 0| \\ |0\ 0\ 0| \\ |1\ 3\ 3| \\ |4\ 5\ 5| \\ |1\ 3\ 3| \\ |4\ 5\ 5|. \end{matrix}
$$

A subsequent vector addition with the expanded "(Bill) on the left" tensor gives us,

$$
\begin{matrix} |3\ 0\ 0| \\ |6\ 0\ 0| \\ |0\ 0\ 0| \\ |0\ 0\ 0| \\ |0\ 0\ 0| \\ |0\ 0\ 0| \end{matrix}
\quad + \quad
\begin{matrix} |0\ 0\ 0| \\ |0\ 0\ 0| \\ |1\ 3\ 3| \\ |4\ 5\ 5| \\ |1\ 3\ 3| \\ |4\ 5\ 5| \end{matrix}
\quad = \quad
\begin{matrix} |\mathbf{3\ 0\ 0}| \\ |\mathbf{6\ 0\ 0}| \\ |\mathbf{1\ 3\ 3}| \\ |\mathbf{4\ 5\ 5}| \\ |\mathbf{1\ 3\ 3}| \\ |\mathbf{4\ 5\ 5}|. \end{matrix}
$$

On this scheme, the tensor representing John loving Mary and the tensor representing Bill calling Paul, i.e., the two tensors in bold, are not semantically related, but they are nevertheless intrinsically connected in virtue of their common 0 components.

NOTES

1. Van Gelder, (1990), proposes that the function from syntactic atoms to syntactic molecules be computable. If, however, real-valued tensors are used in Smolensky's Tensor Product Theory and if van Gelder's definition of functional combinatorialism is to count Smolensky's theory as using functionally combinatorial representations, then we must not take van Gelder's "computable" to mean "Turing computable". Instead, van Gelder's notion of computability must presuppose some broader notion of computation that allows for real-valued arguments.

2. Cf., e.g., van Gelder, (1990), Cummins, (1996b).

3. Fodor & Pylyshyn, (1988), p. 28.

4. Technically speaking, if there is one computer program for doing a task, there are denumerably many. Just take a program that works and add gratuitous steps, like moving the read-write head of a Turing machine back and forth a number of times before getting to the "real work." We ignore this technical point in the discussion.

5. To forestall a possible object, we may not that, for any finite stock of thoughts, there will be some base for the expressing the Gödel numerals such that the base will not entail or nomologically lead to counterfactual dependencies among the thoughts

6. Although Smolensky appears to want to treat the L and R vectors as something like functional categories in transformational grammars, it is not clear that they might not also be thought of as purely syntactic items, such as parentheses.

7. The foregoing exposition ignored certain niceties. One might wonder about what concept of meaning or representation is at work when we claim that the various simple and complex vectors mean such things as John, (John) on the left, (loves) on the left - (Mary) on the right, and John loves Mary. It is doubtful that one notion of meaning or representation is at work here. Then there is the impropriety in the use of quotation marks. These niceties are ignored in order to facilitate the principal points of Smolensky's tensor product theory and because there seems to be little of scientific or philosophical good to be gained by the additional attention that would be needed to formulate these matters properly.

8. This is a highly conservative estimate of the number of nodes required. If the R and L vectors have k components, and the lexical vectors have m components, then just the output layer of a network will need at least kmn components.

9. John Bickle suggested that this feature of the requirement be added.

10. Cf., Smolensky, (1995), pp. 259-260, 248, fn., 24, p.284.

11. Cf., Smolensky, (1995), p. 263.

12. Technically, we do not have a counterfactual dependence of one tensor upon another. The reasoning here is essentially the same as what we saw in our earlier discussion of GN. The loss of the capacity to produce one tensor might not precipitate the loss of the capacity to produce another, since the loss of the one might be due to a component not found in the other. Here we grant to Smolensky, for the sake of argument, that we can generate a true counterfactual dependence between one tensor and another. Even with this quite significant concession, Smolensky cannot use TPT to explain the systematic features of thought.

13. Recall Smolensky, (1995), p. 263.

14. Cf., Smolensky, (1995), pp. 263, 269-271.

CHAPTER 9

AN ALTERNATIVE COGNITIVE ARCHITECTURE

Chapters 3 through 6 examined the bearing of the systematicity and productivity arguments on cognitive architectures that were committed to Representationalism and the Computational Theory of the Attitudes. Chapter 7 extended this examination to two Connectionist models, models that were committed to Representationalism and at least not obviously inconsistent with the Computational Theory of the Attitudes. Chapter 8 extended the argument to two versions of Functionally Combinatorial theories of cognitive representations. Now, in this chapter, we shall consider an alternative cognitive architecture that part ways with both Representationalism and CTA, namely, an architecture based on Robert Cummins's very interesting work on naturalizing meaning in *Representations, Targets, and Attitudes*. While Cummins believes that cognition involves computational processes and representations, he does not accept Representationalism or the Computational Theory of the Attitudes found in Classicism. Insofar as the many kinds of systematicity and productivity are *bona fide* features of human cognition, however, it is relevant to ask how this alternative cognitive architecture, designed to meet other explanatory ends, fares when facing the family of systematicity and productivity arguments. What we find is that, despite Cummins's attempt to find an architectural alternative Classicism, in the end the theory retains hypotheses that attempt to explain systematicity and productivity through recourse to Classical principles implemented in a new ontology.

Because Cummins's approach differs from Classicism in so many fundamental respects, we will have to spend a bit of time motivating this alternative conception. As was explained in Chapter 1, Classicism is committed to the idea that cognitive science will prove to be, in large measure at least, a science of propositional attitudes. It assumes that most, if not all, of cognition is a matter of agents having particular attitudes, such as believing, hoping, fearing, and worrying, toward various propositional contents, such as that it is raining, that George Washington was the first President of the United States, or that the rise of multinational corporations is a threat to world democracy. Classicism divides the labor of accounting for the nature of the attitudes between Representationalism and the Computational Theory of the Attitudes. The doctrine of Representationalism accounts for the propositional contents to which agents have attitudes, while the Computational Theory of the Attitudes has it that properties of a hypothetical computer program of the mind account for the attitudes. Thus, if A believes that p, then there is some representation r in A that means that p and a computational property of A that constitutes A's attitude of believing.

Questions relating to the structure of cognitive representations have been one area of Classical investigation. Another area has been the attempt to provide naturalistic conditions under which the hypothesized syntactic structures in the mind come to have the semantic contents they do.   That is, Classical Representationalists have sought conditions under which some syntactic item r has content p, where those conditions do not involve terms that presuppose semantic notions such as "means," "designates," "refers to," and so forth. Throughout the foregoing discussion we have supposed that molecular representations, if there be such, have the semantic content they do in virtue of some relation they stand in to the atomic representations from which they are derived. For the atomic representations, however, we have simply supposed that there are naturalistic conditions in virtue of which atomic representations have the contents they do without in any way specifying what those conditions might be. Yet, it cannot be that cognitive agents think what they do in virtue of the stipulations or stance-takings of cognitive scientists or other observers. The buck for having cognitive content must stop somewhere, with some cognitive agent who has the thoughts and beliefs she does, not in virtue of another's stipulation or stance-taking. Else, how could the whole project of stipulating and stance-taking get off the ground? At least, so reasons the Classicist.

A leading family of theories of naturalized semantics has been so-called "informational" approaches.[1]   According to these approaches, certain representations, the semantically complex or molecular representations, get their contents in virtue of the meanings of their constituent atomic representations and the way in which those atomic representations are put together. This much is a straightforward part of Classicism. Atomic representations cannot, of course, get their meaning in this way. Very roughly, the idea behind informational semantics is that the atomic representations get the content they do in virtue of the informational, nomological, or causal relations they bear to objects in the external world. Thus, the electrical activity in a set of neurons might have the meaning red if that activity is informationally or lawfully or causally connected to red things in the environment. The electrical activity in another set of neurons might mean horizontal line if that activity is produced as a response to horizontal lines in the environment. The same is supposed to hold *mutatis mutandis* for other objects in the environment.

While the specific variants of the informational approach suffer their specific setbacks, the leading problem for all versions of informational semantics has been the so-called "disjunction problem."[2]   Suppose that an informational approach maintains that electrical activity r in some set of neurons means horse. Presumably, it is possible for a cognitive agent to mistake, say, a dog for a horse. This might happen when the agent sees the dog at a distance under poor lighting conditions. But, it would appear that the electrical activity r might have the same nomological, causal, or informational connection to a dog at a distance under low light as it does to a horse in the middle distance under moderate light. But, given that such a dog and such a horse equally produce r's, it would appear that the information theorist would have to be committed to saying that r means something like horse or dog, rather than horse. That is, r would have the disjunctive content dog or horse, rather than the univocal content horse. Worse still, if r means horse or dog, rather than merely horse, then, contrary to one's initial expectation, a tokening of r in the presence of a dog at a distance under poor lighting conditions is never an instance of mistaking a dog for a horse, hence never an error. In other words, if the agent produces r when presented with the dog at a distance in poor light, rather than mistaking the dog for a horse, the agent appears to be correctly thinking that a horse or dog is present. Indeed, it appears that errors of mistaking one thing for another are not possible on informational semantics.

There have, of course, been numerous attempts to address the disjunction problem while remaining true to the central idea of informational approaches, none of which has been found to be very convincing. Rather than exploring further options within the informational approach, however, Cummins proposes to move in a new direction. Cummins suggests that informational approaches are fundamentally ill-suited to handling the disjunction problem insofar as they do not draw a distinction between the target of a tokening of a representation r and the content of r. The target of r is what r *is supposed to* represent on a given occasion, whereas the content of r is what r actually represents. Error is the consequence of the target of a given token of r differing from the content of r. To put matters in another way, Cummins contends that naturalized theories of content need to recognize two factors in the tokening of a representation: the target to which a particular use of a representation is applied and the content of the representation. Thus, in the horse/dog example just considered, we may suppose that there exists in the agent a system V that is dedicated to representing the contents of the visual field. The agent commits an error when, in the presence of a dog in the local visual field, V tokens a representation r_1 with the content horse, when it should have tokened a representation r_2 with the content dog. To repeat, Cummins maintains that an error is occasioned when target and content diverge.

Having made the case for a need to distinguish between the target of a given token of r and the content of r, Cummins must have an independent theory of each. That is, Cummins needs a theory of content and a theory of target fixation.

As a theory of content, Cummins adopts what he calls the Picture Theory of Representation (PTR). According to this theory, the representation relation is simply an isomorphism relation between one relational structure **R** and another relational structure **C**, where relational structures are understood in the model theoretic sense. In other words, objects, relations, and states of affairs in the structure **R** represent objects, relations, and states of affairs in the structure **C** just in case

    1) for every object in the universe of discourse of **C**, there is exactly one object in the universe of discourse of **R**,

    2) for every relation in **C**, there is exactly one relation in **R**, and

    3) whenever a relation in **C** holds of a given n-tuple in **C**, the corresponding relation in **R** holds of the corresponding n-tuple in **R**.

As a theory of target fixation, Cummins supposes that there exist cognitive subsystems and that such subsystems, or combinations of subsystems, have identifiable functions. These functions might be such things as indicating what is currently in an agent's visual field, determining the syntactic structure of the sentence currently being heard, and calculating the sum of two numbers. These subsystems determine that a given tokening of a representation is aimed at what is currently in an agent's visual field, the syntactic structure of the sentence currently being heard, and the sum of two numbers, respectively.

Prima facie, Cummins's distinction between target and representation and his two subtheories of them could be rendered compatible with much of Classicism. So, to begin with, one might suppose that the Classicist's computer program of the mind, causally sensitive to the structure of cognitive representations and responsible for implementing the various attitudes, might at the same time constitute subsystems of the mind that fix targets. Further, consistent with Cummins's Picture Theory of Representation, Classicists could continue to maintain that there exist atomic and molecular cognitive representations and that the molecular representations mean what they do in virtue of the meanings of the parts and the way in which those parts are put together satisfying the hypothesis of context independence of content. But, whereas a Classicist like Fodor maintains that the atomic mental representations mean what they do in virtue of some informational account, a Classicist could adopt Cummins's approach and maintain that atomic representations mean what they do in virtue of their place in a relational structure **R** that is isomorphic to another relational structure **C**. Thus, rather than "John" meaning John in virtue of "John" standing in an informational, or nomological, or causal relation to John, the alternative would be to have "John" meaning John in virtue of "John" being part of a relational structure **R** that is isomorphic to a relational structure in the world **C** containing John. This approach would respect the Representationalist idea that in order for an agent to

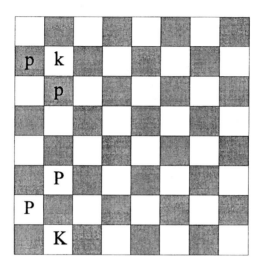

Figure 9.1. A Chessboard layout.

have an attitude to the proposition p, the agent must have a representation r that means that p. Cummins's ideas to this point might, thus, be made consonant with both the Computational Theory of Attitudes and the Classicist form of Representationalism. Cummins, however, chooses to break with Classicism.

Cummins rejects the Representationalist idea that having an attitude toward a proposition that p involves having a representation r that means that p. In essence, his rejection of Representationalism is based on an interpretation of the operation of various computing devices. Imagine a chess playing program Σ that represents the positions of pieces on a chess board using a fixed 8x8 matrix POS(x,y), where the value of a row and column is either one of the chess pieces or a blank. Thus, the chessboard shown in Figure 9.1 is specified with the following assignment of values to POS(x,y):

POS (2,1) := p,
POS (2,2) := k,
POS (3,2) := p,
POS (6,2) := P,
POS (7,1) := P,
POS (8,2) := K,

with the remainder of POS(x,y) being assigned 0s. Further, let Σ have a subroutine CURR_POSS_OPP_KING that takes the POS(x,y) data structure as input and produces as output the current position of the opponent's king. Thus, CURR_POS_OPP_KING writes something like "KR8" or "KB8" on its output tape. Clearly this subroutine has the function of determining the current position of the opponent's king, hence, according to Cummins, this subroutine has as its target the current position of the opposing king. In other words, this subroutine aims to report the current position of the opposing king.

Cummins does not spell out just how a program and data structure will, in general, conspire to determine attitude contents, but does suggest that, were we to attribute some propositional attitude to Σ, it might be that Σ believes that the current position of the opponent's king is KR8. Yet, contrary to Classicism's form of Representationalism, neither the system nor the subroutine contains a representation r that means that the current position of the opponent's king is KR8. The data structure "KR8" evidently means the king rook 8 square on the chess board. On Cummins's theory, therefore, a computer program of the mind and its data structures combine to yield a propositional attitude, but not via the neat division of labor envisioned by Fodorian Classicism. Where Fodorian Classicists maintain that the content toward which an agent has an attitude is determined entirely by properties of the computing device's representational data structures, Cummins proposes to distribute the work of specifying this content over both computer program and data structure.

Although our principal concern here is with the impact of the productivity and systematicity arguments on Cummins's proposed architecture of cognition, it would be a mistake to see these arguments as the leading challenges facing Cummins's theory. Truth be told, the systematicity arguments appear to be among the less fundamental difficulties facing Cummins's proposal. In order to keep a proper perspective on the relative importance of these issues, it might be well to consider just briefly the other relatively more fundamental issues, before turning to the relatively less fundamental.

The most obvious problems facing Cummins's architecture concern the Picture Theory of Representation. Could the representation relation really be a matter of isomorphism? Representation in any familiar conception is an asymmetric relation, where isomorphism is a symmetric relation. The "+" sign represents the addition function, but the addition function does not represent "+". Cummins deals with many more subtle objections to his theory than this one, but does nothing to address the rather traditional sort of challenge to picture theories. Goodman, (1947), for example, objected to picture theories of representation that relied on a notion of resemblance, since resemblance is a symmetric relation, where representation is an asymmetric relation.

A second, less obvious, problem is that representation as isomorphism threatens to lead to what might be called "pansemanticism," where everything has a meaning or everything is a representation. Consider any object that has a property. This will define a relational structure R with a universe of discourse having one object and just one property. Now consider any other object with another property. This will define a relational structure C with a universe of discourse having one object and one just on property. Obviously, **R** and **C** will be isomorphic relational structures, so **R** will represent **C**. In fact, given the symmetry of an isomorphism, **C** will represent **R**. In fact, it also turns out that **R** will represent itself, since a relational structure is trivially isomorphic to itself. This does not strictly show that literally everything is a representation, but it surely makes representation a strikingly pervasive feature of the natural world. For example, every object with a mass constitutes a representation of anything that has a mass. Every object with a velocity constitutes a representation of anything that has a mass. What could fit the usual conception of representation any worse? The problem here is the ubiquity of relational structures. There is simply no such thing as *the* unique relational structure to which a thing belongs. A single object belongs to many definable relational structures. To speak metaphorically, the world does not come parsed into the single relational structure. The relational structure of the world is not a given. Solving the pansemanticism problem would, thus, seem to involve saying that some relational structures count as representational relational structures, where some do not. But, Cummins gives us no hint as to how this might be done.

The foregoing two observations indicate that isomorphism of relational structure leads to a highly counterintuitive notion of representation. In response, Cummins might wish simply to abandon our "folk" conception of representation and all of its attendant intuitions. All that might really matter for cognitive science is isomorphism of relational structures with all of its differences from the "folk" notion of representation. Perhaps cognitive science can dispense with a primitive, antiquated folk notion of representation in favor of the theoretically advanced notion of isomorphism of relational structure.

The foregoing representational eliminativist line will not work, however. Cummins can run from the pansemantic problem, but he cannot hide. Even if we accept the idea that we should eliminate our "folk" conception of representation, Cummins will still have to face the consequences of the ubiquity of isomorphism. The ubiquity of isomorphism still gives rise to what we might call the "loss of epistemic determinacy." Suppose that our chess subroutine CURR_POS_OPP_KING produces as output "KR8". Cummins wants to say that, in tokening "KR8", the chess playing program believes that the opponent's king is at the king rook 8 square. To this end, he apparently presupposes that "KR8" is part of a relational structure **R** having the universe of discourse consisting of the 64 squares of the chess board, along with various properties and relations. Yet, even though "KR8" is a part of some such relational structure, "KR8" is also part of other relational structures. As we noted above, there is no such thing as *the* relational structure of which "KR8" is a part. So, consider a relational structure in which "KR8" is the lone item in the universe of discourse of **R'** and that there is only one property that "KR8" has. Now consider the following 64 relational structures

C_1 : UD = {the king rook 1 square},
      P = the property of being occupied or unoccupied,
C_2 : UD = {the king rook 2 square},
      P = the property of being occupied or unoccupied,
C_3 : UD = {the king rook 3 square},
      P = the property of being occupied or unoccupied,

    ....

C_{64} : UD = {the queen rook 8 square},
      P = the property of being occupied or unoccupied.

Since, **R** is isomorphic to each of C_1, C_2, ..., C_{64}, the Picture Theory of Representation would seem to have no basis for saying that system Σ believes that the current position of the opponent's king is the king rook 8 square, rather than that Σ has the belief that the current position of the opponent's king is any other square of the chessboard. Indeed, the Picture Theory would seem to have no basis for saying that Σ has beliefs about chess, rather than beliefs about any other isomorphic relational structure. The fundamental problem, to reiterate, lies in Cummins's apparent assumption that a given object participates in exactly one relational structure.

The foregoing constitutes simply the opening salvo for the symmetry problem, the pansemanticism problem, and the loss of epistemic determinacy problem. Perhaps they will prove to be more tractable than the old disjunction problem, but their simplicity doesn't bode well for Cummins. Be this as it may, we now can turn to Cummins's hints as to how his theory will accommodate the productive and systematic characteristics of thought. Since Cummins provides no hint as to how the systematicity of inference might be explained, we will skip this. Further, since it is unclear how Cummins's theory will handle the co-occurrence of diachronic and synchronic systematicity, we shall also leave this matter alone.

Cummins believes his theory of targets and attitudes can explain the productivity of thought by appeal to the nesting of subroutines.[3] A cognitive architecture of the sort he envisions is able to generate an unbounded number of representations by making the appropriate number of iterations through recursive subroutines. Although the exact details are omitted, the idea might be reconstructed as follows. Suppose that, in addition to the CURR_POS_OPP_KING subroutine, our chess playing program also has a NEG subroutine which provides the negation of a sentential argument passed to it. With recursive calls, we get the following set of propositional attitudes in our chess program Σ:

When CURR_POS_OPP_KING (POS(x,y)) = KR8, the system believes the opponent's king is at king rook 8,

When NEG(CURR_POS_OPP_KING (POS(x,y)) = KR8), the system believes that it is not the case that the opponent's king is at king rook 8,

When NEG(NEG(CURR_POS_OPP_KING (POS(x,y)) = KR8)), the system believes that it is not that case that it is not the case that the opponent's king is at king rook 8,

. . .

Given that the recursive nesting of subroutines is a perfectly acceptable feature of a Turing-equivalent computational system, the proposal makes use of Classically acceptable apparatus. Since there is no bound on the number of recursive calls to a subroutine, there is no bound on the number of distinct propositional attitudes that this sort of architecture can have. There is, of course, a memory space limitation on the actual number of recursive calls that any physical machine might make, but there remains a finite physical basis, namely, a computer program, that will constitute a device's capacity for generating an unbounded number of distinct representations. Since all the computational apparatus to which Cummins appeals is Classical, Cummins appears to have an account of the productivity of thought that Classicists must accept.

The principal concern one might have with this explanation is the extent to which it constitutes a genuine alternative to the Classical account. Clearly Cummins's architecture rejects the Classical variety of Representationalism according to which having a cognitive attitude toward a content p involves having a representation r that means that p. In other words, Cummins believes that representations are involved in cognition, but not in the way that we have been using the term "Representationalism." Yet, other features of Cummins's theory appear to be Classical. In particular, the parts of Cummins's theory that are invoked to explain the productivity of thought, the combinatorial syntax and semantics, appear to be Classical. Notice that, on Cummins's theory, there is a distinction between atomic and molecular representations. An atomic representation r gets its content in virtue of satisfying the conditions of the Picture Theory of Representation. Molecular representations, by contrast, get their content from atomic representations and the computational subroutines through which they are processed. So, when a representation of the chess board configuration given by POS(x,y) causes the subroutine CURR_POS_OPP_KING to produce a "KR8" as output, Σ will be thinking that the current position of the opponent's king is king rook 8, whereas if POS(x,y) causes the subroutine MY_NEXT_MOVE to produce a "KB, KR8" Σ will be thinking that its next move will take the king's bishop to king rook 8. Now recall the sequence of structures that Σ displays

(*)   CURR_POS_OPP_KING (POS(x,y)) = KR8,
       NEG(CURR_POS_OPP_KING (POS(x,y)) = KR8),
       NEG(NEG(CURR_POS_OPP_KING (POS(x,y)) = KR8)),
       NEG(NEG(NEG(CURR_POS_OPP_KING (POS(x,y)) = KR8)))
       . . .

On this combinatorial scheme, syntactically complex representations contain syntactically simpler representations as proper parts. Further, something like the Classical Principle of Semantic Compositionality is satisfied. The content of a propositional attitude is a function of the meaning of its atomic representations and the way in which those atomic representations are combined to form complex representational states. This is not exactly the Principle of Semantic Compositionality embodied in Classicism, since the Classical principle concerns only the hypothetical representational data structures. Yet, the Classical Principle of Semantic Compositionality is there up to the level of the ontology implementing it, so to speak. Moreover, something like the Classical Principle of Context Independence, according to which each syntactic atom makes the same semantic contribution to every context in which it occurs, also holds. The Classical Principle of Context Independence itself does not hold, since the Classical principle concerns representational data structures. Yet again, we have a principle that is like the Classical principle, differing only in the ontology to which it applies. So, it looks as though Cummins's architecture succeeds in explaining the productivity of thought by virtue of relying on a more or less minor revision of Classicism. The Classical idea is that productivity is possible because of concatenative combinatorialism, but Cummins's idea appears to rely on an alternative implementation of concatenative combinatorialism.

Before we move to the systematicity of cognitive representations, we should consider how the preceding point fares given another possible interpretation of the ontology of Cummins's theory. In the preceding argument, we supposed that the system's beliefs involve representational states containing structures corresponding to the items in (*) listed above. To put the matter in other words, we were supposing that an instantaneous description of the total state of Σ contains structures corresponding to each of the members of (*). But, an alternative supposition is that each member of (*) stands for an act Σ performs, rather than a proper part of a state Σ goes through. Thus, CURR_POS_OPP_KING (POS(x,y)) = KR8 indicates that the CURR_POS_OPP_KING subroutine of Σ tokened "KR8" in response to an input of POS(x,y). On this version, occurrent thoughts, beliefs, desires, and so forth, are to be conceived as acts, rather than as states of constituent components. Thus, insofar as the argument of the preceding paragraph was directed at the "instantaneous descriptions version" of Cummins's theory, one might think it was misdirected.

While this is a reasonable interpretation of Cummins's theory of cognitive architecture, the alternative does not ultimately suffice to avoid the charge that Cummins's account of productivity is a variation on the Classical account. The problem is that acts, just like parts of instantaneous descriptions, satisfy the relevant principles of Classicism. On the acts version, there are still atomic representations that have the meaning they do in virtue of satisfying the principles of Picture Theory of Representation. These atomic representations are used in acts to create propositional attitudes. Thus, when CURR_POS_OPP_KING returns a value of KR8 on an argument of POS(x,y), it produces a complex propositional attitude that means what it does in virtue of the meaning of "KR8" and the way it was produced by the subroutine CURR_POS_OPP_KING in response to an input of POS(x,y). The combinatorialism invoked here involves representations and acts. We might call this a level one act. At the next level, after CURR_POS_OPP_KING produces a "KR8", that token of "KR8" might be passed to the NEG subroutine that produces a "KR8" as output. The resulting complex propositional attitude is that Σ believes that the current position of the opponent's king is not king rook 8. This we might call a level two act. We can now see how the Classical principles apply to this new ontology. A version of the Principle of Semantic Compositionality holds, since the content of a complex propositional attitude, such as Σ's believing that it is not the case that the opponent's king is at king rook 8 is a product of the meanings of the acts and representations from which it is constructed and the way those acts and representations are put together. A version of the Principle of Context Independence holds, since each act or representation that constitutes a complex propositional attitude has the same content independent of its context. Thus, as we saw before, Cummins's theory is still essentially a version of Classicism with a distinct ontology, hence explains the productivity of thought in virtue of its constituting a realization of Classical ideas.

Having addressed the productivity argument, we may ask to what extent Cummins's proposed architecture can address the putative counterfactual dependence of one thought capacity upon another. Let us begin with a *prima facie* reason to think that Cummins's type of architecture can indeed explain this. Rather than consider the existence of a nomologicaly necessary and sufficient connection between the thought capacity for John loves Mary and the thought capacity for Mary loves John, we might recycle an earlier system by supposing that there is a nomologically necessary and sufficient connection between the capacities for the thoughts that it is not the case that the opponent's king is at king rook 8, it is not the case that it is not the case that the opponent's king is at king rook 8, and it is not the case that it is not the case that it is not the case that the opponent's king is at king rook 8. As a system meeting Cummins's specification that might explain this, recall the system having the NEG subroutine and CURR_POS_OPP_KING subroutine. In this system, the capacities for all the thoughts that involve negation, i.e., all but the first of these thought capacities in (*) above, rely on the system's capacity to token KR8, the NEG subroutine, and the CURR_POS_OPP_KING subroutine. The capacities for all the thoughts involving at least one negation involve all and only the same cognitive subcapacities. Therefore, if there were some cognitive cause that lead Σ to lose the capacity to think, say, that it is not the case that the opponent's king is at king rook 8, Σ would thereby lose the capacity to think that it is not that case that it is not the case that the opponent's king is at king rook 8, and so on. So, *prima facie*, there is an explanation of the systematicity of cognitive representations.

As we have come to expect, this account must rely on some unarticulated auxiliary hypotheses. Here is why. Even though there are systems with computer programs that satisfy the conditions of Cummins's theory and have a NEG subroutine that allows an unlimited number of recursive calls, there are other systems with computer programs that satisfy the conditions of Cummins's theory, but which have a subroutine NEG' that replaces NEG. Where NEG allows for an unbounded number of recursive calls, NEG' can only be deployed once. It cannot be recursively or iteratively called. The system with NEG' will think that it is not the case that the opponent's king is at king rook 8, but not think that it is not that case that it is not the case that the opponent's king is at king rook 8, and so forth. So, in order for a system satisfying the conditions of Cummins's theory to succeed in explaining the nomologically necessary and sufficient connection between thought capacities, Cummins's must introduce some additional hypothesis concerning tha nature of the subroutines in the systems. Yet, it would apear that the confirmation of the existence of a subroutine like NEG, rather than NEG', will require the prior establishment of Cummins's approach to cognitive architecture.

One can grant that a "typical" subroutine for NEG will allow an unbounded number of recursive calls. One can grant that the "most useful" version of the NEG subroutine will be the one that allows an unlimited number of recursive calls. Nevertheless, this is not the standard to which Fodor and Pylyshyn have drawn our attention. In "typical" computer programs satisfying the principles of Classicism, we have a syntactically and semantically combinatorial representational system with a set of atoms for terms and a set of atoms for relations and all the relations are defined over all the terms. Further, we might that think the "most useful" syntactically and semantically combinatorial system would be one in which each term could combine with each relation. Yet, in challenging Classicism, our objection turned on the logical existence of the formal languages that satisfy the principles of Classicism, but do not display dependencies among thought capacities. Our objection turned on such "atypical" and "useless" languages as those that allowed one term to combine with only one relation. Thus, the "peculiar" standard we imposed on Classicism is just the "peculiar" standard imposed on Cummins's theory. The allowable defenses against the systematicity arguments must be consistently enforced.

We have just reviewed the potential Cummins's theory has for explaining how one thought capacity might be nomologically necessary and sufficient for another. Now, however, see how the story goes for "weak intrinsic connections." Recall the system Σ which contains the subroutine CURR_POS_OPP_KING that takes the POS(x,y) matrix and produces the name of a position as output. In Σ, the subroutine CURR_POS_OPP_KING underlies many of Σ's putative thought capacities, including Σ's capacity to have the thought that the current position of the opponent's king is KR8, its capacity to have the thought that the current position of the opponent's king is KN8, its capacity to have the thought that the current position of the opponent's king is KB8, and so forth. All of these thought capacities depend on the capacity embodied in the subroutine. This indicates that there is a kind of intrinsic connection between Σ's capacity to have the thought that the current position of the opponent's king is KR8 and its capacity to have the thought that the current position of the opponent's king is KN8. This scheme does not, however, deliver the kind of counterfactual dependencies among thought capacities that have been at the center of our attention, namely, nomologically necessary and sufficient connections, since on this scheme it is possible for Σ to lose one of the thought capacities without losing another. For example, it is possible for Σ to lose its capacity to think the thought that the current position of the opponent's king is KR8 without thereby losing its capacity to think that the current position of the opponent's king is KN8. One capacity might be lost, while the other retained, if the system loses the capacity to generate the KR8 data structure, while retaining the capacity to generate the KN8 data structure. Nevertheless, we can see how a device meeting Cummins's specifications could generate "weak intrinsic connections."

Now review how our familiar concerns arise in the case of this last system with "weak intrinsic connections." Not all systems meeting the conditions of Cummins's theory of cognitive architecture will show such connections. One way this might happen is that the subroutine CURR_POS_OPP_KING is replaced by a family of subroutines that give the current position of an opponent's king only on some proper subset of the possible configurations of the chess board. That is, there are subroutines that are like CURR_POS_OPP_KING except for the fact that they are only defined for a limited range of possible arrangements of pieces on the board. Among these variants of CURR_POS_OPP_KING are ones that are defined only for one board configuration. So, even though there are some systems using Cummins's ideas that have intrinsic connections among the capacities for distinct thoughts, there are other systems using these ideas that do not. If there is to be a collection of hypotheses involving Cummins's theory of cognitive architecture that explains these "weak intrinsic connections" among possible occurrent thoughts, there must be some auxiliary hypothesis that forces the architecture to give rise to such connections. Yet, the confirmation of such hypotheses would appear to presuppose the truth of Cummins's theory of cognitive architecture. By the time one had confirmed the relevant auxiliary hypothesis or hypotheses, one would have already established the truth of Cummins's theory of cognitive architecture. How could one know the putative role of these subroutines in cognition, short of having established Cummins's theory?

Having examined the way in which Cummins's theory fails to handle both "strong" and "weak" intrinsic connections, we might show how it is that Cummins's account of the systematicity of cognitive representations relies on Classical principles of syntactic and semantic concatenative combinatorialism.

Indeed, we should be prepared to conclude that Cummins's theory fails to explain the two notions of systematicity in just the way Classicism does, because Cummins's theory proceeds along Classical lines. We saw how this problem arises in dealing with Cummins's treatment of productivity. Further, we saw that it holds for the combinatorialism run on computational states or on acts. For simplicity, therefore, we will speak neutrally between these two interpretations. Recall that the output of a subroutine is a combination of a data structure, such as "KR8," and a subroutine, such as CURR_POS_OPP_KING(POS(x,y)). Moreover, the syntactic item "KR8" means king's rook eight and contributes this content to every context in which it occurs. The relevant syntactic structure of the CURR_POS_OPP_KING subroutine also contributes the same semantic content to each syntactic object in which it plays a role. So, viewed in this way, Σ satisfies versions of both the Principle of Semantic Compositionality and the Principle of Context Independence. This is not perfectly Classical, insofar as Classicism is concerned with computational data structures, whereas Cummins's architecture involves subroutines and data structures satisfying the relevant combinatorial principles. Yet, in essence, it appears that Cummins's architecture has a story to tell about the systematicity of cognitive representations in virtue of satisfying a version of Classicism.

Next there is the matter of the content relations among the possible occurrent thoughts. Given that the CURR_POS_OPP_KING subroutine can produce the name of any square of the chess board as output, it is not hard to see how there would be at least some contentfully related occurrent thoughts in a system's cognitive repertoire. The system would be able to think that the opponent king's current position is QR1, that the opponent king's current position in QR2, that the opponent king's current position in QR3, and so forth. The weaknesses with this account, however, are just what we saw with the account of systematicity of cognitive representations. Even though the "typical" and "most useful" version of the CURR_POS_OPP_KING subroutine is the one that is defined over all possible board configurations, there are those pesky variants of CURR_POS_OPP_KING in which the subroutine is defined over only a single board configuration. Cummins can, of course, add some hypotheses that ensure that the relevant subroutines are defined over all chessboard configurations, but then is faced with the burden of showing how such an additional hypothesis might be confirmed short of establishing his theory of cognitive architecture. This, we have repeatedly argued, prevents the architecture from having a genuine explanation of compositionality. By this point, we can also simply note that the strategy Cummins's is using to try to explain the semantic relations among thought capacities is essentially Classical. The reasoning from the previous arguments applies.

Finally, we have to consider the possibility that Cummins's architecture can explain the co-occurrence of the systematicity of cognitive representations and semantic relatedness of thought capacities. Given the extent to which Cummins's architecture resembles Classicism, it is natural to consider the possibility that the strategy used by Classicists can also be used by Cummins. So, we should ask whether the minimally successful version of the nested subroutines account of either systematicity of cognitive representations or semantic relatedness is also sufficient to account for the other feature of thought. If so, then the idea of nested subroutines will be in as good a position as is Classicism. There are two cases to consider:

1) Does the minimal account of semantic relatedness of thought capacities lead to one thought capacity being nomologically necessary and sufficient for another?

2) Does the minimal account of one thought capacity being nomologically necessary and sufficient for another lead to the semantic relatedness of possible occurrent thoughts?

Of course, we know that there are systems meeting Cummins's specifications that have both the systematicity of cognitive representation and the semantic relatedness of thought capacities, but must the apparatus necessary to account for one regularity be sufficient to account for the other. The answer to both of these questions is yes.

What makes it the case that the propositional attitudes in a system of the sort Cummins envisions are contentfully related? The case of "weak" and "strong" intrinsic connections are essentially the same, so we will rehearse the argument just for the "weak" connections case. The answer, in short, is common elements that maintain their semantic content across diverse contexts. On Cummins's theory, the common elements can be either a) the syntactic atoms, such as "KR8," that satisfy the principles of the Picture Theory of Representation or b) the subroutines, such as CURR_POS_OPP_KING or CURR_POS_OPP_QUEEN, that operate on the syntactic atoms. Whichever basis gives rise to common contents also leads to systematicity. Take case a) first. The symbol, "KR8," for example, means king rook 8 because of its role in a relational structure **R** and the isomorphism between **R** and another relational structure **C**. This role, however, does not change as "KR8" is tokened by the CURR_POS_OPP_KING or the CURR_POS_OPP_QUEEN subroutine. It is constant across those contexts. "KR8," thus, satisfies the Principles of Semantic Compositionality and Context Independence. Notice that in order for there to be two or more propositional attitudes that have the common content of king rook 8, the "KR8" token must be produced by more than one subroutine. So, Σ's capacity to think that the current position of the opponent's king is king rook 8 and Σ's capacity to think that the current position of the opponent's queen is king rook 8 both require the capacity to token "KR8." If, however, "KR8" is produced by more than one subroutine, such as the CURR_POS_OPP_KING or the CURR_POS_OPP_QUEEN subroutines, then one can see why it is that Σ must also be "weakly connected." The capacity to think that the current position of the opponent's king is king rook 8 and the capacity to think that the current position of the opponent's queen is king rook 8 both depend on the capacity to produce a token of "KR8." Semantic relatedness, thus, brings with it "weak" systematicity in case a). Take case b), where the common content is supposed to be due to diverse propositional attitudes having a common subroutine. In such a case, a subroutine such as CURR_POS_OPP_KING will return more than one type of output given different POS(x,y) matrices as input. So, on one chessboard configuration CURR_POS_OPP_KING will produce "KR8," while on another chessboard configuration it will produce "KB8." Since, however, Σ's capacity for the thought that the current position of the opponent's king is king rook 8 and Σ's capacity for the thought that the current position of the opponent's king is king bishop 8 both rely on the CURR_POS_OPP_KING subroutine, they will be mutually dependent, hence "weakly" systematically related. So, on case b) semantic relatedness leads to systematicity. Thus, we can conclude that on Cummins's theory, semantic relatedness of thought capacities leads to "weak" systematicity. The reason is that both explananda require of Cummins's architecture a certain sort of combinatorialism.

Why is it that the systematicity of cognitive representations in one of Cummins's systems Σ brings with it the semantic relatedness of thought capacities in Σ? Again, the short answer is that both explananda require of Cummins's architecture a kind of syntactic and semantic combinatorialism. Having run through the arguments *ad nauseum*, much less is needed in the way of filling out this answer. On Cummins's theory, it is the sharing of either a subroutine or an "atom" satisfying PTR that gives rise to the systematicity of cognitive representations. But, since both the subroutines and the atoms respect the Principles of Semantic Compositionality and Context Independence, the sharing of common elements necessitates the sharing of common contents. So, we can see how it is that semantic relatedness and systematicity keep such close company.

The foregoing argumentation linking the semantic relatedness of thought capacities and the systematicity of cognitive representations shows just how extensively Cummins's theory relies on Classical ideas. It seems fair to say that Cummins's theory is Classical in principles, though non-Classical in its use of ontology. Cummins's theory, like Classicism, relies on computational processes and representational data structures. Cummins makes different use of this ontology than does the Classicist, but the ontology is shared. Like the Classicist, Cummins imposes a kind of concatenative combinatorial syntax and semantics on this ontology. This enables him to achieve the same degree of explanatory success that Classicism enjoys.

NOTES

1. Cf., e.g., Dretske, (1981, 1988), Fodor, (1990).

2. The original formulation of the disjunction problem is to be found in Fodor, (1986). Fodor's (1990) version for informational semantics suffers from a number of problems discussed in Adams & Aizawa, (1994).

3. Cf., Cummins, (1996a), p. 17.

CHAPTER 10

TAKING THE BRAIN SERIOUSLY

For some supporters of Connectionism, the Classicist's productivity and systematicity arguments are largely misguided efforts, since these arguments do not involve taking the brain seriously. There are numerous permutations on this view. For example, one might think that the arguments rely on a naive or misguided understanding of cognition. Alternatively, one might think that the arguments rely on a naive or misguided understanding of the proper or best scientific methods for studying cognition. For the more radical skeptics about the mind, there are behavioral variants of these views. Thus, one can think that the arguments rely on a naive or misguided understanding of behavior. One can also believe that they rely on a naive or misguided understanding of the proper or best scientific methods for studying behavior. Uniting many of these skeptical reactions to the Classical arguments is the belief that cognitive science should in some sense take the brain seriously. Patricia and Paul Churchland, for example, have developed views in this vein. Having expressed interest in various eliminativist ideas about the mental, they have largely ignored the productivity and systematicity arguments. Certainly anyone who has doubts about the plausibility of the entire conceptual framework of the cognitive will have even greater skepticism about more esoteric features such as its putative productivity and systematicity. Further, the Churchlands have consistently and enthusiastically supported neurobiological and neurocomputational theorizing, in general, and Connectionist theorizing, in particular.

Fodor and Pylyshyn's original critique of Connectionism, of course, addressed some components of the view that there is some conceptual or methodological advantage in Connectionism's "brain style" modeling. Their response was that much of the allure of "brain style" modeling was perfectly consistent with a Classical theory of cognition. Such consistency can be had either through directly incorporating the neurobiologically plausible hypotheses into a Classical model, or through incorporating them into the implementation of a Classical model. So, for example, Fodor and Pylyshyn note that the idea that the brain uses parallel processing is perfectly consistent with Classicism, since there are perfectly well-defined, Turing-equivalent parallel processing digital computers. Here a "brain style" processing idea is directly incorporated into a computational, hence cognitive, level of scientific theorizing. As another example, there is the famous "100 step rule." Connectionists note that reaction time experiments show that the brain is capable of performing many cognitive tasks, such as recognizing faces, objects, and words, in less than 500msec. Yet, the transmission of a signal from a presynaptic neuron to a postsynaptic neuron takes on the order of 5msec. This is supposed to mean that the computer program of the mind can execute no more than 100 steps in these cognitive tasks. The weakness in this well-known argument is that there is no independent motivation for the underlying assumption

that the execution of a hypothetical instruction in the hypothetical computer program of the mind is implemented in the transmission of a signal across a synapse. Classicists are free to reject the implementation theory that is implicit in this argument. So, Classicists can accept the well-established results of reaction time experiments and the theory of synaptic transmission, without having to abandon or even modify Classicism. Classicism avoids apparent conflicts with neurobiological facts in part because of the simplicity of Classicism: it is simply a theory of the causally efficacious structure of cognitive representations. As was noted in Chapter 1, Classicism does not claim that humans are Turing machines or that humans have a von Neumann computer architecture.

Although Fodor and Pylyshyn have offered a point for point rebuttal of components of the Connectionist case for taking the brain seriously, the aim of this penultimate chapter is to take another route to dampening the Connectionist enthusiasm for brain style modeling. Anyone who advocates taking the brain seriously as a means of advancing psychological understanding will, of course, admit that this is a defeasible research strategy. Using neuroscience might help us in making psychological discoveries, but then again it may be lead to dead ends. Nevertheless, the advocate of taking the brain seriously must say that there is some sense in which a methodology that takes the brain seriously in psychological theorizing is superior to a methodology, such as Fodor's, that largely ignores studies about the brain. The aim in this chapter is to offer a kind of inductive argument against the Connectionist version of taking the brain seriously. The first step is to draw attention to what is arguably the fundamental move in neuropsychology, namely, forging a link between some neuroscientific object, state, or process and some psychological object, state, or process.[1] Having taken this step, it will be possible to develop a taxonomy of ways in which using neuroscientific research can mislead psychologists. Historical cases will serve to make this clearer. They will show ways in which a "lower level" theory can misdirect "higher level" theorizing. Finally, it will be possible to draw attention to ways in which the historical cases of misdirections resemble the contemporary situation with Connectionist brain style modeling. The point of these considerations is simply to offer an inductive argument that weakens the sense that taking the brain seriously is the obvious research methodology to adopt. The point is to make vivid the true inductive risk in any method of taking the brain seriously in psychology. Although Connectionism is the focus of these arguments, the scope of our arguments will extend some indeterminate distance beyond Connectionism.

1 THE FUNDAMENTAL NEUROPSYCHOLOGICAL INFERENCE

The first type of scientific inference that counts as clearly neuropsychological consists of forging a link between some neurobiological object, state, or process N and some psychological object, state, or process P. Attempts to link the neurobiological and the psychological can be found throughout the history of Western psychology, neuroscience, and biology from the latest scientific journal articles to the speculations of the early Greek natural philosophers. In order to forge a link between N and P, a neuropsychologist will provide biological evidence that N has property ϕ and further independent psychological evidence that P has property ϕ. Given that N and P both have ϕ, one might link them by inferring that N and P are one and the same thing. To take a contemporary illustration of the idea, we might consider the neurobiological process of long-term potentiation (LTP) and the psychological process of learning some conditioning task. One might find that the drug AP5 inhibits LTP, hence perform an experiment to determine whether AP5 also prevents learning in the given conditioning task. Insofar as both LTP and conditioning have property ϕ, i.e., both are inhibited by AP5, one has some reason to link LTP and conditioning.

This move is primary in this sense: it is the first move one makes when combining results from psychology and neuroscience. One can make all sort of determinations concerning psychological states and processes within the context of psychology alone. This is the kind of work that interests Fodor and Pylyshyn. One can, likewise, make all manner of determinations about the structure and function of the brain and its subcomponents within the context of neuroscience. These separate enterprises come together with the information they independently develop by forging links between the psychological and the neuroscientific. The move is important insofar as it represents a kind of activity we don't find in "pure psychology" or "pure neuroscience". In fact, it seems to be a reasonable basis upon one which one might make the claim that neuropsychology is methodologically superior to "pure psychology" or even "pure neuroscience."

We have said that when it is found that N and P share property ϕ, there is some basis for forging a link between N and P. There is a rationale beyond this choice of metaphor. For many contemporary neuropsychologists, the natural defeasible inference to draw from the fact N and P share ϕ is that P *is* N. Given that AP5 inhibits both the induction of LTP and successful conditioning, the natural defeasible inference is that the process of conditioning is a matter of inducing LTP. Conditioning is inducing LTP. And while it is true that the inference of an identity between N and P is common and natural to many, it is not the only inference that neuropsychologists appear to make. Rather than infer that P is N, functionalist neuropsychologists will infer that P is instantiated or realized by N. The difference here concerns the metaphysics of the mind. Old fashioned type identity theorists will infer an identity between the type P and the type N, where functionalists will infer only a weaker instantiation or realization relation between P and N. Fans of supervenience will infer that P supervenes on N. Substantival dualists, however, will infer only that P and N are correlated.

The first point being made here is that the methodology of relating the neurobiological to the psychological is independent of the metaphysics of the mind. Although some form of identity theory appears to dominate the work of contemporary neuropsychologists, this is not a matter of conceptual necessity. The secondary point to make, however, is that, if we consider the range of those scientists who have a legitimate claim to having taken the brain seriously in their psychological theorizing, we shall find some representation of the diversity of possible metaphysical views here mentioned. So, the rationale for recourse to the metaphor of forging a link between N and P is two fold. It respects the conceptual difference between a scientific methodology and a scientific metaphysics and it respects the diversity of actual practice in the history of what we are here calling neuropsychology.

If the primary neuropsychological move is to link something neurobiological and something psychological, what are the secondary moves? There are at least two sorts. One secondary move is to broaden the evidential base for linking N and P. In other words, having ventured a link between P and N on the basis of some property ϕ_1, one then searches for further properties ϕ_2, ϕ_3, ..., and ϕ_m that can be shared by both N and P. Thus, an experimental result that finds that ϕ_2 applies to some neurobiological structure N will spur an experiment to determine whether or not ϕ_2 applies to the psychological structure P. Similarly, an experimental result that finds that ϕ_2 applies to some psychological structure P will spur an experiment to determine whether or not ϕ_2 applies to N. This provides further evidence for linking N and P. Another secondary move is to extend the range of neurobiological and psychological objects that can be linked. That is, once N_1 and P_1 are linked, one may attempt to link N_2 and P_2, N_3 and P_3, etc. Such further links are forged as before by finding common properties of the neurobiological and the psychological. In these two secondary moves, neuropsychology might be thought to have some virtue in guiding psychology along new lines of investigation. So, the overall conception is that one links N_1 and P_1 in virtue of the evidence that they share properties $\phi_1, \phi_2, ..., \phi_m$, one links N_2 and P_2 in virtue of the evidence that they share properties $\psi_1, \psi_2, ..., \psi_n$, one links N_3 and P_3 in virtue of the evidence that they share properties $\omega_1, \omega_2, ..., \omega_p$. There are at least two virtues in these secondary steps. First, it can extend the range of predictions that one can make. Given that N and P are linked and that N has ϕ, one can infer that P has ϕ. Second, there may be neuroscientific procedures that allow the control of N's having ϕ, but not psychological procedure for controlling P's having ϕ. Thus, neuropsychology may make it possible to extend the range of experimental manipulations.

2 MORE HISTORY OF SCIENCE

In Chapter 2, we used some episodes from the history of science that appear similar to the explanatory strategy Fodor and Pylyshyn use in the systematicity arguments. Here again we turn to the history of science to illustrate ideas in the methodology of science. Here we are exploring ways in which "lower-level" theories have mislead "higher-level" theories. Textbook science and textbook histories of science tend to underrepresent the frequency of failures in science, hence underrepresent the frequency with which lower-level sciences mislead higher level sciences. This means that many cognitive scientists will be less familiar with cases in which lower-level theories were misleading. The history examined here, howevever, draws attention to such cases. It also also suggest some preliminary analysis of when scientists in higher-level sciences should be cautious in following the lead of lower-level sciences.

Through the course of six editions of the *Origin of Species*, Charles Darwin was able to convince the majority of practicing biologists that in fact biological species evolve. He was, however, much less successful in persuading his contemporaries that natural selection was the cause of evolution. The late 19th Century thus saw a rise in the popularity of neo-Lamarckism. Although many factors were involved in this so-called "Eclipse of Darwinism," there are two significant groups of scientific arguments that pitted "lower-level" theories in physics and inheritance against Darwin's theory of natural selection. The first involved the application of principles of thermodynamics to determinations of the age of the earth; the second involved the theory of pangenesis.

During the 1860's, Lord Kelvin carried out a series of calculations in an effort to determine the age of the earth based on the cooling of the Sun and the cooling of the earth.[2] In calculating the age of the Sun, Kelvin began with an estimate of the size of the sun and the amount of energy it produces. He then calculated that, given the most energetic chemical reaction then known, the solar system could be no more than about 100 million years old. If, however, the earth is no more than 100 million years old, then the earth is not old enough for natural selection to have produced the great diversity of life forms we see today. To calculate the age of the earth based on its cooling, he supposed that the earth was initially formed as a molten ball of iron and nickle. If so, then given that there are no internal heat sources in the earth and the heat coefficients of iron and nickel, once again, Kelvin concluded that the earth could be no more than about 100 million years old. While these calculations involved a number of assumptions and rough estimations, by and large the scientific community was more impressed by the physicists's arguments based on thermodynamics than by the geologists's arguments based on erosion. Even Darwin's son, himself a physicist, could find no flaw in Kelvin's arguments, thereby leaving the senior Darwin with little option other than attempting to rationalize a reduced estimate of the amount of time it would take for natural selection to effect changes in organisms.

In the goodness of time, of course, physicists discovered the mistaken assumptions in Kelvin's calculations. They found that the sun is not fueled by a chemical reaction, but by nuclear fusion. They found that, in fact, the earth does contain an internal heat source. Heat is produced by the radioactive decomposition of elements trapped in the earth. Thus, for more than forty years, the more "prestigious" lower-level science of physics lead biologists away from Darwin's theory of natural selection in favor of alternative evolutionary mechanisms. In some areas, there was a return to the earlier Lamarckian idea that morphological characters obtained by prolonged use over several generations might make a character heritable. Perhaps the use of some character by an entire population could lead to large scale evolutionary change within the time frame allowed by physics. Mutation theory was also entertained. Among the virtues of this theory hope was the promise that large mutations could accumulate fast enough to effect macroevolutionary changes in the time allotted by physics. Here we have clear cases where apparently well-evidenced theories in lower level sciences threatened the acceptance of what has ultimately proved to be a viable theory in a higher level science.

Another significant challenge to the theory of natural selection was based on misconceptions about the biological mechanisms of inheritance. During the second half of the 19th Century, biological inheritance was thought to be mediated by some sort of blending mechanism. Darwin's (1872) version of this idea postulated that the material passed from parents to offspring–the gemmules–was a kind of sampling of the tissues of the parents. Thus, a dark haired parent would produce gemmules for dark hair because the gemmules were formed from some of the very components that made the parent's hair dark. Each parent would contribute a stock of these gemmules that would blend together to yield offspring. Thus, as a general rule, a cross between a white haired individual and a black haired individual would produce a gray haired individual, a cross between a gray haired individual and a black individual would produce a dark gray haired individual, and so forth.

Fleeming Jenkin, (1872), made the case that Darwin's theory of natural selection would be unable to effect large scale evolutionary change given blending inheritance. Jenkin supposed that a single white individual might be many times more fit than any black individual and that, in addition, fitness was proportional to whiteness.[3] As a result, of his increased fitness a white individual would have disproportionately many offspring. By assumption, these gray offspring will be fitter than the pure black individuals, although not by as much as the original white individual was fitter than the pure black individuals. Because of their greater fitness, the gray offspring will reproduce at a disproportionately greater rate than the pure black individuals and will still typically mate with black individuals. The gray individuals will interbreed to some extent, but the limited numbers of these gray individuals along with their close familial relations will make it unlikely that they interbreed. Crosses between the gray individuals and the black individuals will produce dark gray individuals that are more fit than pure black individuals, but not as fit as either the pure white or gray individuals. Pursuing this line of reasoning, Jenkin argued that, over many generations, the appearance of a single very fit individual would not be able to make significant changes in populations, since all their beneficial characteristics would be blended away within a very few generations. The beneficial traits of a single individual would be outweighed by the blending away and dilution of the benefits in a large population of less fit individuals. In short, blending inheritance would undermine the effects of natural selection.

Here again we have a case in which a mistaken lower level theory, this time a biological theory of inheritance, misdirected the course of evolutionary thinking. It was almost 40 years before population geneticists began to unravel Jenkins's argument and begin to make progress on a selectionist theory of evolution.   Such an advance required, among other things, the proper appreciation of the non-blending "factors" that Gregor Mendel described in his experiments on the cross-fertilization of peas.

The foregoing examples raise a rather obvious way in which what is known in a lower level theory can mislead a higher level theory: the lower level theory can embody some mistaken assumptions or errors. So, we have a way in which theories about the brain can fail to guide neuropsychology. These, however, are just preliminaries to some *bona fide* neuropsychological examples that illustrate more subtle challenges for neuropsychology. The first neuropsychological example is taken from arguments by Rene Descartes. Although Descartes is frequently caricatured for holding *a priori* views of what appear to be plainly empirical matters, in actual practice, Descartes made ample recourse to the methods of empirical investigation available to him. For our purposes, one of

Descartes's most interesting ideas is found quite clearly in one of his last works, the *Passions of the Soul*. As everyone knows, Descartes linked the soul--a psychological structure P--to the pineal gland--a neurobiological structure N. He argued that the pineal gland was the seat of the soul. His argument was that, if one carefully examines the brain, the pineal gland is the only structure that is unitary (= ϕ). That is, it is the only structure that does not come in pairs, one to each side of the body or hemisphere of the brain. Similarly, the thought of any given thing is unitary (= ϕ). Hence, we have some reason to maintain that the pineal gland is the seat of the soul. Descartes's argument is such a nice illustration of the primary neuropsychological move that it is worth quoting in its entirety. This is Article XXXII of the *Passions of the Soul*:

> **How we know that this gland is the main seat of the soul.**
> The reason which persuades me that the soul cannot have any other seat in all the body than this gland wherein to exercise its functions immediately, is that I reflect that the other parts of our brain are all of them double, just as we have two eyes, two hands, two ears, and finally all the organs of our outside senses are double; and inasmuch as we have but one solitary and simple thought of one particular thing at one and the same moment, it must necessarily be the case that there must somewhere be a place where the two images which come to us by the two eyes, where the two other impressions which proceed from a single object by means of the double organs of the other senses, can unite before arriving at the soul, in order that they may not represent to it two objects instead of one. And it is easy to apprehend how these images or other impressions might unite in this gland by the intermission of the spirits which fill the cavities of the brain; but there is no other place in the body where they can be thus united unless they are so in this gland (Haldane and Ross translation, 1911, p. 346).

The extent to which Descartes's reasoning here follows that sketched is quite striking. The history of science should always so nicely meet up with the philosophy of science.

A second example of neuropsychological theorizing gone wrong is found in a work written about a century later. David Hartley, sometimes claimed to be the first neuropsychologist, also makes the primary neuropsychological move. Consider two examples from Hartley's *Observations on Man, his Frame, his Duty, and his Expectations*. First, in Proposition 1, Hartley claims that the *white* matter of the brain is the seat of sensory and motor function. His argument is that when there is damage to the white matter of the brain, sensory and motor function are impaired. In this case, N = the white matter of the brain, P = sensory and motor function, and ϕ = the property of being damaged. Second, in Propositions 3 and 4, Hartley supports the view that sensations (psychological objects) are vibrations in the substance of nerves (neurobiological objects). He claims, following Isaac Newton, that sensations remain in the mind for a short period of time after their sensory stimulus is removed. In the case of vision, for example, bright lights leave afterimages. Similarly, a vibration is the only motion he can imagine that persists for a period of time after its stimulus is removed. This commonality between sensation and vibrations constitutes Hartley's justification for linking them. To summarize succinctly, N = motion in the white substance of the nerves, P = sensations, and φ = persists after a stimulus is removed.

3 THE INDUCTIVE RISKS OF NEUROPSYCHOLOGY

With the foregoing bits of history before us, we are in a better position to appreciate the inductive risks of neuropsychology. We can articulate more clearly some of the ways in which neuroscience can mislead "pure" psychology.

The most obvious inductive risk is the possibility that the underlying neuroscientific theory is false. Hartley's theory of the nature of nerve action is a vivid case in point. In fact, if we survey Hartley's *Observations*, we will find that it offers about as thoroughly wrong a scientific theory as there has ever been. Kelvin's arguments from thermodynamics and Jenkins's argument from the theory of blending inheritance make this idea vivid. It is not that Kelvin and Jenkins were in some respect "poor" scientists. Far from it. Their arguments were ingenious and well-reasoned. Their weakness lay in false assumptions that were largely unproblematic at the time the arguments were put forward. Radioactivity heating, the downfall of the argument from the cooling of the earth, was not discovered until the end of the 19th Century. Nuclear fusion, the downfall of the argument from the cooling of the sun, was discovered later still. Mendel's work on mechanisms of inheritance languished in obscurity until being independently rediscovered three time in 1900. In fact, then, it was several more years before the early population geneticists began to appreciate how Mendel's results might be made to support, rather than undermine, Darwin's theory of natural selection.[4] So, false lower-level theories, though enjoying some measure of empirical support, can nevertheless steer a higher-level science away from the path to truth.

The more interesting cases where lower-level theories can be a hindrance to higher-level theories are when the lower-level theories are in fact true, but are incorrectly linked to the higher-level theories. A special case of this problem involves the layered structure of the world. Among the lowest levels of structure in the world are the electrons, protons, and neutrons that give rise to chemical atoms. Electrons, protons, and neutrons constitute chemical elements, such as hydrogen, carbon, oxygen, nitrogen, calcium, potassium, and iron. They are the immediate constituents of chemical atoms, if you will. The chemical elements in turn give rise to ions and molecules of greater or lesser complexity. Among the more complex molecules are the proteins making up cell membranes, transmembrane proteins, synaptic vesicles, cell nuclei, mitochondria, ribosomes, and other subcellular structures. Subcellular components obviously give rise to cells of various descriptions. Neurons form circuits in some way supported by glial cells. Neural circuits, in turn, appear to give rise to columnar structures and columnar structures appear to constitute the various regions of the cortex subserving cognitive functions, such as visual, linguistic, and olfactory processing.

Given this layered structure of the world, we might draw a rough and ready distinction between "direct" and "indirect" realizations/implementations of higher -level theories by lower level theories. Electrons, protons, and neutrons directly realize or implement chemical atoms; they are the immediate constituents of chemical atoms. By contrast, electrons, protons, and neutrons indirectly realize or implement proteins, subcellular structures (such as ribosomes, mitochondria, and cell nuclei), nerve cells, neural circuits, columns, cortical regions. So, even though there is no scientific doubt that human psychology is implemented in electrons, protons, and neutrons, this implementation/realization relation is quite indirect. The implementation is indirect in the sense that there are levels of structure between electrons, protons, and neutrons, on the one hand, and thinking about a cold beer, on the other.

This distinction between direct and indirect implementations is relevant insofar as the less direct the implementation, the less the principles of the lower level are likely to reflect the principles at the higher level. Electrons, protons, and neutrons form chemical atoms as determined by the interaction of the strong and weak nuclear forces, as well as laws of electromagnetism. Chemical atoms form molecules according to principles of covalent bonding. In proteins, the order in which amino acids are linked, along with their sizes, their shapes, and their electronegativity, conspire to determine the secondary, tertiary, and quaternary structure of proteins, hence their functional properties. In nerve cells, principles governing ion gradients, potential gradients, membrane permeability, and capacitance, interact to determine neuronal activity. Although these principles are relatively clear at lower levels of organization, as we proceed above the neuronal level things are less much clear. What is clear, however, is that even a true theory of electrons, protons, and neutrons, while constituting a relatively fundamental implementation/realization of human psychology, does not provide us much guidance in theorizing about the mind. Brain chemistry might provide part of the story underling cognitive function, but cannot be the whole story. What is less clear, but what is nonetheless suggested is that one of the risks of using principles of neuronal functional to guide theorizing about cognitive function is that one is using too low a level theory.

In retrospect, we can see that Hartley's neuropsychology had this flaw. He took mechanical principles of vibration as the neurobiological basis for his neurophysiology. This step was, of course, quite in keeping with all that was understood within the physics of Hartley's day. Without the chemical theories of the last two centuries, without the techniques in histology and microscopy of the last century, and without the biochemistry of the last half century, there was no empirical way for Hartley to know of the numerous levels of organizational structure separating the simple mechanical principles of vibrations from the complex, high-level principles of cognition. Hartley was completely ignorant of the levels of structure to be found in chemical elements, macromolecules, nerve cells, and neural networks. In retrospect, we can see that Hartley's enterprise was completely hopeless. He simply had far too low a level theory to bring to bear on the theory of cognition.

A true lower-level theory can be a hindrance to a higher-level theory when the lower-level theory is "too low" a theory. While this is the most philosophically interesting type of case, it is not the only type of case. Even when there is no problem involving multiple levels of structure, a true lower-level theory can be a hindrance if weak evidence leads to a mistaken linkage between the lower and the higher. In other words, a mistaken linkage might be drawn when an inductive argument with true premises simply leads to a false conclusion. Inductive arguments have this annoying feature. Descartes' argument linking the soul to the pineal gland might illutrate this case; it appears that an inductively valid argument with true premises lead to a false conclusion. Perhaps there is some truth to the idea that the pineal gland is the only unitary structure in the head.[5] Perhaps there is also some truth to the claim that there is a unity of consciousness. Even so, Descartes offered only one property ϕ as evidence that the pineal gland is the seat of the soul. Descartes is not offering a fallacious inductive argument, like an *ad hominem*. Nor is there a problem with the pineal gland being "too low" a level structure to be the seat of the soul. Rather, Descartes' argument simply does not provide a robust empirical basis for the linkage between the soul and the pineal gland. He does not appeal to a sufficiently large, diverse set of properties $\phi_1, \phi_2, \ldots, \phi_n$.[6] Of course, a low-level theory that is at too low a level will, one hopes, eventually be shown to lack sufficient empirical evidence to sustain a linkage. So, while the levels problem is distinguishable from the bare inductive problem, it is not entirely indepedent of it either.

The foregoing examples from the history of science, including the history of neuropsychology, lead us to some tentative conclusions. Clearly the strategy of using neurobiology to guide psychology is a defeasible research strategy. Neurobiology could guide us to new insights in psychology, but it can also misguide us, directing us down blind alleys. This would seem to be entirely uncontroversial. Where we have advanced beyond the obvious is in seeing more clearly how a neurobiology might misguide psychology. We have seen three ways: 1) by offering false theories of the neurobiological, 2) by offering (possibly true) theories that are at the wrong level of analysis, and 3) by offering non-robust linkages. This suggests that we carefully scrutinize a proposed neuropsychological theory for potential weaknesses in these three areas. In particular, we should scrutinize the Parallel Distributed Processing brand of connectionism for these potential weaknesses.

4 PARALLEL DISTRIBUTED PROCESSING

Chapter 7 examined the possibility of using the apparatus of nodes with weighted connections between them as a basis for explaining the various systematic features of human cognition. In that examination, the apparatus was applied to cognition without regard to its possible relations to neural structures. If one were interested in relating the mathematical apparatus of what we have called "bare Connectionism" to features in the brain in an effort to understand cognition, there are many ways one might try to try to proceed. The Parallel Distributed Processing brand of Connectionism offers one way. Of course, even within the PDP camp, there is less than complete agreement on this matter, but there is a dominant conception. On this conception, we are supposed to recognize three levels of processing. First, there is the neuronal level of interactions among individual neurons. Second, there is the supraneuronal, subcognitive level of processing, sometimes called the subsymbolic level, at the which PDP strain of Connectionists think their mathematically specified networks apply. Third, and finally, there is the cognitive or symbolic level of processing. This is widely taken to be the level at which Classical computational principles hold. Prominent expositions of this view include Smolensky, (1988a, 1995). Although there are other treatments of Connectionism, this one is the most germane to our principal concern with the systematicity arguments, since this is the form of Connectionism most likely to be adopted as an alternative to Classicism. Further, it embraces the idea of taking the brain seriously as something that makes Connectionism methodologically superior to Classicism.

Perhaps the first thing to notice about PDP Connectionism is that it does not clearly fit the model of using the brain to guide psychology that we have sketched. In the schema described above, one must provide independent evidence that some neuroscientific structure, object, or process N has ϕ and that psychological structure, object, or process P has ϕ. The vast majority of PDP research does not do this. Instead, PDP research makes only opportunistic use of the facts of neuroscience, citing neurobiological evidence that is thought to be supportive of PDP, while avoiding neurobiological evidence that does not readily mesh with PDP. Rather than taking the neuropsychological method described here, PDP research typically focuses on building networks that model various cognitive capacities. Thus, most PDP research resembles other forms of "pure psychological" modeling, except for the fact that it attempts to use the apparatus of nodes with modifiable weighted connections. This suggests that while PDP may have its methodological virtues and its empirical successes, its methodological virtues may not be those of neuropsychology. Consider how the observations earlier in this chapter bear on PDP.

In the first place, there is the possibility that connectionism is based on a mistaken neurophysiology. In this regard, the most problematic Connectionist idea by far is its central idea that synaptic modification is the biological basis of learning and memory. The empirical evidence in support of this view appears to be far weaker than is widely appreciated. A rough, but bold assessment of the current situation would say that, to date, there is no direct *in vivo* neuroscientific evidence that synaptic modification constitutes a naturally occurring process in mammalian brains. The overwhelming majority of evidence in support of the view that synaptic modification is the biological basis of learning and memory comes from analogical studies involving model systems that might resemble what might take place in the mammalian brain, driven by the sense that nothing other than synaptic modification could be the mammalian substrate of learning and memory.

Some sense of the status of synaptic modification might be gained through a thumbnail sketch of the history of the idea. The idea that synaptic modification might constitute the biological basis of learning and memory was articulated hot on the heels of the discovery of synapses in the 1890s. The proposal was simply the obvious modernization of the venerable idea that learning how to do something involves getting better, hence that some physiological process must be getting more efficient. For Descartes in the 17th century, animal spirits became more efficient in their coursing through the matter of the brain. For Hartley in the 18th Century, vibrations in the white matter of the brain became more easily reinstated. For Herbert Spencer in late 19th Century, certain chemical reactions thought to occur within the tubules of the nervous reticulum became more efficient. For Santiago Ramon y Cajal in the late 19th Century, presynaptic cells might have a more powerful effect on postsynaptic cells. In the late 19th Century through to the present, the idea of synaptic modification as the substrate of learning and memory has simply made sense.

Through the first half of the 20th Century, physiological investigation revealed the role of electrical activity in the brain and in nerve action. Further, clinical work in humans showed that deep anaesthesia and epileptic seizures would disrupt electrical activity in the brain, yet not disturb long-term memories. Since electrical activity in the brain could not constitutes long-term memories, what else could do the job other than synaptic modification? This argument falters on the fact that electrical activity and synaptic modifications are not the only logically possible mechanisms that might underlie memory and learning. There is, for example, the possibility that changes in the shape of neuronal cells bodies could constitute the substrates of learning and memory.

By the middle of the 20th Century, various animal models of synaptic plasticity began to appear. One of the early phenomena was so-called post-tetanic potentiation (PTP), studied quite extensively for decades by Sir John Eccles. The basic phenomenon was that if one were to apply a large current, a tetanic stimulus, to the nerve leading into a neuromuscular junction, the effect of the nerve on the muscle could be increased. The principal reason the model fell out of favor as a model of learning and memory was the relatively implausible stimuli needed to induce it and its relatively short-lived effects. Invertebrates models, such as the sea snail *Aplysia*, also proved to be quite experimentally tractable and established that principles of conditioning could be realized by synaptic modification of the circuits involved in the Aplysia's gill withdrawal reflex. While invertebrate models of conditioning are highly suggestive, there is room to doubt that the results transfer to vertebrate models of learning and memory.

At present, the most interesting and intensely studied neurobiological model of synaptic modification is a kind of successor to Eccles's PTP, namely, long-term potentiation (LTP). First described in the early 1970's, the phenomenon is intriguing for many reasons. Like PTP, LTP is a facilitation effect, that is, after induction stimulus, a presynaptic neuron has a more potent effect on a postsynaptic neuron on which it synapses. Second, the phenomenon can be induced in the mammalian brain, rather than in the neuromuscular junction or in some non-human animal preparation. Third, it can be induced with much weaker stimuli than those used to induce post-tetanic potentiation. In fact, it has proved to be possible to induce LTP with a stimulus that appears to mimic an endogenously occurring pattern of electrical activity. Fourth, it is known to persist for much longer than does post-tetanic potentiation. Fifth, it has been possible to pair LTP with a complementary process, long-term depression (LTD), which reduces the effect of a presynaptic neuron on a postsynaptic neuron. For these reasons, LTP and LTD have been the subject of intense study for the past decade, making it the most promising model of the sort of synaptic plasticity that might underlie learning and memory.

Despite the immense promise of LTP and LTD, these neurobiological phenomena provide only modest support for the Parallel Distributed Processing versions of Connectionism. PDP weight change procedures are not embodiments, or mathematical versions, of the neuroscientist's ideas. LTP and LTD are neuronal processes, while PDP weight changes are supposed to be supraneuronal processes. Moreover, there are features of, for example, the PDP backpropagation weight change procedure, and its variants, that do not obviously square with neuroscience. For example, backpropagation allows arbitrary large weights on connections, where LTP and LTD involves changes on the order of 50% in the effect one neuron has on another. Backpropagation allows weights to change from positive to negative, and vice versa, where a given presynaptic neuron has either a positive (excitatory) or negative (inhibitory) effect on a given postsynaptic neuron, but cannot switch between the two. A further long-standing problem has been that backpropagation appears to require that signals move bidirectionally along neuronal chains, whereas the vast majority of the synapses in the brain involve chemical neurotransmitters that allow signals to pass in only one direction across the synapse. Although supporters of PDP often resort to talk of abstraction and idealization, this makes the PDP idea of taking the brain seriously less compelling. It is, after all, the Classicist's view that one must abstract away from the properties of neurons in order to come to an understanding of cognition.

What about the robustness of identifying something neurophysiological with something psychological? How many properties ϕ contribute to psychoneural linkages? Part of what we have been saying about LTP/LTD and PDP weight change procedures is that the linkage between the two is not robust. Although one might identify some properties ϕ that LTP/LTD shares with PDP weight change, one can also show that there are other properties where they part ways. This, however, just concerns the attempt to link the PDP's lower level neuronal properties with the PDP level of mathematically specified nodes and connections. There is, in addition, reasons to worry about the robustness of linkages between the PDP level and cognitive processes. Again, the PDP weight change procedure takes center stage here. Here there are well-known divergences. Humans, and many other mammals, are capable of learning some association based on one exposure to the relevant information. The challenge to PDP here is the so-called problem of "one-shot learning." Another problem is called "catastrophic forgetting." If a network is trained on some task, then trained on subsequent task, the network "forgets" what it learned on the first task. In fact, in many cases, what is learned on the first task inhibits or prohibits learning in subsequent tasks. PDP also faces problems insofar as it relies on "supervised learning," where an agent is given the information as to how it should respond to a given input. All of these are well-known problems in the Connectionist literature, suggesting that there is not a robust link between PDP weight change and learning/memory.

Finally, we might ask of the chances that PDP models might offer an indirect, rather than a direct, implementation of cognitive processes. Perhaps the principles governing the operations of nodes and connections, modeled to some degree on the principles of neurons, are no more relevant to cognitive processes than are principles governing the chemical elements. Insofar as individual nerve cells form more complex structures that differ in their information processing principles from the pairwise interactions of individual nerve cells, we run the risk of being mislead by cognitively irrelevant features of neurons. Insofar as different types of nerve cells have different information processing roles in complex neuronal circuits, we have reason to think there are information processing principles we are missing. Insofar as we do not know the information processing significance of the different layers of cerebral cortex, we run the risk of missing important information processing principles. Insofar as we do not understand columnar structure and function, we run the risk of missing principles important to cognition. Insofar as we are ignorant of the regional specialization of brain tissue for diverse information processing tasks, such as vision, language, olfaction, and cognition, just so far do we run the risk of missing the features of the brain that are important to vision, language, olfaction, and cognition. We have noted that lower level objects and processes typically differ from higher level objects and processes and that there seem to be various levels of structure between the neurons that inspired Connectionism and cognition. Thus, we have some reason to worry that Connectionism is misleading us about the relevant biological basis for cognitive processing.

5 THE RISK OF TAKING THE BRAIN SERIOUSLY

No one doubts that scientific methodologies have to face up to inductive risks. Any methodology that might be called "taking the brain seriously" is no exception to this rule. What this chapter has done is to make vivid the risks there are in a methodology which uses the ideas and results of a lower level science to guide theorizing in a higher level science. We have seen three principal ways in which this might happen. First, the lower level science could advocate a false theory of the lower level. Rene Descartes's and David Hartley's neurophysiology were false. 19th Century applications of the thermodynamics slowed the acceptance of Darwin's theory of natural selection. False 19th Century theories of inheritance had the same effect. The PDP theory of the biological basis of learning and memory could be false. Despite the current promise of LTP/LTD as possible biological mechanisms of learning and memory, there remains some inductive risk that they will not prove to be what they are hoped to be. Further, even where these mechanisms to prove to be *bona fide* naturally occurring processes, they could only be suggestive of PDP weight change procedures such as backpropagation. Second, a possible link between a higher level and a lower level might fail to survive robust testing. Here we have reviewed some of the more familiar problems with linking PDP weight changes with both LTP/LTD, on the one hand, and learning and memory, on the other. Third, we have seen that a lower level theory could turn out to be too low a level theory for the purposes of a given high level theory. We explained the idea by reference to subatomic particles, but we also saw that the many levels of organizational structure above the level of neurally-inspired nodes and connections brought the point home in the context of PDP. The overarching point is that the idea of taking the brain seriously does not constitute a compelling reason to reject a Classical perspective in favor of Connectionism. The PDP way of taking the brain is a mixed bag.

NOTES

1. The term "neuropsychology" is often used for the enterprise of using brain lesion studies as an evidential basis for determining cognitive functions of the brain. So used, the term covers a proper subset of what we here mean by "neuropsychology".

2. The following discussion borrows from J. D. Burchfield's book, *Lord Kelvin and the Age of the Earth*.

3. Jenkins preconceptions about race were clearly in evidence in this argument.

4. For more on this chapter in the history of evolution, see Provine, (2001).

5. This claim is not entirely unproblematic, since there are brain structures like the corpus callosum, anterior commissure, and posterior commissure that are unitary in some sense. If, however, one notes that these structures are not unitary in the sense that they are bilaterally symmetric, there is the annoying fact that the pineal gland is also bilaterally symmetric.

6. Viewed from a distance, this is part of what is at issue in the debates among different theories of functional localization. One theory will charge the other with having insufficient evidence to establish the existence of one function or one localization as opposed to another function or another localization. Then there are those who object to all forms of functional localization. One component of these rejections is that the inductive scientific evidence does not bear the weight of the conclusions drawn from it.

CHAPTER 11

PUTTING MATTERS IN PERSPECTIVE

In a broad outline, the foregoing ten chapters are a partial vindication of Fodor and Pylyshyn's brand of Classicism. Classicism explains some of the systematic relations in thought, where rival theories, such as Connectionism and Functional Combinatorialism do not. Thus, we have some defeasible reason to believe in Classicism, rather than it rivals. While this leaves us in essentially the same position as did Fodor and Pylyshyn's critique, this does not mean that no progress has been made in the present study. This final chapter can now briefly spell out just exactly what progress has been made here. In addition, we can review some of most significant challenges that remain in coming to fully understand and evaluate the significance of the productivity and systematicity arguments.

The feature of the systematicity arguments that we have most strongly emphasized is that they should not be viewed simply as providing explananda for which Classicism has an account and for which non-Classical rivals do not. In many instances, both Classicism and its rivals have a story on offer as a possible explanation of some systematic feature of thought. Yet more is needed that simply an account that fits the data. Not only must a theory have an account of systematic relations in thought, a theory must have an account that does not rely on arbitrary hypotheses. This point has been noted from time to time in the cognitive science literature, but it has not been as extensively developed as it has been here. Working through the consequences of this point has been central to our present discussion. This is not, of course, to say that the systematicity arguments have nothing to do with fitting data to theory. We have, in fact, examined cases where the matter of exactly what systematic relations there are in thought do arise. In Chapter 5, we saw that although there are recursive systems of representation that give rise to *some* systematic relations in thought, these systematic relations are not those typically mentioned in the literature. A system of representation that generates counterfactual dependencies among thoughts because of its recursive structure will not generate counterfactual dependencies, such as that between John loves Mary and Mary loves John. Whatever one thinks about the idea that explanations may involve more than data fitting and whatever one thinks about the particular analysis that has here been offered of these explanations, this feature of the arguments cannot go unaddressed by either Classicists or their rivals.

A second area of progress has involved placing the systematicity arguments into the context of other *prima facie* similar explanatory arguments in the history of science. The history of science provides us with relatively less controversial cases of explanatory confirmation. These cases give us clues as to the way we should analyze the explanatory confirmation that is involved in the systematicity arguments. Further, the historical cases provide constraints on how we understand the possible merits of the systematicity arguments. All of this is to say that the history of science aids us in avoiding armchair philosophy of science. In some methodological discussions in cognitive science, one finds simple bald assertions that one theory better explains something than does another. In other methodological discussions, one finds only vaguely specified explanations. The vague and the unsupported are often so insubstantial that they can hardly be engaged in a constructive manner. With real historical examples of confirmatory explanation in hand, however, we have explanatory standards that merit more serious attention. Moreover, they leave us in a better position to avoid *ad hoc* theories of explanation.

A third area of progress is somewhat more subtle. We have seen reason to doubt Fodor and Pylyshyn's widely accepted suggestions that the systematicity arguments are just like the productivity arguments, only relying on weaker premises.[1] In moving from the productivity arguments to the systematicity arguments, Fodor and Pylyshyn, for the sake of argument, abandon the idealization to an unbounded representational capacity. This is not an abandonment of the competence/performance distinction *per se*, but a refusal to rely on a particular conclusion about the nature of cognitive competence for the space of the systematicity arguments. They abandon the idealization, not because they believe it is false or unsubstantiated; they do it because they believe they can have just as good an argument without it. What we have tried to emphasize, however, is that letting go of the idealization to unbounded capacities leads to a chain of quite significant consequences. In the first place, we see that it generally enables non-Classicists to provide at least a *prima facie* tenable model of the systematic features of thought. This, in turn, means that Fodor and Pylyshyn must invoke a principle for deciding between Classical and non-Classical accounts of the systematic relations in thought. This is where the concern about arbitrary hypotheses enters the debate. Next we observe that it was the requirement that a system of representation be capable of handling an unbounded number of representations that forces formal language theory and computer science to methods that avoid reliance on arbitrary hypotheses. In finite languages and for finite tasks, computation lacks its familiar resources for differentiating between arbitrary and non-arbitrary methods. With the foregoing points on the table and once we clarify the apparent nature of the explanatory principle Classicists want to invoke, we find that existing Classical and non-Classical accounts of the systematic features of thought fail. That is, we have a dilemma. Without some principle of better explanation, one has no basis for choosing between two apparently viable Classical and non-Classical accounts, yet with the principle of better explanation, one appears to have no viable Classical or non-Classical account. The abandonment of the idealization to unbounded representational capacities, thus, leads to greater complications than Fodor and Pylyshyn, and everyone else for that matter, appear to realize

A fourth area of progress, one that arises from the present focus on the "logic" of the systematicity arguments, is in our ability to highlight an argument that appears in Fodor and Pylyshyn's discussion of the compositionality of representations. This argument is much stronger than any of those that have been discussed in the literature. This is the argument that asks why it is that the capacities for thoughts that are mutually dependent are, at the same time, content related. This is the co-occurrence interpretation of the arguments. Given the bare minimum of Classical apparatus one needs to explain the mutual dependence among capacities for thoughts, one finds apparatus that also suffices to explain the content relations among thoughts. This is evidently the potent form of explanation we find at work in Copernican astronomy. In addition, once we are attuned to the virtues of these sorts of co-occurrence explananda, we are encouraged to explore the possibility that there is an equally good co-occurrence argument based on the diachronic and synchronic versions of systematicity.

A fifth development is that we have seen how to meet the claims that particular Connectionist models and certain strains of Functional Combinatorialism can explain the systematic relations in thought. Once we see how the systematicity arguments apply to a simple theory, such as Pure Atomism, we can see in detail how the family of systematicity arguments may be extended, essentially unchanged, to apply to familiar non-Classical alternatives. In fact, we can see in detail how to extend the systematicity arguments to a new kind of architecture that to some extent differs from Classical architecture, namely, Cummins's theory of propositional attitudes. In this area, we see a substantial vindication of Fodor and Pylyshyn's claims. Non-Classical architectures apparently lack the resources to explain the systematic features of thought.

Although some progress has been made in our investigations, there remain a number of issues that have not been resolved. In the interest of future progress, some of these issues are emphasized here. Foremost among the concerns is work in the philosophy of science which will explore the analysis of the structure of the systematicity arguments. The arguments involve defeasible, inductive inferences and philosophers of science have been notably unsuccessful in providing accurate and explicit analyses of what constitutes a good inductive argument. On this basis alone, one should expect counterexamples to the analysis that has been offered here. There are bound to be good confirmatory explanations of empirical generalizations that fail to meet the conditions set forth here as well as accounts that meet the conditions set forth here, but which do not count as good confirmatory explanations. This is especially worrisome, since so very much of the foregoing argumentation could turn on the proper analysis of the nature of these explanations. As we have moved from the case of Classicism and Pure Atomism to the analysis of Cummins's cognitive architecture, we have seen numerous points where the analysis could, in principle, break down. We have seen numerous points where the analogy may be stretched beyond proper limits. On this point, one can only hope that cognitive scientists will not be satisfied with mere counterexamples to the foregoing analysis and analogies, but that they will take on the job of a philosopher of science and carry out further investigations and explore better analyses. Philosophers of science, for their part, should not give up hope on trying to say what, if anything, there is to the sense that Copernicus had a better explanation than did Ptolemy of the coincidence of the retrograde motions of the superior planets with their being in opposition to the sun. Philosophers of science should not give up on the project of trying to say why evolution provides a better explanation of biogeographical, morphological, embryological, and taxonomic regularities than does creationism.

A second area for further research concerns the further development of options for non-Classical cognitive architectures. In part because of ambiguities and vagaries in the specifications of the explananda in Fodor and Pylyshyn's exposition, non-Classical responses to the productivity and systematicity arguments have often been wide of the mark. Non-Classicists have missed the explananda and failed to appreciate the explanatory standard that has been at work. For a very simple theory of cognitive architecture, such as Pure Atomism, it is possible to see just how limited are the responses to the challenge of explaining the productivity and systematicity of thought. Yet, as we extend the analogies and analyses that serve to compare Classicism and Pure Atomism to more complicated cognitive architectures, such as Connectionism and Functional Combinatorialism, we find that it is less than completely obvious how these theories might attempt to come to grips with the explananda. We have ventured more or less reliable conjectures about these matters, but there is always room for alternative developments that might meet the challenges. In particular, it is always possible that new methods of generating empirical evidence will show how hypotheses that were once thought to be untestable are in fact testable. With our better understanding of what the productivity and systematicity arguments involve, it is certainly reasonable for non-Classicists to continue to seek new possibilities.

A third area, with many subareas, concerns the empirical basis of the alleged explananda. This study has focused on the logic of the productivity and systematicity arguments. It has tried to dispel misconceptions about possible "tricks" in the arguments. It has tried to clarify what constitutes productivity, what constitutes the systematicity of inference, and so forth. The cognitive science literature amply documents the need for this sort of work. Still, this sort of work merely sets the stage for reviews of the existing psychological literature and for the conduct of future research. Several areas of empirical research are potentially fruitful here.

1) Lars Niklasson and Tim van Gelder, and following them, Robert Cummins, have drawn attention to the literature on human reasoning. While the results they brought forward did not establish that inference is not systematic in the way Fodor and Pylyshyn allege, there remains the possibility that there are other results that do.

2) Work on learning and memory is another area that is certainly relevant to the investigation of the extent to which thought is both systematic and compositional in the sense Fodor and Pylyshyn articulated. Here the literature is vast.

3) Research on the extent to which non-human animals display productivity and the various kinds of systematicity. This bears most significantly on arguments that the productive and systematic features of thought are somehow connected with the productivity and systematicity of natural language. One such connection is that the features of thought are artifacts of the features of the natural language we use to ascribe thoughts. Another connection is that the productivity and systematicity of human thought are a product of the productivity and systematicity of the natural language humans speak. In both of these applications, it would appear that the productivity and systematicity of thought would have to be the same as the productivity and systematicity of natural language, which is a problematic conclusion. Dennett, (1991), has hinted that research on vervet monkeys goes against Classical estimates of animal systematicity and productivity, but his claims do not have sufficient detail to enable an easy assessment of the matter.

4) Study of language-less adults promises significant results to complement research on non-human animals. Stereotypically, these individuals are congenitally deaf and are raised in environments without access to sign language. As a result, these individuals do not have what linguists think of as a natural language, although they typically do possess the ability to communicate through mime. Further, they appear to be in many respects quite normal in their intelligence, certainly far and away more cognitively gifted than any non-human animals. Thus, insofar as their cognitive abilities do not differ from those of users of natural language, the case for productivity and systematicity of thought as intrinsic features of cognition is strengthened.

The upshot, of course, is that while some progress has been made in attempting to determine the significance of the productivity and systematicity arguments, there remain a number of conceptual and empirical issues that are worthy of exploration. Then, of course, there remains the broader, and ultimately more important, issue of the final determination of the nature of human cognitive architecture, and of cognitive architecture in general.

NOTES

1. Cf., e.g., Fodor & Pylyshyn, (1988), p. 33, fn. 22, p. 37.

REFERENCES

Adams, F., & Aizawa, K. Fodorian semantics. In Warfield, T., & Stich, S. (Eds.). *Mental Representation: A Reader*. (1994). (pp. 223-242).

Aizawa, K. (1997a). The role of the systematicity argument in Classicism and Connectionism. In O'Nuallain, S. (Ed.). *Two Sciences of Mind: Readings in Cognitive Science and Consciousness*. Amsterdam, The Netherlands: John Benjamins. (pp. 197-218).

Aizawa, K. (1997b). Exhibiting versus explaining systematicity: A Reply to Hadley and Hayward, *Minds and Machines, 7*, 39-55. *(1997)*.

Aizawa, K. (1997c). Explaining systematicity. *Mind and Language, 12*, 115-136.

Braddon-Mitchell, D., & Fitzpatrick, J. (1990). Explanation and the language of thought, *Synthese, 83*, 3-29.

Burchfield, J. D. (1975). *Lord Kelvin and the Age of the Earth*. Chicago, IL: University of Chicago Press.

Chalmers, D. (1990). Syntactic transformations on distributed representations. *Connection Science, 2*, 53-62.

Cheney, D. & Seyfarth, R. (1990). *How Monkeys See the World*. Chicago, IL: University of Chicago Press.

Chomsky, N. (1957). *Syntactic Structures*. The Hague: Mouton.

Chomsky, N. (1965). *Aspects of the Theory of Syntax*. Cambridge, MA: MIT Press.

Chomsky, N. (1980). *Rules and Representations*. New York, NY: Columbia University Press.

Chomsky, N. (1995). *The Minimalist Program*. Cambridge, MA: MIT Press.

Churchland, P. M. (1989). On the nature of theories: A PDP approach. In Churchland, P. M. *A Neurocomputational Perspective*. Cambridge, MA: MIT Press.

Clark, A. (1988). Thoughts, sentences, and cognitive science. *Philosophical Psychology, 1*, 263-278.

Clark, A. (1991). Systematicity, structured representations, and cognitive architecture: A reply to Fodor and Pylyshyn. In Horgan, T., and Tienson, J. (Eds.). *Connectionism and the Philosophy o Mind*. Kluwer.

Cummins, R. (1996a). *Representations, Targets, and Attitudes*. Cambridge, MA: MIT Press.

Cummins, R. (1996b). Systematicity. *Journal of Philosophy, 93*, 591-614.

Darwin, C. (1859). *The Origin of Species*. London: John Murray.

de Swart, H. (1998). *Introduction to Natural Language Semantics.* Palo Alto, CA: CSLI Publications.

Dennett, D. (1991). Mother nature versus the walking encyclopedia: A Western drama. In Ramsey, W., Stich, S., and Rumelhart, D. (Eds.). *Philosophy and Connectionist Theory.* Hillsdale, NJ: Lawrence Erlbaum Associates. (pp. 21-30).

Dennett, D. (1993). Learning and labeling. *Mind and Language, 8,* 540-547.

Dretske, F. (1981). *Knowledge and the Flow of Information.* Cambridge, MA: MIT Press.

Dretske, F. (1988). *Explaining Behavior.* Cambridge, MA: MIT Press.

Elman, J. (1990). Finding structure in time. *Cognitive Science, 14,* 179-212.

Evans, G. (1982). *The Varieties of Reference.* Oxford: Oxford University Press.

Fodor, J. (1981) *RePresentations.* Cambridge, MA: MIT Press.

Fodor, J. (1985). Fodor's guide to mental representation: The intelligent auntie's *vade-mecum. Mind,* 94, pp. 76-100. Reprinted in Fodor, J. *A Theory of Content and Other Essays.* Cambridge, MA: MIT Press. (pp. 3-29).

Fodor, J. (1987) *Psychosemantics.* Cambridge, MA: MIT Press.

Fodor, J. (1998) *Concepts: Where Cognitive Science Went Wrong.* Cambridge, MA: MIT Press.

Fodor, J. (1996). Connectionism and the problem of systematicity (continued): why Smolensky's solution still doesn't work. *Cognition, 62,* 109-119.

Fodor, J. & Lepore, E. (1999). All at sea in semantic space: Churchland on meaning similarity. *Journal of Philosophy, 96,* 381-403.

Fodor, J., & McLaughlin, (1990). Connectionism and the problem of systematicity: Why Smolensky's solution doesn't work. *Cognition, 35,* 183-204.

Fodor, J., & Pylyshyn, Z. (1988). Connectionism and cognitive architecture: A critical analysis. *Cognition, 28,* 3-71.

Garson, J. (1994) Cognition without Classical architecture. *Synthese, 100,* 291-305.

Glymour, C. (1980). *Theory and Evidence.* Princeton, New Jersey: Princeton University Press.

Goodman, N. (1976). *Languages of Art.* Indianapolis, IN: Hackett Publishing.

Goschke, T., & Koppelberg, D. (1991). The concept of representation and the representation of concepts in connectionist models. In Ramsey, W., Stich, S., and Rumelhart, D. (Eds.). *Philosophy and Connectionist Theory.* Hillsdale, NJ: Lawrence Erlbaum Associates. (pp. 129-161).

Griggs, R.A., & Cox, J. R. (1982). The elusive thematic materials effect in the Wason card selection task. *British Journal of Psychology*, 73, 407-420.

Hadley, R. (1994). Systematicity in Connectionist Language Learning. *Mind & Language, 9*, 247-272.

Hadley, R. (1997a). Explaining systematicity: A reply to Kenneth Aizawa. *Minds and Machines, 7*, 571-579.

Hadley, R. (1997b). Cognition, systematicity, and nomic necessity. *Mind & Language, 16*, 137-153.

Hadley, R., and Hayward, M. (1997). Strong semantic systematicity from Hebbian Connectionist learning. *Minds and Machines*, 7, 1-37.

Hempel, C. G. (1965). *Aspects of Scientific Explanation*. The Free Press: New York.

Hempel, C. G., and Oppenheim, P. (1948). Studies in the logic of explanation. *Philosophy of Science, 15*, 135-75.

Horgan, T., & Tienson, J. (1996), *Connectionism and the Philosophy of Psychology.* Cambridge, MA: MIT Press.

Hull, D. (1973). *Darwin and his Critics*. Chicago, IL: University of Chicago Press.

Jackendoff, R. (1994). *Patterns in the Mind*. New York, NY: Basic Books.

Johnson-Laird, P. N. (1975). Models of deduction. In Falmagne, R.J. (Ed.). *Reasoning: Representation and Process in Children and Adults*. Hillsdale, NJ: Lawrence Erlbaum Associates. (pp. 7-54).

Karmiloff-Smith, A. (1992). *Beyond Modularity*. Cambridge, MA: MIT Press.

Kern, L.H., Mirels, H.L., & Hinshaw, V.G. (1983). Scientists' understanding of propositional logic: an experimental investigation. *Social Studies of Science*, 131-146.

Kuhn, T. (1957). *The Copernican Revolution*. Cambridge, MA: Harvard University Press.

Loewer, B., and Rey, G. (1991). Editors' Introduction to *Meaning in Mind: Fodor and his Critics*. Oxford: Blackwell Publishers. (pp. xi-xxxvii).

Matthews, R. (1994). Three-concept Monte: Explanation, implementation, and systematicity. *Synthese, 101*, 347-363.

Matthews, R. (1997). Can Connectionists explain systematicity? *Mind & Language, 12*, 154-177.

McLaughlin, B. (1993a). The classicism/connectionism battle to win souls. *Philosophical Studies, 70*, 45-72.

McLaughlin, B. (1993b). Systematicity, conceptual truth, and evolution. In Hookway, C., and Peterson, D. (Eds.). *Philosophy and Cognitive Science.* Cambridge: Cambridge University Press.

Niklasson, L., and van Gelder, T. (1994). On being systematically connectionist. *Mind and Language, 9,* 288-302.

Pollack, J. (1990). Recursive distributed representations. *Artificial Intelligence, 47,* 77-105.

Provine, W. (2001). *The Theoretical Origins of Population Genetics.* Chicago, IL: University of ChicagoPress.

Rowlands, M. (1994). Connectionism and the language of thought. *British Journal for the Philosophy of Science, 45,* 485-503.

Ruben, D. (1990). *Explaining Explanation.* New York: Rutledge.

Rumelhart, D., Hinton, G., & McClelland, J. (1986). A general framework for parallel distributed processing. In Rumelhart, D., & McClelland, J. (Eds.)., *Parallel Distributed Processing: Explorations in the Micro structure of Cognition.* (pp. 45-76).

Smolensky, P. (1987). The constituent structure of connectionist mental states: A reply to Fodor and Pylyshyn. *Southern Journal of Philosophy, 26, Supplement: Spindel Conference 1987: Connectionism and the Philosophy of Mind,* ed. Horgan, T., and Tienson, J. Kluwer.

Smolensky, P. (1988a). On the proper treatment of connectionism. *Behavioral and Brain Sciences, 11,* 1-74.

Smolensky, P. (1988b). Connectionism, constituency, and the language of thought. University of Colorado Technical Report. Reprinted in Loewer, B., & Rey, G., (Eds.), *Meaning in Mind: Fodor and his Critics.* Oxford: Blackwell Publishers.

Smolensky, P. (1990). Tensor product variable binding and the representation of symbolic structures in connectionist systems. *Artificial Intelligence, 46,* 159-216.

Smolensky, P. (1995). Reply: Constituent structure and explanation in an integrated Connectionist/Symbolic cognitive architecture. In MacDonald, C., & MacDonald, G. (Eds.). *Connectionism: Debates on Psychological Explanation.* (pp. 223- 290).

Sterelny, K. (1990). *The Representational Theory of Mind: An Introduction.* Oxford: Blackwell.

van Gelder, T. (1990). Compositionality: A connectionist variation on a Classical theme. *Cognitive Science, 14,* 355-384.

van Gelder, T., and Niklasson, L. F. (1994). Classicism and cognitive architecture. *Proceedings of the Sixteenth Annual Conference of the Cognitive Science Society,* Atlanta, GA, pp. 905-909.

INDEX